Benjamin Britten
Peter Grimes

Compiled by
PHILIP BRETT

CAMBRIDGE UNIVERSITY PRESS

Cambridge
London New York New Rochelle
Melbourne Sydney

Published by the Press Syndicate of the University of Cambridge
The Pitt Building, Trumpington Street, Cambridge CB2 1RP
32 East 57th Street, New York, NY 10022, USA
296 Beaconsfield Parade, Middle Park, Melbourne 3206, Australia

First published 1983

Printed in Great Britain at the University Press, Cambridge

Library of Congress catalogue card number: 82-14627

British Library Cataloguing in Publication Data

Brett, Philip
Britten, Benjamin, Peter Grimes – (Cambridge opera handbooks)
1. Britten, Benjamin. Peter Grimes
I. Title II. Series

ISBN 0 521 22916 2 hard covers
ISBN 0 521 29716 8 paperback

ME

Cambridge Opera Handbooks

Benjamin Britten
Peter Grimes

A page from the composition sketch showing the crisis of the quarrel between Peter and Ellen in Act II scene 1, not yet in its final form (see below, pp. 75-8)

CAMBRIDGE OPERA HANDBOOKS

General preface

This is a series of studies of individual operas, written for the serious opera-goer or record-collector as well as the student or scholar. Each volume has three main concerns. The first is historical: to describe the genesis of the work, its sources or its relation to literary prototypes, the collaboration between librettist and composer, and the first performance and subsequent stage history. This history is itself a record of changing attitudes towards the work, and an index of general changes of taste. The second is analytical and it is grounded in a very full synopsis which considers the opera as a structure of musical and dramatic effects. In most volumes there is also a musical analysis of a section of the score, showing how the music serves or makes the drama. The analysis, like the history, naturally raises questions of interpretation, and the third concern of each volume is to show how critical writing about an opera, like production and performance, can direct or distort appreciation of its structural elements. Some conflict of interpretation is an inevitable part of this account; editors of the handbooks reflect this – by citing classic statements, by commissioning new essays, by taking up their own critical position. A final section gives a select bibliography, a discography and guides to other sources.

Books published

Richard Wagner: *Parsifal* by Lucy Beckett
W. A. Mozart: *Don Giovanni* by Julian Rushton
C. W. von Gluck: *Orfeo* by Patricia Howard
Igor Stravinsky: *The Rake's Progress* by Paul Griffiths
Leoš Janáček: *Kát'a Kabanová* by John Tyrrell
Giuseppe Verdi: *Falstaff* by James A. Hepokoski

Other volumes in preparation

In loving memory of E. M. Forster
and for Don Clark and George Haggerty
who helped me turn skies back and begin again

Contents

Illustrations

Preface

The inspiration for this book came from the publisher's original idea of modelling the series on the literary 'case-books'. In casting around I was surprised at the extent and variety of good critical writing on an opera still so young, and I was encouraged by this to explore its history in greater detail. The opening of the Britten–Pears Library at Aldeburgh came at an opportune moment: it was exciting to find, as material was uncovered or arrived there bit by bit, that an attempt could be made to follow the evolution of the work step by step.

The plan of the book follows exactly the main concerns of the series outlined in the General Preface. The historical matter comes first, beginning with E. M. Forster's 1941 radio talk, which prompted Britten and Pears, unhappy in their self-imposed exile in the United States, to think of returning to Britain, and which sent them to the works of the Suffolk poet George Crabbe. Forster's second, less well known essay provides greater insight into the poem from which Britten and Pears drew the main material for the opera. In an annotated interview with the librettist's widow, Donald Mitchell throws new light on Montagu Slater and his relationship with the composer and also on many other aspects of the opera's early history. My own documentary study of the opera and its growth is followed by a chapter on stage history in which I have included a discussion of the critical reception of the work at the immediate level of the newspaper or magazine review.

The second part of the book comprises Hans Keller's analytical synopsis – one of his most perceptive essays on Britten – and a specially commissioned analytical account of Act II scene 1, the crux of the opera, by David Matthews, one of the new generation of writers on Britten's music.

The section of criticism opens with Britten's own introduction to the work and with an explanation of its main dramatic themes that Peter Pears wrote for a radio performance in 1946. Since these are to some extent statements of intention by those with whom the idea of the opera originated, it seemed only right to place them here together; and readers approaching the opera for the first time and with no knowledge of its history might like to turn to Britten's account before starting the book, since it also tells the story of the work's inception. After this the arrangement is chronological. Among the reviews of the first performance, that of Desmond Shawe-Taylor stands out (almost alone) as being of more than ephemeral interest. In addition to its interesting musical perceptions, it raised an ethical question about the nature of the protagonist which, expressed in a variety of forms, has preoccupied a number of critics of the work, especially in Britain. In a later essay, J. W. Garbutt pursues this question to its furthest point, finding the figure of Grimes 'self-contradictory', a 'neurotic failure'. An initially unwilling witness of the first production, the distinguished American critic Edmund Wilson, wrote what must be one of the most eloquent accounts of this or of any other opera, exploring its symbolic meanings in a way that musical critics seemed reluctant to attempt. Peter Garvie, looking back on the opera from the vantage point of the early 1970s, examines its themes in relation to those of the later stage works, and develops a Christian interpretation of Britten's operas in the process. My own essay, written just before the composer's death, took issue with such views of the character of Grimes as those of Shawe-Taylor and (though I had not yet discovered it) J. W. Garbutt, and went on to explore the influence of Britten's sexuality and his sense of 'roots' upon the shaping of the work. It seemed important to discuss just what reverberations lay behind those often-repeated catch-phrases, 'the outcast' and 'the individual against the crowd', which the composer himself in talking to Murray Schafer had already related to his status and feelings as a conscientious objector; and I have taken the opportunity to pursue this inquiry in a Postscript.

I make no claim to have exhausted the possibilities. There are accounts, notably the one by Peter Evans, that I would gladly have reprinted had they not appeared so recently; and there are others that I have singled out in a note to the bibliography. One thing is certain: *Peter Grimes*, whatever history's ultimate judgment, has had a strong and disturbing effect upon its first-generation audience; it is a musical drama of particular relevance to our present age, and one that may well reveal further levels of meaning to future generations.

I should like to thank all the contributors to this book. To one of them I owe an apology and a promise to make amends: in spite of a thorough search I have been unable to identify J. W. Garbutt. Peter Garvie and David Matthews have both given further aid, and I am also grateful for help of various kinds to Joan Cross, Eric Crozier, Tanya Moiseiwitsch, O. W. Neighbour, Andrew Porter and Wayne D. Shirley. Without the encouragement of Rosemary Dooley I should have taken much longer to finish the book; and Ruth Smith made several important contributions while ostensibly editing it. Sir Peter Pears has been unfailingly gracious and informative: to him as one of the finest musicians of our time I already owed more than I could express, and he has increased the debt by his friendliness. My greatest thanks in working on *Peter Grimes*, however, go to Rosamund Strode and Donald Mitchell; if my work on the opera's origins and development begins to match the extraordinary extent of their enthusiasm and generous co-operation I shall be very gratified indeed.

Riverside, California Philip Brett
and Sheringham, Norfolk
Spring 1982

Acknowledgments

The publishers gratefully acknowledge permission to reprint the following: E. M. Forster's 'George Crabbe – the Man and the Poet' (chapter 1) by permission of King's College, Cambridge, and the Society of Authors as the literary representatives of the Estate of E. M. Forster, and his 'George Crabbe and Peter Grimes' (chapter 1) from *Two Cheers for Democracy* by permission of Edward Arnold (Publishers) Ltd; chapter 5 (Dr Hans Keller); chapter 7 (by kind permission of the Executors of the Britten Estate); chapter 8 (Sir Peter Pears); chapter 9 (Mr Desmond Shawe-Taylor); chapter 10, reprinted from Edmund Wilson's *Europe without Baedeker* (copyright © 1947, 1966 by Edmund Wilson, copyright renewed © 1975 by Elena Wilson) by permission of Farrar, Straus and Giroux Inc.; chapter 11 (*Music and Letters*); chapter 12 (Mr Peter Garvie); and chapter 13 (*Musical Times*). The frontispiece (© 1945 Boosey & Hawkes Ltd) and Figs. 1, 3, 4 (© The Britten Estate) and 5 (© 1945 Boosey & Hawkes Ltd), from the Britten–Pears Library (photographs Nigel Luckhurst), appear by courtesy of the Britten Estate; Fig. 2 has kindly been made available by Mrs Enid Slater; Figs. 6, 10 and 11 appear by permission of the Harvard Theatre Collection (Angus McBean photographs); Fig. 7 is taken from Charles Stuart's *Peter Grimes* (London, 1947); and Fig. 8 appears by permission of the photographer, Stuart Robinson, and Fig. 9 by permission of the photographer, Donald Southern.

HISTORY

1 *Two essays on Crabbe*

E. M. FORSTER (1941, 1948)

The first of the two essays reprinted here is in a literal sense the source of the opera. Benjamin Britten and Peter Pears, who had left England for the United States in 1939, were staying with friends in Southern California in the summer of 1941 when they came across a back issue of *The Listener* containing Forster's radio talk. As the composer himself explains (see chapter 7), it was reading these very words that first sent him in search of Crabbe, and led him in particular to *The Borough*, the poem that includes the story of Peter Grimes and provided most of the characters for the opera. Forster later revised this essay for inclusion in the booklet that accompanied the original production,[1] but I have chosen to reproduce the original in view of its special role in the inception of the opera.

The second essay, a lecture delivered at the first Aldeburgh Festival in June 1948, was written after the opera had enjoyed its first great success. Forster returned to his themes about Crabbe without this time quoting from his earlier writings. This essay is a much more profound statement about the poet, it gives a penetrating account of the poem, and in addition it serves the reader of this book by including a substantial amount of quotation. (Couplets and lines that Forster left out I have included, as in the first essay, in square brackets.) In a postlude, Forster gives his own rather terse account of the opera, dissociating it from Crabbe, and interpreting its moral in an authoritative way.[2]

It is instructive to compare Forster's reading of the poem, and that of Britten and the librettist Montagu Slater, with other views. An almost line-by-line commentary is given by Peter New, who reaches the conclusion that 'as the humane representation of a barely human consciousness it has few rivals in English literature' (p. 100). In a challenging new look at Crabbe emphasising the social criticism implied in his work, Ronald B. Hatch sees in the poem the same condemnation of society that Forster, in speaking of the opera, had felt – but for different reasons. Crabbe's Grimes, according to Hatch, merely takes advantage of what the law allows him: for unlike the typical villain of the Gothic novel, he does not have to resort to kidnapping to place another person under his complete control; he has only to apply to the nearest workhouse. The townspeople are convincingly shown to be implicated in the maltreatment of the boys:

> Some few in town observed in Peter's trap
> A boy, with jacket blue and woollen cap;
> But none inquired how Peter used the rope,
> Or what the bruise, that made the stripling stoop;
> None could the ridges on his back behold,
> None sought him shiv'ring in the winter's cold;
> None put the question – 'Peter, dost thou give
> 'The boy his food? – What, man! the lad must live:
> 'Consider, Peter, let the child have bread,
> 'He'll serve thee better if he's stroked and fed.'
> None reason'd thus – and some, on hearing cries,
> Said calmly, 'Grimes is at his exercise.' (XXII, 67-78)

And when they finally turn on Peter after the death of the third apprentice, they do so only to find a scapegoat, not to examine their own consciences. For the most part,

> Grimes does not think he is doing anything out of the ordinary: nor do his fellow citizens. And in fact he is not. He is taking advantage of an accepted system. His individual savagery reflects the savagery of the society. Where he differs is that he takes advantage of the system to do what it permits, instead of availing himself of the system and modifying his behaviour through moral considerations (pp. 108-9).

Here, then, we might suggest, lies the essential difference between Crabbe's Grimes and that of Britten, a difference that rings deeper (and perhaps truer) than the usual distinction drawn – in the first instance by the librettist himself[3] – between the poet's harsh 'eighteenth-century' realism and the composer's Byronic figure. Crabbe's Peter is an embodiment of the dark side of an uncaring and morally enfeebled society, whereas Britten's is the victim of that society and a symbol of its oppression.

Where Crabbe differs from the social reformer, as both Hatch and Forster would agree, is in not urging change. He is a pessimist, who presents rather than persuades. Thus he is able, as Hatch points out, to come close 'to achieving the impossible, writing social criticism which does not place all the onus for the trouble on "society", but which reveals that the economic forces of society are themselves rooted in man's perception of himself' (p. 113).

Hatch's account is the most stimulating recent study of Crabbe's poetry; the standard modern biography is still that of Huchon. As Forster pointed out, Crabbe was fortunate in having his life written well (if not with complete accuracy) by his son, and *The Life of Crabbe* has achieved the status of a minor classic. There is also a more recent and very readable biography by Neville Blackburne. Further information can be found in the valuable annotated bibliography by Bareham and Gatrell, and Pollard's volume in the Critical Heritage series provides an interesting selection of reviews and opinions.

George Crabbe: The Poet and the Man

To talk about Crabbe is to talk about England. He never left our shores and he only once ventured to cross the border into Scotland. He did not even go to London much, but lived in villages and small country towns. He was a clergyman of the English Church. His Christian name was George, the name of our national saint. More than that, his father was called George, and so was his grandfather, and he christened his eldest son George, and his grandson was called George also. Five generations of George Crabbes!

Our particular George Crabbe was born (in the year 1754) at Aldeburgh, on the coast of Suffolk. It is a bleak little place: not beautiful. It huddles round a flint-towered church and sprawls down to the North Sea – and what a wallop the sea makes as it pounds at the shingle! Near by is a quay, at the side of an estuary, and here the scenery becomes melancholy and flat; expanses of mud, saltish commons, the marsh-birds crying. Crabbe heard that sound and saw that melancholy, and they got into his verse. He worked as an unhappy little boy on the quay, rolling barrels about and storing them in a warehouse, under orders from his father. He hated it. His mother had died; his father was cross. Now and then he got hold of a book, or looked at some prints, or chatted with a local worthy, but it was a hard life and they were in narrow circumstances. He grew up among poor people, and he has been called their poet. But he did not like the poor. When he started writing, it was the fashion to pretend that they were happy shepherds and shepherdesses, who were always dancing, or anyhow had hearts of gold. But Crabbe knew the local almshouses and the hospital and the prison, and the sort of people who drift into them; he read, in the parish registers, the deaths of the unsuccessful, the marriages of the incompetent, and the births of the illegitimate. Though he notes occasional heroism, his general verdict on the working classes is unfavourable. And when he comes to the richer and more respectable inmates of the borough who can veil their defects behind money, he remains sardonic, and sees them as poor people who haven't been found out.

He escaped from Aldeburgh as soon as he could. His fortunes improved, he took orders, married well, and ended his life in a comfortable west country parsonage. He did well for himself, in fact. Yet he never escaped from Aldeburgh in the spirit, and it was the making of him as a poet. Even when he is writing of other things, there steals again and again into his verse the sea, the estuary, the flat Suffolk coast, and local meannesses, and an odour of brine and dirt – tempered occasionally with the scent of flowers. So remember Aldeburgh when you read this rather odd poet, for he belongs to the grim little place, and through it to England. And remember that though he is an Englishman, he is not a John Bull, and that though he is a clergyman, he is by no means an 'old dear'.

His poems are easily described, and are easy to read. They are stories in rhymed couplets, and their subject is local scenes or people. One story will be about the almshouses, another about the Vicar, another about inns. A famous one is 'Peter Grimes': he was a savage fisherman who murdered his apprentices and was haunted by their ghosts; there was an actual original for Grimes. Another – a charming one – tells of a happy visit which a little boy once paid to a country mansion, and how the kind housekeeper showed him round the picture gallery, and gave him a lovely dinner in the servants' hall; Crabbe had himself been that humble little boy. He is not brilliant or cultivated, witty or townified. He is provincial; and I am using provincial as a word of high praise.

How good are these stories in verse? I will quote some extracts so that you can decide. Crabbe is a peculiar writer: some people like him, others don't, and find him dull and even unpleasant. I like him and read him again and again; and his tartness, his acid humour, his honesty, his feeling for certain English types and certain kinds of English scenery, do appeal to me very much. On their account I excuse the absence in him of a warm heart, a vivid imagination and a grand style: for he has none of those great gifts.

The first extract is from 'Peter Grimes'. It shows how Crabbe looks at scenery, and how subtly he links the scene with the soul of the observer. The criminal Grimes is already suspected of murdering his apprentices, and no one will go fishing with him in his boat. He rows out alone into the estuary, and waits there – waits for what?

When tides were neap, and, in the sultry day,
Through the tall bounding mud-banks made their way,

[Which on each side rose swelling, and below
The dark warm flood ran silently and slow;]
There anchoring, Peter chose from man to hide,
There hang his head, and view the lazy tide
In its hot, slimy channel slowly glide;
Where the small eels that left the deeper way
For the warm shore, within the shallows play;
Where gaping muscles, left upon the mud,
Slope their slow passage to the fallen flood. [XXII, 181-91]

How quiet this writing is: you might say how dreary. Yet how sure is its touch; and how vivid that estuary near Aldeburgh.

Here dull and hopeless he'd lie down and trace
How sidelong crabs had scrawl'd their crooked race;
Or listen sadly to the tuneless cry
Of fishing gull or clanging golden-eye;
What time the sea-birds to the marsh would come,
And the loud bittern, from the bull-rush home,
Gave from the salt-ditch side the bellowing boom:
He nursed the feelings these dull scenes produce,
And loved to stop beside the opening sluice. [XXII, 192-200]

Not great poetry, by any means; but it convinces me that Crabbe and Peter Grimes and myself do stop beside an opening sluice, and that we are looking at an actual English tideway, and not at some vague vast imaginary waterfall, which crashes from nowhere to nowhere.

My next quotation is a lighter one. It comes from his rather malicious poem about the Vicar of the Parish 'whose constant care was no man to offend'. He begins with a sympathetic description of Aldeburgh church, and its lichen-encrusted tower, and now he turns, with less sympathy, to the church's recent incumbent. Listen to his cruel account of the Vicar's one and only love affair. He had been attracted to a young lady who lived with her mother; he called on them constantly, smiling all the time, but never saying what he was after; with the inevitable result that the damsel got tired of her 'tortoise', and gave her hand to a more ardent suitor. Thus ended the Vicar's sole excursion into the realm of passion.

'I am escaped', he said, when none pursued;
When none attack'd him, 'I am unsubdued';
'Oh pleasing pangs of love', he sang again,
Cold to the joy, and stranger to the pain.
Ev'n in his age would he address the young,
'I too have felt these fires, and they are strong';
But from the time he left his favourite maid,
To ancient females his devoirs were paid;
And still they miss him after morning prayer. [III, 55-63]

He was always 'cheerful and in season gay', he gave the ladies presents of flowers from his garden with mottoes attached; he was fond of fishing, he organised charades, he valued friendship, but was not prepared to risk anything for it. One thing did upset him, and that was innovation; if the Vicar discerned anything new, on either the theological or the social horizon, he grew hot – it was the only time he did get hot.

> Habit with him was all the test of truth,
> 'It must be right: I've done it from my youth.'
> Questions he answer'd in as brief a way,
> 'It must be wrong – it was of yesterday.'
> Though mild benevolence our priest possess'd,
> 'Twas but by wishes or by words express'd:
> Circles in water, as they wider flow,
> The less conspicuous in their progress grow;
> And when at last they touch upon the shore,
> Distinction ceases, and they're view'd no more.
> His love, like that last circle, all embraced,
> But with effect which never could be traced. [III, 138-49]

The Vicar's fault is weakness, and the analysis and censure of weakness is a speciality of Crabbe's. His characters postpone marriage until passion has died; perhaps this was his own case, and why he was so bitter about it. Or they marry, and passion dies because they are too trivial to sustain it. Or they drift into vice, and do even that too late, so that they are too old to relish the lustiness of sin. Or like the Vicar they keep to the straight path because vice is more arduous than virtue. To all of them, and to their weaknesses, Crabbe extends a little pity, a little contempt, a little cynicism, and a much larger portion of reproof. The bitterness of his early experiences has eaten into his soul, and he does not love the human race, though he does not denounce it, nor despair of its ultimate redemption.

But we must get back to the Vicar, who is awaiting his final epitaph in some anxiety.

> Now rests our Vicar. They who knew him best,
> Proclaim his life t'have been entirely rest; –
> [Free from all evils which disturb his mind,
> Whom studies vex and controversies blind.]
> The rich approved, – of them in awe he stood;
> The poor admired, – they all believed him good;
> The old and serious of his habits spoke;
> The frank and youthful loved his pleasant joke;
> Mothers approved a safe contented guest,
> And daughters one who back'd each small request:
> [In him his flock found nothing to condemn;

Him sectaries liked – he never troubled them;]
No trifles fail'd his yielding mind to please,
And all his passions sunk in early ease;
Nor one so old has left this world of sin,
More like the being that he enter'd in. [III, 150-65]

For the Vicar died as a child, who retains his innocence because he has never gained any experience.

Well, the above quotations from 'Peter Grimes' and from 'The Vicar', one about scenery, the other about character, should be enough for you to find out whether you have any taste for the story-poems of George Crabbe. Do not expect too much. He is not one of our great poets. But he is unusual, he is sincere, and he is entirely of this country. There is one other merit attaching to him. The George Crabbe who was his son wrote his life, and it is one of the best biographies in our language, and gives a wonderful picture of provincial England at the close of the eighteenth century and the beginning of the nineteenth. Even if you are not attracted as much as I am by Crabbe's poetry, you may like to get hold of his life, and read how the poor little boy who rolled barrels on the quay at Aldeburgh made good.

George Crabbe and Peter Grimes

Before I come to George Crabbe or to Peter Grimes the poem, or to Peter Grimes the opera, I must speak of Aldeburgh.

The situation of this place is curious. A slight rise of the ground – I'll call it a hill, though the word is too emphatic – projects from the fenlands of Suffolk towards the North Sea. On this hill stands the church, a spacious Gothic building with very broad aisles, so that it has inside rather the effect of a hall. At the foot of the hill lies the town – a couple of long streets against which the sea is making an implacable advance. There used to be as many as five streets – three of them have disappeared beneath the shallow but violent waters, the house where Crabbe was born is gone, the street that has been named after him is menaced, the Elizabethan moot hall, which used to be in the centre of the place, now stands on a desolate beach. During the past twelve months the attack has been frightening. I can remember a little shelter erected for visitors on the shingle. Last autumn it was at the edge of a cliff, so that fishermen at the high tide actually sat in it to fish. This spring it has vanished, and the waters actually broke into the High Street – huge glassy waves coming in regularly and quietly, and each exploding when it hit the shore with the sound of a gun. This sort of attack went on a hundred and fifty

Fig. 1: An aerial view of Aldeburgh and the curious estuary of the Alde. The Moot Hall, marked by its tall double chimney-stack, stands slightly set apart in the lower foreground; the church lies directly inland from it and is not visible. Crabbe Street extends roughly from the Moot Hall to the Y-shaped intersection higher in the picture; No. 4, Crag House, where Britten and Pears moved soon after the initial triumph of *Peter Grimes*, is the second of the first block of three houses on the sea-front side

years ago, when Crabbe was alive, but the zone of operation lay further out. To-day, only the hill is safe. Only at the church, where he preached, and where his parents lie buried, is there security and peace.

North and south of the hill lie marshes. The marshland to the north requires no comment, but that to the south is peculiar, and I had it in mind when I called the situation of Aldeburgh 'curious'. It is intersected by the river Alde which flows due east, – but when it is within fifty yards of the sea it turns due south, and does not reach the sea for twelve miles, being divided from it by a narrow ridge of shingle [see Fig. 1]. Here again the waves are attacking, and are trying to break through the barrier that keeps them from the river. If they succeed – and they have had some success – Aldeburgh will be menaced on its flank and the valuable town grazing lands will disappear into the slime of the estuary.

It is with this estuary of the Alde that we are mainly concerned to-day. It is here, and not on the open sea or the sea front, that the action of the poem of 'Peter Grimes' takes place. There used to be a little port on the estuary, Slaughden Quay. It was important in Crabbe's day, and was well defined even in my own earlier visits to the district. It is now battered and derelict and the sea may wash across into it at the next great storm. Here Crabbe worked as a boy, rolling casks of butter about, and much he hated it. Hence Peter Grimes set out to fish. The prospect from Slaughden, despite desolation and menace, is romantic. At low tide the great mud flats stretch. At high tide the whole area is a swirl of many-coloured waters. At all times there are birds and low woodlands on the further bank, and, to the north, Aldeburgh sheltering among a few trees, and still just managing to dominate her fate.

I wanted to evoke these sombre and touching scenes as best I could, in order to give a local habitation and a name to what follows. Crabbe without Aldeburgh, Peter Grimes without the estuary of the Alde, would lose their savour and tang. Now for my story, and the first point I have to make is that Crabbe disliked his native town. Born here in 1754, he grew to manhood in straitened circumstances. He was afraid of his odd rough father who made him roll the casks about; then he was apprenticed to an apothecary; he hated that too, he couldn't even handle a boat properly, he was no use at all. One grim day in the winter of 1779, he walked to the bleak and cheerless Marsh Hill, gazed at a muddy stretch of water called the Leech Pond, and decided to clear out. Leaving these shores 'where guilt and famine reign',[4] he set out to seek his fortune in London as a poet. He nearly died of starvation first, and he was rescued not by his fellow townsmen, but by the generosity and insight of Edmund Burke. Burke recognised his genius and had faith in his integrity.

From that moment his fortunes were assured; he abandoned medicine and turned to the church for his profession, took orders, and returned to Aldeburgh three years later in the unexpected rôle of a triumphant curate.

Again he was unhappy, and no wonder. For he had not concealed his opinions on his home-town, and had indeed described it to Lord Shelburne as a venal little borough in Suffolk. He knew what he thought of his parishioners and they, for their part, regarded him as an ill-tempered intellectual who, having failed to heal men's bodies, proposed to interfere with their souls. The emotions are recorded with which he mounted the pulpit of Aldeburgh church for the first time. 'I had been unkindly received in the place – I saw unfriendly countenances about me, and, I am sorry to say, I had too much indignation – though mingled I hope with better feelings – to care what they thought of me or my sermon.'[5] The tension only lasted a few months. He got transferred. He was appointed domestic chaplain to the Duke of Rutland, moved away inland into Leicestershire, where he was happy or anyhow cosy. But his distaste for his native town had been confirmed. Everything seemed to incommode him there. Even his hopes of discovering a new species of trefoil on the beach were dashed. 'If I can once more shake off my complaints,' he writes, 'and gain a little life and spirit, I verily believe I shall publish an account of my plant.'[6] But Sir Joseph Banks reported that the trefoil had been catalogued already. And when towards the end of his life, he indulged in a visit of sentimentality, what were the results?

> Beccles is the home of past years and I could not walk through the streets as a stranger. It is not so at Aldeburgh. There a sadness mingles with all I see or hear; not a man is living whom I knew in my early portion of life; my contemporaries are gone, and their successors are unknown to me and I to them.[7]

Beccles, Leicestershire, Wiltshire – anywhere else. It is rare to discover in his writings a reference to his native town that is neither melancholy nor satirical.

Crabbe's antipathy to his birthplace was to play an essential part in the creation of 'Peter Grimes'. It was not a straightforward antipathy. It was connected with a profound attraction. He might leave Aldeburgh with his body, but he never emigrated spiritually; here on the plane of creation was his home and he could not have found a better one. This Borough made him a poet, through it he understood Suffolk, and through East Anglia he approached England. He remains here, however far he seems to travel, whatever he says to the contrary. His best work describes the place directly – *The Village*, *The Parish Register*, *The*

Borough – and its atmosphere follows him when he attempts other themes.

> The few dull flowers that o'er the place are spread
> Partake the nature of their fenny bed;
> Here on its wiry stem with rigid bloom
> Grows the salt lavender that lacks perfume;
> Here the dwarf sallows creep, the septfoil harsh
> And the soft slimy mallow of the marsh.
> Low on the ear the distant billows sound
> And just in view appears their stony bound;
> No hedge nor tree conceals the glowing sun . . .[8]

Dull, harsh, stony, wiry, soft, slimy – what disobliging epithets, and yet he is in love with the scene. And the love becomes explicit in a prose footnote which he appends to the passage.

> Such is the vegetation of the fen when it is at a small distance from the ocean; and in this case, there arise from it effluvia strong and peculiar, half saline, half putrid, which would be considered by most people as offensive and by some as dangerous; but there are others to whom singularity of taste or association of ideas has rendered it agreeable and pleasant.

The sights and the sounds are not beautiful, the smells are putrid, yet through the singularity of his taste and the associations they bring to him he loves them and cannot help loving them. For he had the great good luck to belong to a particular part of England and to belong to it all his life.

This attraction for the Aldeburgh district, combined with that strong repulsion from it, is characteristic of Crabbe's uncomfortable mind. Outwardly he did well for himself, married money and ended up as a west country pluralist. Inwardly he remained uneasy, and out of that uneasiness came his most powerful poems. It is natural to remember Wordsworth in connection with him. They were contemporaries, and they had this in common, that they were regional and that their earliest impressions were the most durable. But there the resemblance between them ends. Wordsworth – his superior genius apart – had a power of harmonising his experiences which was denied to Crabbe. He could encircle them with the sky, he could overawe them with tremendous mountains. Crabbe remains down amongst them on the flat, amongst pebbles and weeds and mud and driftwood, and within earshot of a sea which is no divine ocean. Thus based, he is capable of considerable achievements, and the contradictory impulses possessing him generated 'Peter Grimes'.

We know how this sombre masterpiece originated. When Crabbe was trying to be a doctor he came across an old fisherman who had had a succession of apprentices from London and a sum of money with each. The apprentices tended to disappear and the fisherman was warned he would be charged with murder next time. That is the meagre material upon which a poet's imagination worked. According to Edward Fitzgerald – who was a persistent student of Crabbe – the fisherman's name was Tom Brown. Anyhow, he is transformed into Peter Grimes.

The poem occurs in the series of 'The Borough,' which was written for the most part away from Aldeburgh, and finished there in 1809. As a narrative, it is one of the best of the series, and it is prefaced by quotations from *Macbeth* and *Richard III* which fix the emotional atmosphere and warn us that the murdered apprentices will live again. It opens with a father-motive; like Crabbe himself, Peter Grimes hates his own father – a pious old fisherman who makes him go to church – and breaks away from him abusively, on one occasion striking him on the head and felling him. Murder is not done, but the wish to murder has been born.

> The father groan'd 'If thou art old' said he,
> 'And hast a son, thou wilt remember me.' [XXII, 28-9]

Peter was indeed to beget sons, though not in the flesh. For the present he gets drunk, and when his father passes away, indulges in maudlin grief. It is a prelude to the main tragedy.

Freed from control, the young fisherman proposes to enjoy life – 'the life itself' he has called it exultantly – and gambles and drinks. But money is required for such joys, so he develops into a poacher and trespasser, a rustic Ishmael. Then come the sadistic lines:

> But no success could please his cruel soul
> He wish'd for one to trouble and control;
> He wanted some obedient boy to stand
> And bear the blow of his outrageous hand;
> And hoped to find in some propitious hour
> A feeling creature subject to his power, [XXII, 53-8]

and the first of the apprentices arrives, a product of the eighteenth-century workhouse system. Everyone knows he is being mishandled and starved, no one protects him,

> and some on hearing cries
> Said calmly 'Grimes is at his exercise' [XXII, 77-8]

– a phrase which is effectively introduced into *Peter Grimes* the opera.

Thus lived the lad in hunger, peril, pain,
His tears despised, his supplications vain:
Compelled by fear to lie, by need to steal,
His bed uneasy and unblessed his meal,
For three sad years the boy his torture bore,
And then his pains and trials were no more. [XXII, 89-94]

The second apprentice follows, also with premium, and he too dies. Peter's explanation is that he was playing on the main mast at night, fell into the well where the catch was kept and hit his head. The jury exonerate him. The third apprentice is a delicate well-mannered child, who rouses the townsfolk to pity and charity and whom Peter dares not beat too hard. He disappears during a voyage at sea. Peter had his fish and wanted to sell it in the London market. They encountered a storm, the boat leaked, the boy fell ill and before Peter could make harbour both the fish and the boy had died. Such anyhow was Peter's account. But

The pitying women raised a clamour round
And weeping said 'Thou hast thy prentice drown'd.'
[XXII, 153-4]

The mayor forbade him to hire any more apprentices (as in the opening of the opera) and none of his neighbours would help him, so henceforward he carried on his trade alone, and melancholy invades him.

Now begin the depths, and I would add the flats of the poem – using 'flat' in no derogatory sense, but to indicate the glassy or muddy surface upon which the action now proceeds and through which at any moment something unexpected may emerge. Nothing is more remarkable, in the best work of Crabbe, than the absence of elevation. As a preacher, he may lift up his eyes to the hills. As a poet he was fascinated by

The bounding marsh-bank and the blighted tree;
The water only, when the tides were high,
When low, the mud half-cover'd and half dry;
The sun-burnt tar that blisters on the planks,
And bank-side stakes in their uneven ranks;
Heaps of entangled weeds that slowly float,
As the tide rolls by the impeded boat. [XXII, 174-80]

That is what attracts him – flatness – and upon it the most tragic of his poems deploys. The idea of regeneration, so congenial to Wordsworth and the Lake District, does not appeal to this son of the estuary. Those who sin on the lines of Peter Grimes must sink and sink – incapable ever of remorse, though not of fear, incapable of realising the sun except as a blistering heat, and incapable of observing the stars.

When tides were neap, and, in the sultry day,
Through the tall bounding mud banks made their way,
There anchoring, Peter chose from man to hide,
There hang his head . . .
Here dull and hopeless he'd lie down and trace
How sidelong crabs had scrawl'd their crooked race
Or sadly listen to the tuneless cry
Of fishing gull or clanging golden-eye . . .
He nursed the feelings these dull scenes produce,
And loved to stop beside the opening sluice . . .[9]

The hanging of the head, the dullness, the nursing of dullness, the lying down motionless in a motionless boat, the dreary contemplation of nature in her trickling exhaustion, the slow downward bending paralysis of the once active man – they present what the poet too had experienced and the clergyman had combated or ignored. They spring from the attraction and from the repulsion exercised on Crabbe by the surrounding scenery, from the dual feeling which I analysed earlier.

We must consider Crabbe's sensitiveness to dreams in a moment – we are not quite in the world of dreams yet. Peter is still sane and awake. The only sign of abnormality is that he avoids three particular places in the estuary of the Alde; when near them he rows away whistling until they are out of sight. It would seem that here and there the surface of the water is thinner than elsewhere, more liable to be broken from below. He becomes a solitary, seeks men and curses them, and they curse him and he retires to his boat. For a whole winter no one sees him. Next summer, he is afloat as before, but no longer fishing. He is gazing, hypnotised by the three places in the stream. 'Dost thou repent?' he is asked. The words have a crystallising effect and shatter him. Quitting his boat, he goes raving mad, rushes over the countryside and is caught and carried to the parish infirmary. Here, half nightmare, half vision, the story culminates. Grimes himself takes up the tale in the sedate eighteenth century couplets and the formal diction which Crabbe could not and perhaps did not desire to forgo.

'I'll tell you all,' he said, 'the very day
When the old man first placed them in my way:
My father's spirit – he who always tried
To give me trouble, when he lived and died –
When he was gone he could not be content
To see my days in painful labour spent,
But would appoint his meetings, and he made
Me watch at these, and so neglect my trade.

‘ ’Twas one hot noon, all silent, still, serene,
No living being had I lately seen;
I paddled up and down and dipp’d my net,
But (such his pleasure) I could nothing get, –
[A father’s pleasure, when his toil was done,
To plague and torture thus an only son!]
And so I sat and look’d upon the stream,
How it ran on, and felt as in a dream:
But dream it was not: No! – I fix’d my eyes
On the mid stream and saw the spirits rise:
I saw my father on the water stand,
And hold a thin pale boy in either hand;
And there they glided ghastly on the top
Of the salt flood, and never touch’d a drop:
I would have struck them, but they knew th’ intent,
And smiled upon the oar, and down they went.

‘Now, from that day, whenever I began
To dip my net, there stood the hard old man –
He and those boys: I humbled me and pray’d
They would be gone; – they heeded not, but stay’d:
Nor could I turn, nor would the boat go by,
But, gazing on the spirits, there was I:
They bade me leap to death, but I was loth to die:
And every day, as sure as day arose,
Would these three spirits meet me ere the close;
To hear and mark them daily was my doom,
And “Come,” they said, with weak, sad voices, “come.”
To row away, with all my strength I tried,
But there were they, hard by me in the tide,
The three unbodied forms – and “Come,” still “come,” they
cried. [XXII, 290-327]

‘There were three places, where they ever rose, –
The whole long river has not such as those –
Places accursed, where, if a man remain,
He’ll see the things which strike him to the brain;
And there they made me on my paddle lean,
And look at them for hours; – accursed scene!
When they would glide to that smooth eddy-space,
Then bid me leap and join them in the place;
And at my groans each little villain sprite
Enjoy’d my pains and vanish’d in delight.

‘In one fierce summer-day, when my poor brain
Was burning hot, and cruel was my pain,
Then came this father-foe, and there he stood
With his two boys again upon the flood:

There was more mischief in their eyes, more glee,
In their pale faces when they glared at me:
Still did they force me on the oar to rest,
And when they saw me fainting and oppress'd,
He, with his hand, the old man, scoop'd the flood,
And there came flame about him mix'd with blood;
He bade me stoop and look upon the place,
Then flung the hot-red liquor in my face;
Burning it blazed, and then I roar'd for pain,
I thought the demons would have turn'd my brain.

'Still there they stood, and forced me to behold
A place of horrors – they can not be told –
Where the flood open'd, there I heard the shriek
Of tortured guilt – no earthly tongue can speak:
"All days alike! for ever!" did they say,
"And unremitted torments every day" –
Yes, so they said' – But here he ceased, and gazed
On all around, affrighten'd and amazed;
[And still he tried to speak, and look'd in dread
Of frighten'd females gathering round his bed;]
Then dropp'd exhausted, and appear'd at rest,
Till the strong foe the vital powers possess'd;
Then with an inward, broken voice he cried,
'Again they come,' and mutter'd as he died. [XXII, 338-75]

Crabbe is explicit on the character of Peter Grimes, and appends an interesting note. 'The mind here exhibited is one untouched by pity, unstung by remorse and uncorrected by shame.' And he shrewdly observed that 'no feeble vision, no half-visible ghost, not the momentary glance of an unbodied being nor the half audible voice of an invisible one would be created by the continual workings of distress on a mind so depraved and flinty.' Grimes is tough, hard and dull, and the poet must be tough with him, tougher than Shakespeare had to be with Macbeth, who possessed imagination. He must smash him up physically with penury, disease and solitude, and then place indubitable spectres in his path. Physical sufferings have their effect on any nature:

and the harder that nature is, and the longer time required upon it, so much the more strong and indelible is the impression. This is all the reason I am able to give why a man of feeling so dull should yet become insane, and why the visions of his distempered brain should be of so horrible a nature.

The poet sees his literary problem very clearly. A sensitive Grimes would mean a different poem. He must make him a lout, normally impervious to suffering, though once suffering starts it is likely to take a strange form.

Grimes in a normal state would be inarticulate. He can only address us effectively through nightmares, and skilful use is made, at the close, of that dream state with which Crabbe was himself too familiar for his own happiness. He recognised its value for his work. He once told Lady Scott, Sir Walter's wife, 'I should have lost many a good bit, had I not set down at once things that occurred in my dreams,'[10] and he kept a lamp and writing material by his bedside in order to record them before they were forgotten. Many of them were unpleasant. He suffered himself from a recurrent one, induced perhaps by opium. He would dream that he was teased by boys who were made of leather so that when he beat them they felt nothing. 'The leather lads have been at me again,' he would remark in fatigued tones at the rectory breakfast table.[11] Dreams of all types occur in his work. 'The World of Dreams' and 'Sir Eustace Grey' are terrifying. There is a poignant one at the close of 'The Parting Hour' where a desolate man dreams that his wife and children are with him in an enchanting tropical land. And there is a nightmare, rivalling Grimes' in terror and exceeding it in subtlety, where an imprisoned highwayman, condemned to death for murder, dreams that he is innocent and is walking in exquisite weather down to the sea with the girl he loves, and with his sister. The three young people pass through the lanes and over the sheep walk, 'Where the lamb browses by the linnet's bed,' cross the brook and behold

The ocean smiling to the fervid sun –
The waves that faintly fall and slowly run –
The ship at distance and the boats at hand:
And now they walk upon the sea-side sand,
Counting the number and what kind they be,
Ships softly sinking in the sleepy sea. [XXIII, 311-16]

On it flows, with a gentleness and sensuousness unusual with Crabbe, in order that the awakening may be the more terrible. They admire

those bright red pebbles that the sun
Through the small waves so softly shines upon:
And those live lucid jellies which the eye
Delights to trace as they swim glittering by;
Pearl-shells and rubied starfish they admire,
And will arrange above the parlour-fire –
Tokens of bliss –

Then the nightmare asserts itself, the surface is broken:

Oh! horrible! a wave
Roars as it rises – save me, Edward! save!

She cries: – Alas! the watchman on his way
Calls and lets in – truth, terror, and the day! [XXIII, 323-32]

This famous passage is more dramatic and more sensitive than anything in 'Grimes'. More human values are involved, so there is more to lose, the sudden reversal in fortune is only too typical of sleep, and the wave joins the horrors of imagination to those of fact. We are back in the prison which we had forgotten. Truth re-establishes itself, the more relentless for its withdrawal when the criminal walked with those he had loved and lost.

As for Peter Grimes. He has gone to hell and there is no doubt about it. No possibility of mercy intervenes. A simple rough fisherman over whom some would have sentimentalised, he is none the less damned, the treacherous flatness of the estuary has opened at last. He will sink into the fire and the blood, the only torments he can appreciate. His father has brought him to disaster – that is his explanation, and the father-motive which preluded the tragedy has re-emerged. To push the motive too hard is to rupture the fabric of the poem and to turn it into a pathological tract, but stressed gently it helps our understanding. The interpretations of Freud miss the values of art as infallibly as do those of Marx. They cannot explain values to us, they cannot show us why a work of art is good or how it became good. But they have their subsidiary use: they can indicate the condition of the artist's mind while he was creating, and it is clear that while he was writing 'Peter Grimes' Crabbe was obsessed by the notion of two generations of males being unkind to one another and vicariously punishing unkindness. It is the grandsire–grandson alliance against the tortured adult.

The other motive – also to be stressed cautiously – is the attraction-repulsion one. Peter tries to escape from certain places on the stream, but he cannot, he is always drifting back to them. Crabbe is always drifting back in the spirit to Aldeburgh. The poet and his creation share the same inner tension, the same desire for what repels them. Such parallels can often be found between the experiences of a writer, and the experiences of a character in his books, but the parallels must be drawn lightly by the critic, for the experiences have usually been transformed out of recognition and the moral climate changed. To say that Crabbe is Peter Grimes would make that prosperous clergyman indignant and would be false. To say that Crabbe and Grimes share certain psychological tensions might also make him indignant, but it would be true.

And now let us consider *Peter Grimes* the opera; or rather the libretto, for we shall not be much concerned with its music.

The circumstances of its creation are remarkable. The composer, Benjamin Britten, a Suffolk man, was away in the United States, and read there with feelings of nostalgia the poems of Crabbe. They recalled his own country to him, they inspired him, and commissioned by the American conductor, Koussewitzky, he wrote the opera. It has been accepted as a great work; it has become a national possession and been performed all over the world, and it is a work for which I myself have deep affection.

Now since it bears the same title as the poem people often assume that it is Crabbe set to music. This is not the case. The opera diverges widely from its original, and it is interesting to examine the changes which the composer and his librettist, Mr Montagu Slater, have thought fit to make. They had every right to make them. A composer is under no obligation to stick to his original; his duty is to be original himself. Sometimes he chooses to stick. Verdi's *Otello*, for instance, follows Shakespeare closely – the only addition being the credo introduced for Iago. Bizet's *Carmen*, on the other hand, diverges from Prosper Mérimée's story of the same name, and Donizetti's *Lucia di Lammermoor* owns only the wildest obligations to Sir Walter Scott.

The plot of *Peter Grimes* and the character of its hero are closely interwoven. The curtain rises on the trial of Peter for murdering an apprentice. The scene is the Moot Hall, and the date is 1830 – about fifty years later than the presumable date for the action of the poem. Peter is let off with a warning and we gather that he was innocent. Ellen Orford, the schoolmistress – who is introduced, with much alteration, from another poem – believes in him, and he hopes to make good and marry her; he hates being an outcast. Then the scene changes to the beach and to that music of the work-a-day sea which always brings tears into my eyes, it is so lovely, the townsfolk gather, the pleasant time-serving rector (borrowed from another poem) passes, Auntie and her dubious if desirable nieces appear out of another poem at the entrance of the Boar. Peter cannot get help with his boat, people shun him, but he hears of a possible apprentice in the Ipswich workhouse, and Ellen goes off to fetch the boy. The weather turns to storm and the scene to the interior of the Boar. There, in a terrific moment, Peter bursts in on the riotous company. There is silence and he meditates aloud on the Great Bear, the Pleiades, the impossibility of deciphering fate upon the revolving sky. He is revealed as the exception, the poet. The uproar resumes, Ellen enters with the new apprentice, and Peter takes him 'home' amongst cries of derision.

'Home' is an upturned boat on the edge of a cliff. Much has happened by the time we reach it – much gossip about Peter's brutality and some evidence of it. The ill-assorted pair enter – the boy terrified, Peter now irritable, now gentle, trying to make friends, dreaming of marriage with Ellen. The neighbours are heard approaching to look into the rumours of cruelty. Peter, enraged, hurries the boy off to their fishing, pushes him out through the cliff door, he slips, falls, and is killed. The next act is a manhunt; there is evidence of murder, voices shout through the fog. Peter realises that all is up. He launches his boat, sails out into the darkness in it, and sinks it. The new day begins and with it the music of the work-a-day sea. Someone sights a sinking boat, but it is too far off to be rescued or identified, and no one is interested, and all is as if nothing had ever been. The chorus gathers, the curtain falls slowly, the opera is over.

It amuses me to think what an opera on Peter Grimes would have been like if I had written it. I should certainly have starred the murdered apprentices. I should have introduced their ghosts in the last scene, rising out of the estuary, on either side of the vengeful greybeard, blood and fire would have been thrown in the tenor's face, hell would have opened, and on a mixture of *Don Juan* and the *Freischütz* I should have lowered my final curtain. The applause that follows is for my inward ear only. For what in the actual opera have we? No ghosts, no father, no murders, no crime on Peter's part except what is caused by the far greater crimes committed against him by society. He is the misunderstood Byronic hero. In a properly constituted community he would be happy, but he is too far ahead of his surroundings, and his fate is to drift out in his boat, a private Viking, and to perish unnoticed while work-a-day life is resumed. He is an interesting person, he is a bundle of musical possibilities, but he is not the Peter Grimes of Crabbe.

You remember the words in which Crabbe describes his hero. He is hard and dull, flinty, impervious to sensations, and it was a problem to Crabbe to make such a character suffer. 'The mind here exhibited is one untouched by pity, unstung by remorse, and uncorrected by shame.' And he gazes downward. Whereas Grimes in the opera is sensitive, touched by pity, stung by remorse, and corrected by shame, he needs no apparitions to remind him of his errors and he lifts up his eyes to the stars. We leave him with the knowledge that it is society who sinned, and with compassion.

The community is to blame. That is one implication of the opera, and Mr Montagu Slater in his introduction[12] suggests that the implication is to be found in Crabbe himself and that the poet-clergyman was ahead of his times. And the date of the action is put forward into 1830, the year of revolution, and extracted from the placid eighteenth century where it was originally embedded. There is benefit in this operatically, but it cannot be justified from Crabbe. Crabbe satirised society. He did not criticise it. Doctrinally he was a Tory parson, equally averse to idleness and to enthusiasm, and he ascribed human miseries to human frailties and to fate. As his biographer Huchon remarks, 'he had nothing of the radical or rebel in him. To make him a sort of early Cobbett is to take a strangely mistaken idea of his character and his ideas . . . He remained essentially bourgeois.'[13] The implication of a social problem combines with the changes in the action and the transformation of Grimes' character to make the opera very different from the poem. The first time I heard it, this worried me rather. I knew the poem well, and I missed its horizontality, its mud. I was puzzled at being asked by Grimes to lift up my eyes to the stars. At the second hearing my difficulty disappeared, and I accepted the opera as an independent masterpiece, with a life of its own.

It is time to leave both the opera and the poem behind. I would like in conclusion to go beyond them and revert to the obscure person, who lived at Aldeburgh about two hundred years ago, and whose name was perhaps Tom Brown. He got apprentices from London, they kept disappearing, and he was warned. That is all we know. But he caught the attention of a young surgeon who afterwards specialised in poetry and turned him into Peter Grimes. Two centuries pass. A young musician out in America reads 'Peter Grimes'. It catches his attention, and inspires him to create an opera. Is that how works of art are born? Do they all depend on a Tom Brown? No, they depend on the creative imagination which will find a Tom Brown somewhere or other, and will accrete round him until he is transformed. So I do not suggest that Aldeburgh need raise a statue to this obscure and unattractive citizen. Still the fact remains that he happens to be genesis in the whole affair. He is the first step in a series of creative events which has produced your Festival, and if he could ever see anything and if he can see anything now he is feeling surprised.

2 *Montagu Slater (1902–1956): who was he?*

An annotated interview (1981) with Enid Slater, with interpolations from Christopher Isherwood, Bridget Kitley (née Slater), Peter Pears, Eric Crozier and Kenneth Green

DONALD MITCHELL

Montagu Slater occupies a paradoxical position in the Britten landscape. He was the librettist of *Peter Grimes*, the opera which established Britten as a leading musical dramatist of the century on the international stage; and yet we know less about him than almost any other of Britten's librettists.

This annotated interview represents a first attempt at documenting the gifted and unusual man who played an important role in Britten's creative life, not only at the time of *Grimes* but in the immediately preceding decade. It is indeed the evolution and continuity of the relationship between about 1935 and 1945 that I wish to emphasise and untangle. I should like most warmly to thank Slater's widow, Mrs Enid Slater, herself a noted photographer, for her willing collaboration.

Slater was a prolific writer and active in many spheres, as novelist, poet, propagandist, journalist, dramatist, film-scripter, critic and editor. This is not the place for the systematic survey which his output clearly warrants; I would only mention his association with, and for a time, editing of, the *Left Review*. This influential journal, published from October 1934 to May 1938, could be described as one of the most serious – not to say earnest – centres of the literary and dramatic activities of the Left which characterised the thirties: it was closely associated with *Left Theatre* and *Left Revue*, which are also mentioned in the following interview. In assessing the posture taken by the *Left Review* in its early years, Stuart Laing discusses the term 'reportage' as used in a review by Stephen Spender, and comments: '"Reportage" was here defined [by Spender] in terms of a naturalistic style of *presentation* rather than of "things as they are" in the sense of historical accuracy. It is a question of *realism* as a style, not, pre-eminently, of giving the verifiable facts, although clearly these might go together.'[1] '*Realism* as a style' might be said adequately and fairly to sum up an over-riding trend in Slater's aesthetic, a trend he believed in and helped to create in his own literary environment. It was an aesthetic that belonged particularly to the thirties. *Grimes*, of course, belongs to the post-war forties, and the music, self-evidently, transformed – or transcended – the work and the aesthetic of the librettist. Nonetheless, '*realism* as a style' remained, I am convinced, a potent and influential force, a legacy – in the very person of Slater – from the thirties and one that made its own powerful appeal to the realistically minded composer of *Peter Grimes*. Without the past that Slater represented for Britten, some highly characteristic and telling features of the opera would not have taken the shape they did.

I should like to thank Mr Christopher Isherwood, Mrs Bridget Kitley (née Slater), Mr Kenneth Green, Sir Peter Pears, Mr Eric Crozier and Mr Leonard Thompson for allowing the use of their memories and documents to amplify the interview which follows.

DONALD MITCHELL: I wonder, for a start, if you could tell me a little about your husband's life. What were his circumstances? What family was he born into, and so on?

ENID SLATER: Montagu's family came from the north of England, from Cumbria. Millom is by the sea, but was a coal-mining town. His father was the village postmaster and also had a tailor's shop. It was a big corner shop, and the Slaters lived over it. Montagu had three sisters [Doris, Bessie and Rosa] and one younger brother [John]. The family was not hard-up, but they had to be careful. His father was a Methodist, and he was one of those awful Methodists – on Sunday he pulled all the blinds down, you weren't allowed to read anything but the Bible. I went and stayed there [laughing], and it was ghastly. Montagu went to the local grammar school, got a scholarship to Magdalen, Oxford, and left home very thankfully. Then his sister, Rosa – who was also very bright – she left home too. He kept her for years, while she went through university and until she got a job.

DM: What did he make of Oxford?

ES: He did pretty well there.

DM: Did he read English?

ES: English and philosophy, I think. [Slater graduated in 1924.] Then he got a job, in Liverpool, which is where I met him. He was on the *Liverpool Post*, and we were both members of a very nice club for painters and writers and everyone with an interest in the arts. The club used to do very inexpensive lunches, everybody used it for meeting, and that's where I got to know Montagu well. My parents, I ought to explain, didn't come from the north, but my father was an ex-naval man and he was in charge of the port of Liverpool. Montagu had also joined the University Social Club – what you'd call a 'do-gooders' club' . . .

DM: . . . a kind of welfare organisation?

ES: It ran a youth club, for example.

DM: That, in those days, was a form of social work?

ES: It was, yes.

DM: So he became aware of the problems of the unemployed, of young people, and so on?

ES: Yes. Montagu got well into that. Then he got a job on the *Morning Post* in London [in 1928] and I used to go up to see him, and return to Liverpool. He lived with a painter friend of his in Fitzroy Street, I think it was, off Charlotte Street.

DM: Who was that? Do you remember?

ES: Carl Thompson. Montagu knew a lot of London painters. Montagu knew our next-door neighbour, who died the other day, Claude Rodgers . . . [James] Boswell [who was also closely associated with the *Left Review*] . . . oh lots of them, you know, the people of that time, the Euston Road Group: Montagu knew them all. He was very interested in painting. Then, when we got married, we lived in a small flat at the top of a large Georgian house in Primrose Hill. Later, we had to have my sister-in-law [Rosa] with us, so we moved to a larger house in Haverstock Hill. By then we'd had one child and Montagu was with the Sunday *Observer*: he was with them for ages . . .

DM: As a reporter or features writer?

ES: He was writing a lot of features, and, when there wasn't anything particular they wanted him for, just routine journalism.

DM: Was this something he had wanted to do when he came down from university?

ES: Oh yes, yes. He wanted to write, he always wanted to write. But he knew he couldn't just write and not earn a living. He much enjoyed being on the *Observer*. Then he accepted quite a good offer from the *Daily Express*. But he didn't like that at all. So he went on to the *New Statesman* to do the drama for them, and he did that for some time. But those were occasional contributions because by then Montagu was freelancing. The rest of the time he was on *Reynolds News* – long gone now.

DM: The Sunday Co-op paper?

ES: Yes. It was very left in its views.

DM: If you took the *Daily Herald* in the week, you might take *Reynolds News* on Sunday?

ES: Yes. It wasn't a bad paper. Indeed, it had an outstanding cartoonist who became a great friend of ours, Carl Giles, who's now on the *Express*. And Montagu was working for *Reynolds News* when war broke out.

DM: Doing what? General features?

ES: He was sub-editing, the whole time. And then still doing drama for any publication that would accept work from him.

DM: That takes us up to 1939.

ES: Yes, we had a cottage in Princes Risborough, in Buckinghamshire. Because Montagu's father had died, his mother came and lived there. We bought a cottage, to be near her, because we were all very fond of her – luckily so, because it came in very handy when war broke out. We kept our flat in Hampstead and moved the children to my mother-in-law's.

DM: Can I ask you more about the pre-war days, when your husband was very much committed to left-wing theatre, to left-wing politics. When did his political interest start? Was that at Oxford, or later?

ES: I think at Oxford, yes. He was certainly very left-wing when I knew him first in Liverpool.

DM: Was he a member of the Communist Party?

ES: Not then.

DM: But he joined the Party?

ES: Oh yes, he did. [Probably in 1927, the year after the General Strike.]

DM: And he remained a member?

ES: He remained a member. I was surprised because I didn't agree with him, but we didn't fight over it. We agreed to disagree. I think he joined about the time he moved to the *Express*. He certainly carried a card. And occasionally he used to send things in to the *Daily Worker*, as it used to be called in those days. When we were in Hampstead, which was the period you're interested in – that would be from 1930 onwards – we were in a house, we had a maisonette. It was awfully nice, right up by the Heath. And there used to be lots of 'cells' – that's what they called them then – and the house was always full of Party members. I never liked them. Couldn't get on with them at all, with a few exceptions. It was then that Montagu was working on and off for Crown Films.

DM: I think you mean the GPO Film Unit?

ES: I can't remember which was which.

Fig. 2: Princes Risborough, *c* 1942–3: Montagu Slater with his daughters (left to right) Bridget, Carol and Anna, photographed by Enid Slater

DM: The Crown Film Unit was a later development, I think. It grew out of the GPO Film Unit and during the war made propaganda films for the Ministry of Information. But before the war the GPO Film Unit had made documentaries – films like *Coal Face* and *Night Mail*, films that Britten and Auden worked on together. In fact, your husband too did something for the GPO Film Unit?

ES: Yes, he did. I know he worked on *Coal Face*, and another film. Because that was where he met Ben, who was looking after the sound effects and music. Montagu was terribly intrigued because Ben would shake chains, persuade some sort of music out of them.

DM: Britten certainly had an extraordinary facility for putting to musical use whatever was lying around the studio.

ES: Montagu brought Ben home with him – Ben was then living with Beth [the younger of his two sisters] in, I think, West End Lane [in fact, West Cottage Rd, NW2] – he brought Ben home with him for supper one night. You know, we both took to him so much – and he really was having quite a tough time. So he used to come back – come to the house – an awful lot. It was all very well living with a sister, but you know – and they're dears, I know them both, and they are awfully sweet – I think that he liked to get away; and Montagu would have tickets for the theatre, because he could get them free, and we'd all go to the theatre or the cinema. We saw quite a lot of him at that time. Then he and Montagu might work at night, and try out different ideas, different suggestions.

DM: Britten wrote quite a bit of incidental music before the war for some of your husband's plays.

ES: Yes.

DM: One of those plays was *Stay Down Miner*. [See Mitchell and Evans, *Pictures from a Life*, no. 91.] Do you remember anything about it? The circumstances in which it was written, or the performance? Did you go to the performance? And did it make an impression on you?

ES: Yes, it did. Oh yes, I was very impressed with it. I thought it was extremely good.

DM: Was it a protest against conditions in the pre-war mining industry?

ES: It was, yes. Because they were pretty dreadful. [*Stay Down Miner* was about the sit-ins in South Wales in 1935, hence its title. Eric Crozier suggests that G. W. Pabst's famous film about a mine disaster, *Kameradschaft* (1931), may have influenced Slater.] Montagu got to know quite a few miners in Millom – to his family's horror, because that wasn't the sort of thing that was done. So he knew quite a lot about mining. And for *The Brave Don't Cry* – do you remember that film? – he got hold of people in the coal-mining industry and went down mines and so on.

DM: What film was that?

ES: It was a film that he made with Phil [Philip Leacock], our son-in-law, about a mine in Scotland.

DM: Made after the war?

ES: Yes. Just after. They went and lived in the mining village and went down the mine for a month or more. They both became fascinated by the whole thing. It was more or less the same idea as before, you know, an exposure of the bad, terrible conditions. In those days, if there was a disaster, nobody was really organised to do much about it.

The Brave Don't Cry (1952), about a Scottish mine disaster, was made by Group Three, an organisation set up under the National Film Finance Corporation. One of its vice-presidents was the guiding spirit of British documentary film, John Grierson. Some of the ideas of Group Three, and indeed the character of some of its films, clearly relate to the ideals and practice of documentary and thus to the great pre-war days of the GPO Film Unit. As Basil Wright remarks in his history of film, *The Long View* (p. 334), Grierson's role in Group Three 'was seen to be as much a new extension of the documentary idea as Free Cinema. And, like Free Cinema, it didn't last . . . the Group Three experiment quietly faded.'

DM: Do you remember your husband working for groups like the *Left Revue*? That group's speciality was political satire, political cabaret, and so on, and your husband and Britten collaborated in contributions to some of the *Revue*'s shows. Any memories?

ES: No, I don't remember anything about that. I remember they did it. But I don't even remember the theatre.

I have not traced a single mention of *Left Revue* except in letters of Britten's from 1937 in which he variously refers to *Left Review*, *Left Revue* and *Left Theatre* without making much distinction between any of them; and probably there was none in his mind. It was *Left Theatre* which had produced Slater's *Stay Down Miner* in May 1936: André van Gyseghem in his invaluable contribution to *Culture and Crisis in Britain* describes Slater as 'about the only British writer of stature who was consistently writing for the new realistic theatre of social conscience and working-class interests' (p. 214). One might now interpret *Left Revue* as the Left's answer to C. B. Cochran's famous and opulent revues for the West End of the same period.

DM: Your husband and Britten were very busy deflating political pretensions and deceits and attacking . . .

ES: . . . they were, yes . . . they were at it all the time . . .

DM: . . . from a particular left-wing point of view. Baldwin, appeasement, rearmament: these were some of their local targets.

ES: Yes, they worked together an awful lot. They used to have rehearsals in the flat. I made myself scarce because the children were very young then and kept me pretty busy. But the rehearsals used to go on sometimes until quite late at night, when they were going through things, routines and so on. My husband played the piano very often. Sometimes Ben wanted to make noises or do something, so my husband played the piano, while he was making noises.

DM: Your husband was musical, then?

ES: Very. He played the flute too, very well. Oh yes, he was very keen on music. It was a great thing he had in common with Ben. And it was Ben who started one of my daughters off at the piano and she too is really very good, though she only does it for fun. He was marvellous with children. We owe Ben Bridget's start at the piano; and something else too. He would never let the children swear. And they don't swear to this day. You see, they never, never got over him ticking them off. They adored him. They've never forgotten him. The children can tell you much more about the things they used to do together. He always seemed to find a circus somewhere. When we came up to London, which we did occasionally, there might be a children's play on somewhere, even during the war, and he'd insist on taking them.

DM: Children responded, didn't they, to the child in Britten?

ES: They did, they used to *play* together. And even when they were being difficult he could sort them out in no time at all – it was no problem to him.

Bridget Kitley, née Slater, formerly Britten's piano pupil, proves her mother's point by kindly writing down for me her childhood memories of Britten. They show, charmingly, how much the Slater family must have meant to the composer – they clearly provided the kind of companionable family life that he so much enjoyed, perhaps because it reflected his own happy childhood – and at the same time that his own geniality could often alternate with darker, sharper moods. It would not have surprised Britten, I think, to learn that he had been so candidly observed by a child.

My sisters and I were always careful to be good girls when Ben came to stay. I was impressed by his unpredictability and his irritability. I was never sure when he would turn in a fractious fury or gently join us in a game. My mother was in loving awe of him and I was often irritated by her concern for him and her determination that he shouldn't be bothered by 'mosquitoes' (my sisters and me). Peter, the equable partner, was a constant. With him we always knew that we had a gigantic ally. I can remember Ben mostly in musical terms – which is fitting I suppose. Once I was playing 'sevens' against the side wall of our newly built pebble-dash house and did not know Ben was watching. When I got to the bit where the player has to bounce the ball off the wall and clap before it is caught, Ben came forward and asked if he could do it. His way was to clap after the ball hit the wall instead of simultaneously, as I had been doing. He was clapping, as it were, on an off-beat. This change of rhythm fascinated me and we both bounced and hummed and felt friendly again and peaceful. When I saw *Albert Herring* there was a moment when the children do this – 'Bounce me high / Bounce me low. . .' – and I was quite sure that this was from a musical note that he had made that day.

I can remember being stopped in mid-whistle by Ben before breakfast one morning and being asked to repeat what I had just done. I did my double whistle again and he tried to copy it. I was surprised and gratified that he found it quite hard – that I could do something that he couldn't and I only ten or whatever. He did master it eventually, having reversed our roles so that I was the teacher. Then I heard the whistling in the *Spring Symphony* and it felt like a secret dedication.

Much later – it must have been in 1946 because there was a rift between Ben and my father after that (something to do with my father's disapproval of Ben becoming, as he called it, a 'court musician') – we were having supper at Kent Terrace [Regent's Park, the Slaters' home], and Ben filled the wine glasses with water to make a complete – if off-key – scale when tapped by teaspoons. Ben conducted and we played (I think it was 'God Save the King'); and we, after having disciplined ourselves for a while, fell about laughing: my father in gasps as if it were forced out of his nose, my mother caught up in gales of smoker's cough, and my sisters and I in the paroxismic, abandoned, teenage way of laughter. And I think it was the same evening that Ben conducted his sneeze. Each person was allotted a 'hish', a 'hosh', a 'hash' and a 'rats'. Ben's conductor's arm fell and this giant's sneeze shook the kitchen.

I can remember St John's Wood, and Peter in the kitchen serenely making cauliflower cheese. Ben was playing Haydn and in a bad temper. I felt threatened by his black mood; and now it comes to me, I must have been quite small because the only place to hide was under the piano and his thunderous and probably impeccable playing was dangerously delicious.

Later, in St John's Wood – I must have been thirteen because I was having hopeless loves – I can remember feeling dowdy, overweight, sluggish, at odds with my body; and there was Marion Stein in red velvet, poised for a visit to a concert, and there were Ben and Peter, my composite love, leading her, so courtly, to a waiting taxi.

DM: Did you have much contact with Wystan Auden at all?

ES: At that time, quite a bit, because he was a friend; and Ben was a friend of Bill Coldstream [Sir William Coldstream, the painter] who was also a great friend of ours.

DM: Coldstream was another member of the GPO Film Unit team.

ES: He was. And Auden was often at the Coldstreams'. Several times he and I used to babysit for the Coldstreams together.

DM: Auden a *babysitter*?

ES: Well, the children were difficult and it took two of us to manage. Auden was very good, he really was. I liked him a lot. Oh yes, he was around all the time, more or less.

DM: Did you ever run into someone called Randall Swingler?

ES: Indeed, yes. His wife – Geraldine Peppin [the pianist] – died recently. One of the nicest people, she really was. I always liked Randall, very much. He and Montagu were great friends. They were in and out all the time.

DM: Would you say that Montagu and Randall Swingler – just to use him as an example – were members of a coherent, cohesive group of creative people?

ES: Oh yes, very much so. There was a real solidity among them, you know. [Swingler became editor of the *Left Review* in 1937. Britten set texts by him in *Advance Democracy* (1938) and *Ballad of Heroes* (1939).]

DM: Do you remember anything about the other Slater–Britten pre-war collaborations, apart from *Stay Down Miner*? An item that has interested me is *Pageant of Empire*, which was one of the *Left Revue* shows that I was telling you about. [Slater wrote a series of pageants for the Co-operative Movement, of which this may have been one. See also van Gyseghem.] Your husband wrote some words for it and Ben wrote the music. It was satirical in intent, anti-imperialist, anti-colonial and above all anti-war. But of course it was a relatively marginal theatrical enterprise. There were other, more important things . . .

ES: . . . for example, *Easter 1916*, about the Irish troubles . . .

DM: . . . that are still with us. Montagu would have been horrified, wouldn't he, by what's going on in Ireland now? And then were there not pieces for the puppet theatre, *The Seven Ages of Man* and *Old Spain*, for which Britten also wrote some incidental music? [These were performed by the Binyon Puppets at the Mercury Theatre, London, in 1938.]

ES: My husband was very keen on puppets. I know he did do quite a bit for them, but I don't remember the details. I have a horror of puppets, so I never went to see them. I don't know why, but I just can't look at them at all, which is stupid, because I'm sure they can be very good. But, you know, some people feel like that about mice, or spiders, or something. I feel that way about puppets. But I know Montagu felt differently.

DM: Could we move on to the outbreak of war in 1939? Was he surprised by that?

ES: No, no. He knew it was coming a long time off, and always said so. And that was why he thought it was a good idea for us to buy the cottage at Princes Risborough, three, four years before, because we knew it was coming.

DM: To get out of London?

ES: Get the children out, anyway. But I mean he wouldn't get out, except for weekends. He used to do firewatching on the roof of *Reynolds News*.

DM: So he felt committed to the war effort in some way?

ES: Oh yes. He did, I didn't. I did plane-spotting in the country, and that was about all.

DM: Did either of you – or both of you – have a view of Auden and Isherwood when they left England for America in 1939?

ES: Montagu was very upset. Very upset. He felt they shouldn't have done it.

DM: That it was in some sense a betrayal or a retreat?

ES: Yes. He felt very strongly about it.

DM: Did he feel the same about Britten and Peter Pears's departure, later the same year?

ES: Yes. Very strongly. I thought Ben was just being sensible, getting out of it quick. He felt as I did about it: that the whole thing was useless, a waste of time, a waste of lives, a waste of everything. Why not get away and go on working and do something worthwhile? But Montagu didn't agree, he felt very strongly about it.

DM: So there was some friction there?

ES: Yes, but it went.

DM: Did you hear from Britten and Pears in America? They kept in touch?

ES: Oh yes, regularly. The whole time.

DM: May I ask you two other questions? Were you aware of Peter's arrival on the scene as a factor affecting Ben's life and his relationship with other people?

ES: Very much so. Because I had known of – and in one case become involved in – some of Ben's other relationships. One relationship had got difficult before he went to America and I used to go and try and sort things out a bit. And when Peter came on the scene, I must say I was very relieved. I liked Peter at once. And I thought this relationship is right, you know, this is absolutely perfect.

DM: Why did you think that?

ES: I liked Peter so much and I knew he was right for Ben. He just was. Both my husband and I agreed that this was right, let's hope it lasts, while some of the other affairs, the ones my husband didn't know about, you know I could tell they were wrong, that they wouldn't work out. But Peter, yes.

DM: Did many women fall for Britten?

ES: [laughing] Oh yes, all over the place. I had to help him with that problem too, several times. He used to get terrified. 'Can I come round? So-and-so's chasing me.' He was terrified. Ben was so innocent, he never could think the worst of people, always the best, and that was fatal. Perhaps his charm was his undoing. We used to get violent SOSs and he used to rush down to Risborough when we were there, or rush round to Hampstead when we were there, hiding from whoever it may have been. Oh dear, it was very funny, it really was.

DM: This 'innocent' aspect of Ben's character, I'm sure it was there; but by friends like Wystan Auden it was felt to be not so much innocence as reserve, aloofness, an unwillingness to involve himself physically in his relationships: that he held himself back.

ES: I think that was the case.

DM: Was that your impression of Britten's relationships with whomever he was bound up with at a particular moment? Do you think these were 'affairs' in the sense that we would understand the word, or were they just very intense friendships?

ES: Do you mean with men or women?

DM: With men.

ES: Until Peter arrived on the scene. Before that he didn't want to get involved. His work came before everything, and he felt that it would be detrimental if he got too involved with one sex or the other. He just didn't want to be landed with this situation, you know what I mean. He didn't have a feeling strong enough to make him commit himself, which he was to do, to Peter.

DM: Were you and your husband during these years particularly conscious of Britten's homosexuality?

ES: Well, we knew he was homosexual, yes. And we knew Wystan was, and we knew Isherwood was. I don't think we ever thought much about it, we just took it for granted. I mean Bill Coldstream wasn't, and MacNeice wasn't, and various people weren't. I don't think we ever discussed it. It was just one of those things, you know.

DM: Were there patterns of behaviour that particularly brought Britten's homosexuality to your attention?

ES: Oh no, no. He was very discreet about all his relationships, very. Again, until Peter arrived, and then it was different.

DM: Because they fell in love?

ES: Oh yes, definitely, quite definitely. And I think everybody, all his friends who wished him well, were thankful, because a lot of them didn't know about the other problematic relationships but could sense that he was searching around a bit, that he wanted some sort of stable relationship in his life. And then I think the thing was that his mother died, you know [in 1937]. That upset him quite incredibly much. He could not get over it. It took him an awfully long time. He was a bit at sea after that, for quite a while. He hadn't got anything stable: I mean, he'd got his two sisters and they were fine and very supportive and good, but it was not the same. Ben missed his mother appallingly, he really did. He used to talk about her such a lot. She sounded such a nice person, too.

DM: I take it that your husband kept on working as a writer during the war?

ES: He never stopped.

DM: How old was he? Was he eligible for conscription?

ES: Montagu was called up and he went off to some camp or other. He was there for a day and they threw him out, hastily. He always had a bad digestion. He wasn't a very strong man ever, and I think they thought with his age and the various ills he had, he'd be no good to anybody, so he came back almost at once. I think he was quite sorry. I wasn't, but I think he was.

DM: The war continued; and then in 1942 Britten returned because he felt he couldn't stick it out any more in the United States.

ES: And by then he'd had the *Peter Grimes* idea.

In fact in the very first instance Britten had invited Christopher Isherwood to collaborate with him (and Peter Pears) on the libretto for *Peter Grimes*. Isherwood had left England for the USA with Auden four months before the departure of Britten and Pears on the same journey and was now resident there. The approach to Isherwood makes perfect sense in the context of Britten's collaboration with him and Auden in the pre-war Group Theatre days in London (on *The Ascent of F6*, and

On the Frontier) – a characteristic example of his turning to friends from the past who had the appropriate experience to participate in a new project. (His *not* turning to Auden can be understood in the light of the unsuccessful first performance of their *Paul Bunyan* in New York in 1941 and the difficulties Britten had begun to encounter with Auden in his role as librettist.) The same attachment to the past would of course have been responsible for the later approach to Slater, again a valued and above all a familiar collaborator from the thirties.

I am very much obliged to Christopher Isherwood for generously allowing me here to reproduce the full text of the letter in which he responded finally and negatively to Britten's suggestion that he should take on the libretto of *Grimes*. That he remarks to Britten on a collaboration 'with you and Peter' is a significant indication of how much pre-planning, selection and rejection had already been carried out by Britten and Pears at this early stage in the evolution of the opera. As Pears remarked in his broadcast on *Grimes*, 'Birth of an Opera', 'by the time we came back to London, the whole story of *Peter Grimes* as set in the opera was already shaped and it simply remained to call in a librettist to write the words'.

834 Buck Lane. Haverford. Pennsylvania.
February 18. [1942]

My dearest Benjy,

Thank you for your letter. I'm sorry, but I don't see any possibility of collaborating with you and Peter on the PETER GRIMES libretto. I have thought it over carefully: it surely is good melodramatic material, and maybe something more than that: the setting is perfect for an opera, I should think. But the real point is that I am quite sure I shan't have the time for such work for months or maybe years ahead; and frankly, the subject doesn't excite me so much that I want to *make* time for it; I mean, to use every available spare moment out of a life like the one I lead at present, or in a work camp, or somewhere even more strenuous. Also, I doubt very much if collaborators can work so far apart as we seem likely to be. So let's drop it, regretfully but finally.

I wish we weren't going to be parted by so much water and so many U-boats. Of course, I may quite possibly come to England; you never know. I don't have to say that I wish you both every kind of success and happiness. If you really leave within ten days and can't get down here, we shan't meet again; as I simply cannot leave right now. Glad you saw Harvey. Wish you could have seen more of and been more to him. Maybe you are the only one who could help.

God bless you both. I'll be thinking of you very often.

Crabbe returns under separate cover.

As always,
CHRIS

In 1981 – nearly forty years on – Isherwood added a gloss on his rejection of Britten's invitation and a clarifying word on 'Harvey':

How fortunate that I *didn't* attempt to write the opera! I was absolutely convinced that it wouldn't work. And, when I saw it on stage, I was astonished – I mean, of course, as a dramatic piece – I never doubted that Ben, as a composer, could rise to *any* occasion!

'Harvey' was a mutual friend – more mine than Ben's. The reference to him in my letter to Ben sounds overly dramatic – I don't think he was in any desperate difficulty. Anyhow, at that point in the war, nearly everybody had serious worries and problems.

DM: What do you remember of Britten's return? Did he write, do you remember, to tell you that he was coming back?

ES: Yes, he wrote and told us he was coming back and why, and Montagu got frightfully interested at once. It was the sort of thing that really roused him. So we were impatiently awaiting him, practically on the dockside.

DM: You heard about *Grimes* in advance of Britten's arrival at Liverpool?

ES: Oh yes, because he was full of it. He wrote to us about it, and he rushed down to Risborough, the second weekend he was home. The first weekend he spent with his sisters and then he came down to us and I couldn't get a word in edgeways for days. Ben and Montagu used to go for long walks, tramping together and talking the whole time. I never saw anything of him.

DM: So any feeling of discomfort that Ben had left for America . . .

ES: . . . had gone. I think that went when he was writing to us from the States. And you know Montagu was very fond of him, he really was.

DM: Was Montagu the older man?

ES: Yes, he was born in 1902.

DM: So he'd have been almost exactly eleven years older than Britten?

ES: Yes. But Montagu was awfully fond of him, always very fond of him, you know; and I think he missed him. I think half the trouble about his going to America was that Montagu was so cross that he was no longer about, you know. They really had got on so well.

DM: Did your husband feel that *Peter Grimes* was also an extension of his own work in the realist theatre? After all, the opera does have a strong social theme.

ES: That's why he liked doing the libretto so much. It was really the very thing for him. It was made to measure, as it were. Ben had bought the Old Mill at Snape and we used to go over from Risborough. It wasn't really that far. It was a lovely drive – we had a car. And we used to spend a long time there. They used to work together the whole day and then we'd go for a walk in the evening, because it was such lovely country round there. And I decided that Ben's garden needed attention. He was delighted and so we re-did the garden.

DM: While Britten got on with planning the opera?

ES: It was great fun. And he had a young nephew, Sebastian, who was the same age as my youngest daughter. My other two were at boarding school. It all worked awfully well.

DM: These were the occasions, no doubt, when you took your photographs of Britten by the marshes with Sebastian? [See Mitchell and Evans, no. 178; see also nos. 79-81, 90, 107-110, 179, 181.]

ES: We really enjoyed those visits.

DM: So the collaboration mainly worked through meetings, either at your cottage or at the Old Mill?

ES: One or the other. Every weekend they worked.

DM: How did your husband find working with Britten?

ES: They got on so well. There was never any trouble at all. Never. The only trouble came at the actual rehearsals – then there was a bit of trouble, not with Ben, not with Peter – Montagu was very fond of Peter, he got on with Peter awfully well – or with Joan Cross, but sometimes one of the other members of the cast wouldn't sing the words as Montagu wanted them. Ben often agreed with him – nine times out of ten he agreed with him – and the problem was straightened out. But I know several times that Montagu came back and said, 'It's no good, he won't sing it right.' And then Ben would come round and say, 'Well, let's work on it'; and they'd work on it, they'd work it out, and the next day it was all right. They worked hard, they really did; they never seemed to stop.

Eric Crozier, the producer of *Peter Grimes* in 1945, has vivid memories of his substantial participation in working meetings on the libretto in London, held perhaps as often as twice a week over a period of months. Slater, Crozier, Britten and sometimes Pears would forgather at St John's Wood High Street, where Britten and Pears were living, or at Kent Terrace, the Slaters' home, and after an evening meal there would be a four- to five-hour session in which the libretto was gone over line by line, scene by scene, and character by character, and suggestions for revisions were put to Slater and attempts made to persuade him to rewrite where necessary. Crozier recalls a largely silent, pipe-smoking Slater, not exactly unco-operative in the matter of revisions but (to use Crozier's own phrase) not showing 'active collaboration' either. As a result, those parts of the libretto that were found not to work when music rehearsals started were largely rewritten by Crozier, Britten and Pears. Something that may also have added to everybody's problems was Slater's method of working (at least at this time). He rose early and wrote first thing in the day, before leaving for his job. This meant that, for him, the long discussions into the night followed a very early start and a day at his office. It cannot always have been easy for him, with this schedule, to produce at a late hour great reserves of flexibility and improvisation.

DM: It was a very big work to get done. You don't remember any specific passages in the opera that were particularly difficult to get right? The mad scene, do you remember, when Grimes has his great solo cadenza, do you remember any special problems about that?

ES: No, I don't, I'm afraid. Sometimes Ben would come up with something that he thought wasn't right for some reason and then they would spend an entire weekend rewriting it. But I don't remember the precise passages. [See, however, Duncan, pp. 37-9 and 49, and below, p. 61.]

DM: It was a happy collaboration?

ES: Oh, very.

Peter Pears, in his broadcast interview about the making of *Grimes* in 'Birth of an Opera', recalls that the collaboration was not 'unhappy' but 'it certainly was tense, the whole situation'. In referring to what must have been Britten's impatient awaiting of revisions of the typescript draft of Slater's libretto (identified by Philip Brett as *La*, see chapter 3) – revisions which would have enabled the composer to progress with the music – Pears remarks that it turned out to be

> hard work one way and another because Montagu was not very prolific. He was a very slow writer and found it very difficult to produce what Ben wanted, so the actual work of the libretto was often well behind the work of the music, and [Ben] was really sort of writing music ahead and waiting for the words to come along by the next post and there were obviously tensions and things. Also Montagu was a busy man and hadn't got all of the hours of the day to work on an opera libretto.

That Slater's natural pace of invention was somewhat slower than Britten's seems to be well established; and undoubtedly he found it difficult at times to accept the kind of modifications to his text mentioned by Mrs Slater above and arrived at in the way she describes. The very fact that Slater published his text of *Peter Grimes* as a poem, independent of the opera libretto and free of the 'corruptions' imposed by the working conditions of the opera house, makes its own point. Slater had strong feelings about the integrity of his text as something distinct from the needs of the music, and Eric Crozier remembers one occasion when those feelings unmistakably erupted. It was a week or so before the first performance at Sadler's Wells, and in a nearby café at the Angel, Islington, surprise was expressed by Slater's collaborators (Britten, Pears, Crozier and Joan Cross) at his announced intention to publish as it were an alternative (and in some sense competing) text. Slater's response was uncharacteristically explosive – 'But this is *my* work, this is *my* work', he repeated, and banged the table to emphasise the point. It was almost the only occasion Crozier can recollect on which the normally phlegmatic Slater lost his temper. But whatever the tensions and frictions, the achievement far outweighs them; and indeed the disagreements sometimes led to a fruitful result. An example was the retention of the women's ensemble in Act II scene 1. Withdrawing his agreement to the loss of the quartet in a long letter (3 December 1944), from which Philip Brett quotes extensively (see chapter 3), Slater apologises to the composer for being 'so difficult and argumentative', and Britten may have found him so from time to time. Nonetheless, it was Slater's articulate doggedness that carried the day on this occasion. Without it, the opera might have lacked one of its finest inspirations.

DM: What about the actual first night, which proved to be a famous first night in English theatrical and operatic history?

ES: We all went, the children went, everybody went.

DM: The entire Slater family?

ES: We all went. It was fascinating, yes.

DM: Were you amazed at what the two of them had created? Had you heard a lot of it at the piano?

ES: I'd heard a lot of it at the piano. And one thing I was responsible for – the boy, the apprentice. They had terrible trouble getting a boy. There was quite a lot written for that boy, do you know? Words.

DM: Words?

ES: Yes, there were.

DM: You mean that at some stage Montagu wrote a spoken part for the boy?

ES: Yes, but they couldn't get a boy that pleased them both. For some reason there was always something that was the matter with him. So I got fed up. I lost my temper and said, 'For God's sake, make the boy a dumb role.' And they said, 'If we make him dumb, he needn't sing, need he?' But it only happened because I lost my temper. They'd been at it all day, and there are limits, you know. I apologised afterwards, but Ben said, 'It's one of the best ideas you have ever had.'

It is my belief that here Mrs Slater may have combined a number of recollections or incidents from different times.

For a start, it is clear that Britten and Pears had already been aware of the boy's role as something of a problem even at a very early planning stage. This is made clear in the course of a draft in Pears's hand of the proposed action of the opera (the 'Amityville' draft described early on in chapter 3), where he writes at the opening of what was then to have been Act II scene 2: 'Ellen with boy – Singing to him old stories – (*Boy is dumb – learnt for 1st time*). She pities him for not being able to speak – wants to take him to church . . .'. Making the boy as it were constitutionally dumb (not of course what Mrs Slater had in mind) was perhaps an ingenious way of securing and explaining the boy's silence and at one stroke getting rid of the necessity of finding a boy actor/singer, which must have seemed more of a problem in the 1940s than it might today. But this particular idea was not pursued, for which one is grateful. To cause the death, however inadvertently, of a *dumb* boy would have been to pile on the agony with a vengeance. First and foremost, Grimes would have been beyond anyone's sympathy. But there would have been other practical consequences: for example, we would have been denied the boy's chilling scream as he slips and falls down the cliff at the end of Act II.

From Slater's earliest drafts (see chapter 3, n. 6), however, it is clear that he considered that the boy might (or should?) speak (sing). In one of these the boy has a line, addressed to Ellen: 'When are you going to marry Peter Grimes?', which sufficiently indicates that for Slater at least the issue of his speaking (singing) or not was for a while an open one. Possibly Slater was as 'difficult and argumentative' about the apprentice as on some other occasions, in which case – since it is fairly clear what Britten and Pears had already decided in principle – it is not surprising that there were altercations.

But I believe them to have been altercations about the vocal role of the boy in which Mrs Slater so dramatically and usefully intervened (small wonder the composer was patently relieved), not arguments about the choice of boy for the part. There may have been difficulties about getting the right-looking (i.e. cowed) apprentice for later productions of the opera and perhaps it is these Mrs Slater recalls. For the first production, conventional auditions were not held. The original apprentice, Leonard Thompson, remembers being given 'voice lessons' by Herbert Scott, at the instigation of the producer, Eric Crozier – although, writes Thompson, 'as my voice was just beginning to break there were not many of them'; but Crozier thinks that these were not part of any preparation for the production of *Grimes* but belong to another and later period when he may have lent a helping hand to the first John in the further development of his career. (See also Mitchell and Evans, nos. 185, 187.)

DM: Did you expect – or Montagu – did you expect the opera to be as successful as it was, or were you surprised?

ES: Well, he was always a bit pessimistic, because so many of his other things had not been successful; and I think he took a very pessimistic view of the opera's chances. But he hoped, because he knew it was to date definitely the best thing he'd ever done, and he had a lot of faith in Ben. He knew how good Ben was, so he did have a certain amount of hope. But, you see, it was a funny, dark time in history to launch the opera, wasn't it?

DM: It was a very dark opera.

ES: Yes. So Montagu was terribly bothered. Well, we both were, but I was sure it was going to succeed. I kept on saying: 'This is absolutely something that will go on and on and on.' Montagu couldn't always believe that: I was certain.

DM: Did he come on stage, take a bow?

ES: Yes.

DM: Was he a very shy man?

ES: Yes, terribly.

DM: So it was agony for him to get on the stage?

ES: Ben had to pull him on. I'll never forget it. Oooh, he couldn't bear it. He was terribly shy with everybody.

DM: Was there a party after the first performance? Did you go off and celebrate?

ES: There was a small party [at the Savoy Hotel, given by Britten's publishers]. I think it went off all right; but I had the children with me, you see, and the youngest was quite small.

DM: Did you go to see the opera often?

ES: Practically every performance. In fact, I think it was every performance. I don't think we missed one. I go now when I can, but it's getting a bit expensive. The family go. They love it.

DM: What about some of the others who made major contributions to the first production of *Grimes*? I know you and your husband much liked Eric Crozier, the producer. But what about Kenneth Green, the designer? Do you remember him?

ES: Yes. Yes, I liked him, very nice, very talented. He used to be around quite a bit.

Kenneth Green was himself a Suffolk man. His father indeed had been a patient of Britten's father (who was a dentist in Lowestoft), but it was not until after Britten's return from the USA in 1942 that Green met the composer – in consequence of a chance meeting on Long Island between Britten and Green's son, Gordon, who was a wartime evacuee. Green and Britten got on well together and it seemed to the composer that here was a sympathetic personality with the necessary experience (Green had had some pre-war connections with Glyndebourne) with whom he might work on *Grimes*. The commission came after Green, at the instigation of Joan Cross, had designed *Così* for Sadler's Wells (the production in which Pears was Ferrando), which Green remembers as a practical test of his capabilities before he was finally asked to undertake *Grimes*.

Green sometimes stayed with Britten at the Old Mill at Snape while the opera was being composed. He recalls long walks during which the composer discussed his specific design needs and, above all, how Britten nagged him at a very early stage to be specific in a quite particular way:

He begs me to give some visual ideas about the look of the stage – just a rough idea! . . . Ben seemed helped by what visual vague scenery I conjured up . . . This was long before Eric Crozier really got down to brass tacks in St John's Wood High Street [Britten and Pears's London flat].

I reproduce here for the first time the sketch to which Green refers (Fig. 3). Our black and white reproduction, though it does not convey the delicacy of the colours of the original, admirably makes manifest the concreteness of what Green supplied. That this early sketch was soon superseded by designs more nearly related to the needs of the opera is neither here nor there: its significance rests in the immediate and pressing need the composer felt to have something visual in front of him while he was composing. To have the *locale* of *Grimes* made 'real' in this way was obviously an aid to Britten's invention and inspiration. (Beneath the sketch is a pencil lay-out of the stage for a scene from *Grimes*, though, as Green points out, the finished design bore little relation to it.)

Britten thought of *Grimes* as his most 'realistic' opera; and the work was indeed in part born out of the tradition of social realism with which Slater was so closely associated and of which he was a leading proponent. Green's preliminary sketch makes clear Britten's own preoccupation with the realistic, naturalistic aspect of *Grimes*; at the same time it provides further evidence of what we already know to be the case – the prime importance for Britten generally in his stage works of the relationship between his musical conception, the decor and the details of stage movement and action. (It is of some significance that on the first surviving draft of any part of the plot in Britten's own hand there exists at the top of the sheet an indication of the physical setting which is accompanied by a rudimentary but perfectly clear lay-out of the stage, see Fig. 4.) The extent of Green's commitment to getting every Suffolk detail right can be gauged from his recollection that the fishing nets for the original production were brought from Lowestoft. (See also Mitchell and Evans, nos. 182-7, 231, 235.)

DM: Let me just ask you one or two other things. Why do you think it was that Ben didn't go on working with your husband? They had this great success with *Peter Grimes* and then . . .

ES: I don't know. Montagu was awfully disappointed.

DM: Disappointed?

ES: Oh, frightfully disappointed. Because it was assumed by everybody that they would do two or three operas together, certainly two, and then Ben suddenly chose [Ronald] Duncan as his next librettist. He was terribly disappointed, he really was.

Fig. 3: Sketches for the first production (Sadler's Wells, 1945) by Kenneth Green. Above, the first sketch of the 'look of the stage' (see p. 42); below, an early lay-out of the stage

DM: Your husband was hurt by that? Did it colour their future relationship?

ES: Yes, it did. Oh yes, it did. There's simply no doubt about it. Montagu meanwhile had got another job. He had left *Reynolds News* and taken a job with the Ministry of Information [as Head of Scripts in the Film Division], which was then in Baker Street. We bought the lease of one of the Nash terrace houses in Regent's Park – you could do it easily then because the war hadn't finished. At the time Ben was living in St John's Wood High Street and sharing the flat with the Steins [Erwin Stein was then working at Boosey & Hawkes, the publishers of *Peter Grimes*] and so we saw him quite often. But it wasn't the same. You know, there wasn't that same pleasant, easy relationship, when he would just open the front door and shout out – and I always left it open for him – 'I'm here' or something of the sort. It felt all wrong.

DM: You can't tie this change of temperature to a specific conflict of opinion or personality?

ES: No, no. I think Ben felt bad about it in a way, and Montagu felt very bad about it, while I just didn't know what to do. I couldn't do anything for either of them.

DM: So after *Grimes*, rather ironically, after its enormous success, the old friendship lapsed?

ES: It went. Absolutely went, yes, there's simply no doubt about it. And it had been so good when Montagu had his first operation for cancer, when we were still in Risborough, just before the war. I was so shocked and worried when he'd been to Harley Street and come back again and the doctors had told him what it was. I was really terribly shaken, and I rang Ben up. And he said, 'I'm coming up, I'll come up and see you.' And he came straight away and stayed with me while they did the operation, because he knew I was in a state – he was in a state too – and he couldn't have been nicer, you know. It was such a pleasure to have somebody there that you could talk to – I couldn't talk to the children because I didn't want to worry them. He came back again when Montagu came out of hospital and was very shaky. It was a big abdominal operation: they had to remove most of the stomach. And Ben was terribly good: he did all the shopping and all the running about. He was absolutely wonderful.

DM: It was a rather sad ending of the relationship? There was the huge success of *Grimes* and then some intermittent, occasional meetings. But I suppose that when Britten finally went to live in Aldeburgh – gave up being a Londoner so to speak – the friendship ceased altogether?

ES: We used to see Ben at concerts. When he gave a concert, we always went, generally with Barbara and Beth [Britten's sisters], to see him. And I used to get news of him through Barbara. Because Barbara and I used to meet every week. We went to the Times Book Club to change our library books and then go and have a cup of coffee, every week at Yarner's in Upper Regent Street. Sometimes Barbara brought a message from Ben and I sent one back. That was all there was to it. Montagu never saw him at all.

DM: When Montagu died, you heard from Ben and Peter?

ES: Oh yes, both of them wrote. I let them know at once, and they both wrote very nice letters.

DM: How did your husband feel about Britten's meteoric career in the theatre, from *Grimes* onwards? How did he react to it?

ES: He was very pleased. He wanted him to be a success. He was delighted. Ben might have been a son, you know. Montagu was very proud of him – you'd think he'd invented him at times. But he really was awfully pleased about the success he had. That's why we went to all Ben's concerts. Montagu used to love him being successful.

DM: Was there a feeling that in some sense Britten had abandoned the political principles that he had once shared with your husband and to which your husband continued to adhere?

ES: No.

DM: A feeling that the old radical spirit had gone?

ES: No, I don't think so. I think he thought that it was best that Ben got on with his work, was not distracted. No, he didn't feel that at all, at least not after the initial disappointment of his going off to America. And Montagu was never one to impose his own ideas on anyone. Not on me and never on Ben. People had their own ideas: that was fine for Montagu. [On the other hand Slater's daughter does remember (see above, p. 30) a 'rift' between her father and Britten and attributes it to Slater's feeling that the success of *Grimes* had detached Britten from his former circles. This may have been his conviction. But it must also have been Britten's conviction that the experience of working with Slater on the libretto of the opera did not provide a basis for further collaboration. The friendship seems to have failed with that realisation.]

DM: Did your husband feel as a committed Communist and politically engaged writer that the opinions he held and expressed had had an adverse effect on his own career?

ES: Oh yes, there's no doubt about it. He was turned down right, left and centre.

DM: For political rather than literary reasons?

ES: Yes, there was a very strong objection to him.

DM: Pre-war or post-war?

ES: Before and after. A very strong feeling. Oh yes, he was very aware of it. There was nothing he could do, really. He wasn't going to give up his ideas. It was especially noticeable in television, which he would have liked to have been involved in. He felt that there was a lot to be done with the medium – plays and so on. But they wouldn't have anything to do with him. It was a shame really. Some of the little theatres still do *Easter*: one or two in Wales and in Scotland, odd places like that. They suddenly write to me and say, could they?, and I put them on to the right person. But just lately there's been much more interest in the thirties and in that whole group of writers of whom Montagu was one.

3 'Fiery visions' (and revisions): 'Peter Grimes' in progress

PHILIP BRETT

Some of the most important revelations about the great works of the past or the circumstances surrounding their composition have arisen from close study of the original documents. One has only to think of the new dating of Bach's works during the Leipzig period to realise how radically such evidence can affect critical opinion. With more recent works, comment, whether authentic or hearsay, tends to supplant documentary evidence, which is often more difficult to obtain and to evaluate. There is a great deal of comment about *Peter Grimes* available: those associated with its growth and original staging have been generous with their memories and commentaries, and even the normally reticent Britten had more to say about this opera than any other single work of his output. But comment, though helpful when accurate, is of its very nature selective and partial. Documents, on the other hand, are impartial records which allow the critic or historian to be the one who selects and interprets. There are, fortunately, a fairly large number of documents surrounding the early history of *Grimes*, most of them housed in the Britten–Pears Library at The Red House, Aldeburgh.[1] They include everything from the source of the libretto – the copy of Crabbe's *Works* bought by Peter Pears in Southern California in 1941 – to the finished composition sketch itself, written in Britten's neat and expressive pencil. They are very revealing, and their study throws new light on the finished work. This chapter discusses them in some detail, charting the creative birth-pangs and pinpointing a number of issues that may open the way for a deeper engagement with the work itself.

Peter Pears has said in an interview that 'while Ben Britten was writing *A Ceremony of Carols* and *Hymn to St Cecilia*, which he wrote on board this ship [the *Axel Johnson* in March–April 1942] . . . I was planning the original shape of the *Peter Grimes* libretto'.[2] Work must in fact have begun earlier, when the two men returned to the East Coast from California. While awaiting a passage to England they lived not in the Bohemian establishment in Brooklyn Heights presided over by

Auden (whence they had fled to California in summer 1941) but once again with Elizabeth Mayer and her family at Amityville on Long Island.[3] Among the papers they left with her before sailing in March 1942 are a sheet in Britten's hand with an outline of the main events of Act I of *Peter Grimes*, and four sheets in Pears's hand containing a complete synopsis and an attempt at drafting a short passage of the libretto.[4]

In both drafts of the outline of Act I, the present sequence of seashore (scene 1) and pub (scene 2) already occurs, together with such elements as the storm and the opening chorus. Britten's version brings us immediately face to face with his vivid theatrical imagination: it begins with a stage sketch and a description of the scene (see Fig. 4). Pears, on the other hand, begins with a diagram of opposing forces in the drama:

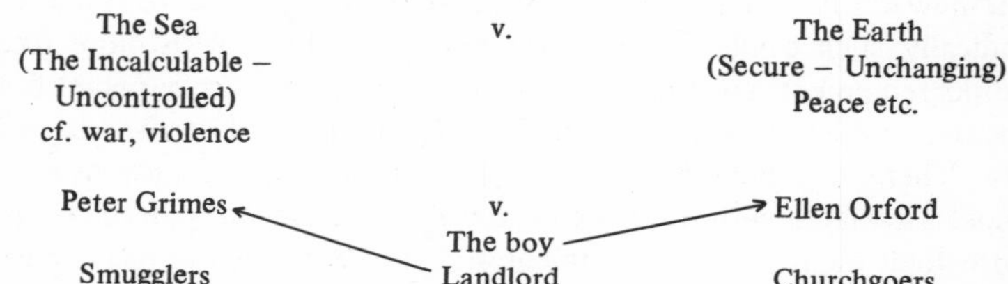

(The word 'Sailors', written below 'Landlord', is crossed out; the arrows denote sympathies or friendships.) The smugglers were the first to go. The suggestion in Pears's draft that the landlord of the pub is Grimes's connection to a contraband ring does not appear in Britten's version. But Britten (who may have broken off before the end of the act) concludes the pub scene without the new apprentice, whereas Pears has Ellen bringing the boy in as a survivor from a ship wrecked in the storm.

The remainder occurs only in Pears's draft. Act II consists of three scenes. The first serves much the same purpose as the present scene 1 so far as Peter, Ellen and the boy are concerned. The church background is postponed until scene 2, when Ellen asks for help from the landlord, whom she encounters as she rushes in late for morning service. Refusing to be alarmed, he nevertheless eventually promises to visit Grimes. Scene 3 opens with Peter's monologue to the boy (originally placed by Pears at the end of Act II scene 1) and ends with the 'accidental murder' and with the landlord (accompanied, on second thoughts, by Ellen) entering to find the apprentice's body. Act III scene 1 is a 'local scene' with 'women collecting sticks or such, or Chorus of fishers or both'. Ellen wants to reach Grimes before the village is roused; the Chorus

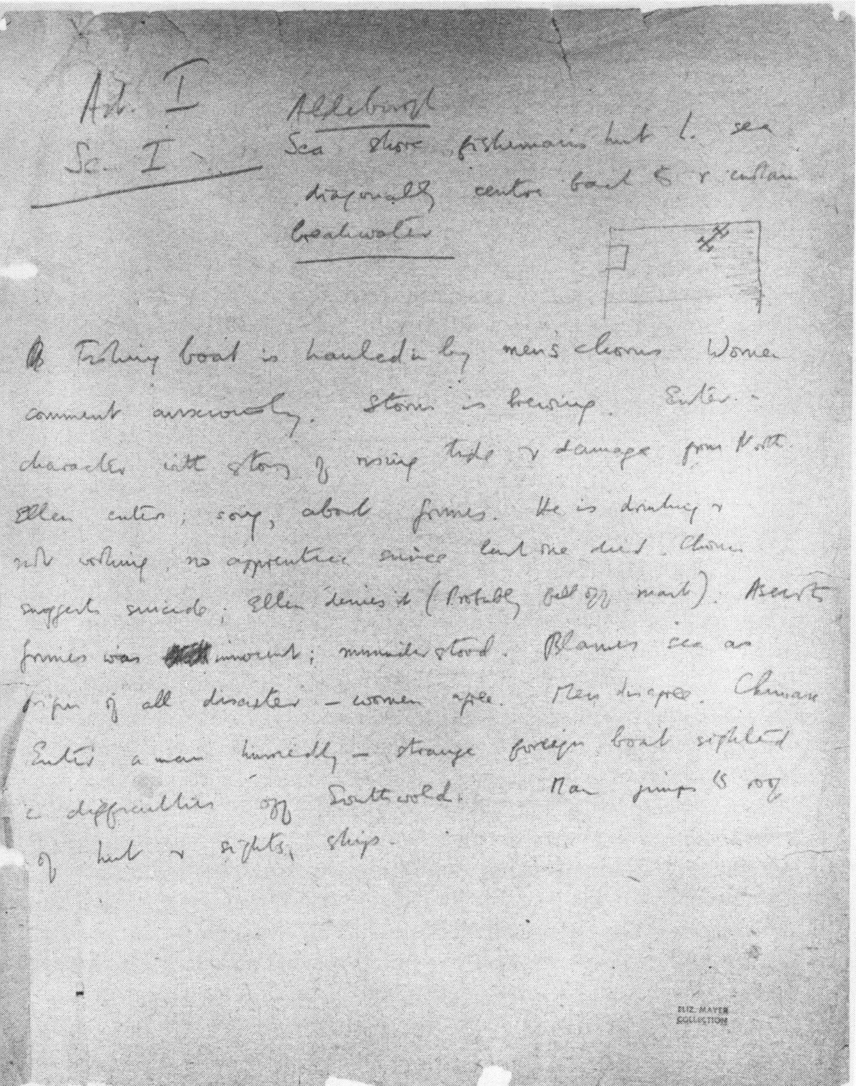

Act I Sc. I

Aldeburgh
Sea shore fisherman's hut L. sea
diagonally centre back & r. curtain
breakwater

A Fishing boat is hauled in by men's chorus. Women comment anxiously. Storm is brewing. Enter character with story of rising tide & damage from North. Ellen enters; song, about Grimes. He is drinking & not working, no apprentice since last one died. Chorus suggests suicide; Ellen denies it (Probably fell off mast). Asserts Grimes was innocent; misunderstood. Blames sea as origin of all disaster – women agree. Men disagree. Climax. Enter a man hurriedly – strange foreign boat sighted in difficulties off Southwold. Man jumps to top of hut & sights ships.

Fig. 4: The earliest draft of the scenario for Act I scene 1, in Britten's own hand, with a sketch of the stage setting at the top (Elizabeth Mayer Collection)

decides to help in the chase. After this, Grimes enters 'near crazy'. The cryptic words 'ghosts scene' presumably indicate a hallucinatory appearance of the two apprentices and father Grimes in the manner of Crabbe. Subsequently, 'the Sea calls him. Just as he is about to leap in, enter Ellen, ahead of crowd. She calls to him. Too late, he says, & jumps in.' There is as yet no resumption of ordinary life at the end.

In this rough scheme, Peter is still very much closer to Crabbe's ruffian than he is in the finished opera, but already in Britten's version of Act I scene 1 there emerges, in Ellen's account, a misunderstood man whose drinking is the result of his not being able to work. The most detailed part of Pears's scheme is Grimes's 'monologue to the boy' (Act II scene 3), which must be quoted in full:

> Admits his youth hurts him, his innocence galls him, his uselessness maddens him. He had no father to love him, why should he? His father only beat him, why should not he? 'Prove yourself some use, not only pretty – work – not be only innocent – work do not stare; would you rather I loved you? you are sweet, young etc. – but you must love me, why do you not love me? Love me darn you.'

There are elements here – an obsession with the father figure and homoerotic feelings – that will be seized on by those who like to discern one or the other in the finished work. But whatever latent power they retained, they were (as we shall see) slowly but surely purged from the surface of the opera as it grew towards maturity. Furthermore, the demand for love by an unlovable man from a terrorised object almost certainly derives from the story of Walter Jones in Letter VIII of *The Borough*; a self-made man, who might well fit the bill as the creature of Peter's fantasy 'that wealthy merchant Grimes', he forfeits the love of his wife and children, whom he confronts in much the same terms as Grimes confronts the boy in this early draft.[5] Perhaps, though, we can also discern in this passage an interesting ambiguity. Looked at one way, Grimes here descends to his lowest point, preying on a young innocent; looked at another, he shows toward the child an honesty and tenderness that elicit greater sympathy for him than Ellen's pleading on his behalf could ever have done.

The next items in this series of early documents date from the journey back to England in March and April 1942. There are three sheets (two of them ship's notepaper of the Johnson Line) on which Britten and Pears set down their ideas of the scenario.[6] Two of them are in Pears's hand, one a number-by-number summary of the opera, the other a fuller account of Acts II and III (a sheet covering the rest is presumably missing); the third, in Britten's hand, presents a very terse outline.

'And to start with', Pears continues in the interview, 'we had a Prologue in which Peter Grimes's father appeared on his death-bed, in which he solemnly cursed the boy – the young man – Grimes.' Pears's number-by-number *Axel Johnson* draft does indeed call for Peter to enter drunk and to be rude to his father, who is attended by Ellen. After the elder Grimes's last speech and death, Ellen and Peter sing their duet – the only part of this particular episode that has a place in the finished work.

The other main differences between this document and the Amityville drafts are: the appearance of Grimes in Act I scene 1 giving his tale of the first boy's death; the addition of a scene between this and the pub scene for 'Grimes' Apostrophe of the Sea' and 'appearance of old Grimes' ghost' (in parentheses with a question mark); an entrance for Grimes half-way through the pub scene (he had previously been envisaged by Britten 'sitting sullenly drinking' from its start); a trio of gossipers overheard by Ellen at the opening of the church scene (still Act II scene 2); no mention of Ellen or the landlord in the 'murder' scene following; and the addition of a lament for Ellen and a 'Fisherman's Song' at the end, though it is not clear as yet whether this last recapitulates the one in Act I scene 1.

Though one can marvel at the sure sense that ultimately led Britten out of certain of these notions – how obvious a final lament for Ellen must have seemed and how disastrous it would have been – to the best dramatic and musical solutions, indecision and unsureness were at this stage still the order of the day. The other draft scenario from the *Axel Johnson*, in the composer's own hand, shows how he began to find his way:

Version I
Prologue Court – [deleted] Magistrate scene
P.G. having 'done away with' boy, is let off with a warning.
Act I Sc. I Seashore
Hauling in of boats. Chorus working.
Storm rising. P.G. has monologue about everything.
Sc. II Pub scene Storm
arrival of Ellen & Boy.
Act II Sc. I P.G's Hut
Ellen comes for boy. P.G. refuses to let him go.
Sc. II Church scene. Ellen disturbed
seeks advice from villagers (Rumour chorus?)
Sc. III P.G's Hut. Murder.
Act III Beach. Finding of Boy's coat – Fury of Villagers
Ellen's Lament.
Night
PG's Mad scene & death.
Chorus as Act I sc I

Version II
Act I as Ver. I
Act II as Ver. I
Act III Terrific court scene. P.G. forbidden ever to have boy again. P.G. is dismissed in disgrace.
Epilogue. P.G. on marshes, goes mad & dies.

This comes closer to the finished work in many important respects – the Prologue, the reduction of Act I to two scenes, the sequence of events in Act III. Yet the alternative version of the last act shows that nothing could yet be called settled; and we suddenly realise that what this document represents is an attempt to come to grips with the main actions of the plot – its architectural skeleton without Pears's glosses – to see what options remained. One can imagine what the composer would have made of that 'terrific court scene'. More important, in the Epilogue of Version II (a scene directly related to Crabbe's poem) there emerges what was to become an increasingly important issue for Britten – the loneliness and isolation of his non-hero.

We can now turn to the third of these *Axel Johnson* sheets, representing those glosses of Pears. It must be quoted *in extenso*, not to show what needed altering so much as to reveal the fullest state of thinking about detail and characterisation on that voyage. It is perhaps important to bear in mind when reading it that some ideas, most notably the quarrel in Act II scene 1, were probably so firmly embedded by this time that Pears may have felt no need to spell them out so fully as the new elements. The less specific language of the scene between Peter and the boy at the hut, however, can only be interpreted as a sign of a change of heart on that issue – a change that heralds the eventual neutralising of all explicit emotion in the relationship between man and boy.

Act 2 Scene I Ellen & the boy.
Grimes enters; he must have the boy for fishing (News of a shoal). Ellen lets him have him – says as he will be out all day she will go over to friends at Snape (?)

Act 2 Scene II
Outside the Church: with the pub opposite.
The church service is just coming to an end, but there's just time for the landlord to emerge in front of his pub & have an aria, before the last hymn starts. The people come out & start talking to one another, Ellen among them. The three gossips talk about Grimes. Ellen overhears and when they go asks landlord about these rumours. The landlord is sceptical, & advises her to leave Grimes to himself; he's not worth the trouble. [Ellen] Has an aria about her doubts of Grimes, & her determination to win. The landlord shrugs & says he will help if he can, and as some men come in to drink he welcomes them. Exit Ellen.

Act 2 Scene III

The hut, empty. Grimes & the boy come back from fishing, Grimes is furious: through the stupidity and carelessness of the boy nets have been lost and fish gone. He blames [him] & his anger grows (as he drinks). He finally drives the boy back to the door over the cliff & in terror the boy opens it: dashes out – onto the rocks.

Act III Scene I

By the sea. The women are picking up sticks, & combing the beach after the storm. Ellen is there, mourning; the chorus stops, and she sings her song over the little cap or coat. Enter the Landlord who goes up to Ellen and tells her he has done what she asked him to. He has seen Grimes, but Grimes refused to come with him, he was very afraid of the village & in a bad state (I would say, Ellen, he was nearly crazy) – 'but he wanted to see you & would meet you by the shore here before dawn tomorrow morning. He said – It was an accident, Ellen. I did not kill him'. Ellen is thankful, promises to meet Grimes & exits – the chorus slowly go off and night falls – the fog comes up – at last enter Grimes, worn out, half mad, falls down. Slowly wakes up & has his mad scene – hallucinations – ghosts of two boys & father – calls for Ellen – completely crazy – and as dawn breaks he staggers up & throws himself off breakwater into sea, as Ellen enters. She dashes up but too late – She weeps over him, has her lament, blaming herself & submitting to God's will, asks God to let his soul rest in peace. He was very weak not bad. As she ceases, the fishers' chorus can be heard slowly coming to work, and when they enter, she joins them to help with the boats.

If this extended synopsis catches something of the resonance of the tale, it also shows how the exigencies of plot have begun to close in upon characterisation and idea. But there must still have been passages and nuances from Crabbe lingering in the composer's mind above and beyond what was required to cement the dramatic action. For clues about these less tangible matters, we may turn to the copy of Crabbe's *Works* bought in California.[7] Against certain passages, ranging from a single line to almost a pageful of verse, there appear vertical pencil marks in the margin; some verses are emphasised by a double line or by red pencil. There is a danger of reading too much into these marks, for the assumption that they all belong to the very earliest stages is not justified. In fact we cannot know exactly who made them, or when, or in what spirit; but they do reveal connections to Crabbe in the opera that might not otherwise be fully appreciated or in some cases even suspected.

Most of the passages marked in Letter I, the 'General Description' of *The Borough*, are those that Montagu Slater adapted for the chorus of Act I scene 1 and the Epilogue.[8] Yet there are also two sea pictures, one of which is surely the literary equivalent of Interlude I (*Dawn*):

Turn to the watery world! – but who to thee
(A wonder yet unview'd) shall paint – the Sea?
Various and vast, sublime in all its forms,
When lull'd by zephyrs, or when roused by storms,
Its colours changing, when from clouds and sun
Shades after shades upon the surface run;
Embrown'd and horrid now, and now serene,
In limpid blue, and evanescent green;
And oft the foggy banks on ocean lie,
Lift the fair sail, and cheat th'experienced eye. (I, 163-72)

The other is the poetical counterpart of Interlude II (*Storm*):

Yet sometimes comes a ruffling cloud to make
The quiet surface of the ocean shake;
As an awaken'd giant with a frown
Might show his wrath, and then to sleep sink down.
View now the Winter-storm! above, one cloud,
Black and unbroken, all the skies o'ershroud;
Th'unwieldy porpoise through the day before
Had roll'd in view of boding men on shore;
And sometimes hid and sometimes show'd his form,
Dark as the cloud, and furious as the storm.
All where the eye delights, yet dreads to roam,
The breaking billows cast the flying foam
Upon the billows rising – all the deep
Is restless change; the waves so swell'd and steep,
Breaking and sinking, and the sunken swells,
Nor one, one moment, in its station dwells:
But nearer land you may the billows trace,
As if contending in their watery chase;
May watch the mightiest till the shoal they reach,
Then break and hurry to their utmost stretch;
Curl'd as they come, they strike with furious force,
And then re-flowing, take their grating course,
Raking the rounded flints, which ages past
Roll'd by their rage, and shall to ages last. (I, 190-213)

Later on, in the Letter devoted to 'Amusements', a passage has been singled out that portrays the atmosphere of Act III scene 2, and may even have suggested to Britten the ghostly off-stage voices that haunt Peter's last moments:

The ocean too has Winter-views serene,
When all you see through densest fog is seen;
When you can hear the fishers near at hand
Distinctly speak, yet see not where they stand . . . (IX, 111-14)

Another set of marked passages later in the poem pertains to the minor characters. In the case of the Vicar and Bob Boles (an anonymous 'Calvinistic Enthusiast' in Crabbe) couplets have been chosen that encapsulate their operatic characters.[9] Swallow and Ned Keene, however, emerge less obviously from the passages singled out for them.[10] Another passage raises the question about the timing and intent of these marginal marks. In the section of *The Borough* devoted to 'Inns', the following has been highlighted:

> Shall I pass by the Boar? – there are who cry,
> 'Beware the Boar,' and pass determined by:
> Those dreadful tusks, those little peering eyes
> And churning chaps, are tokens to the wise.
> There dwells a kind old Aunt, and there you see
> Some kind young Nieces in her company . . . (XI, 165-70)

The passage goes on to cast doubts on the morals of these ladies. But since in all the early plot summaries it is, as we have seen, the land*lord* who figures so prominently, and in the very first of Slater's drafts the pub is 'The Green Man', not 'The Boar', then it is entirely possible that this mark, and perhaps others as well, were made at a much later stage.

The opera gives us Ellen Orford in her middle years, after she has overcome the appalling misfortunes Crabbe heaps upon her and before the blind and penurious old age during which she recounts her tale in the poem. Her story is not as germane to the opera as certain aspects of her character. And it is not surprising to find that the lines marked here are few, and describe her trusting and loving nature, her fortitude and her submissiveness.[11]

The lion's share of marked passages occurs of course in 'Peter Grimes' (Letter XXII). Interestingly, though, these begin with the quarrel between the young Peter and Grimes senior and the general description of Peter's villainy in the early stages of the poem, and then they recur only at the point of Peter's dying hallucinations.[12] It is tempting to surmise from this, and from the Pears synopses, that Britten's initial attraction to the story had more to do with the struggle between father and son than one would ever guess from the completed opera. The brilliant development of Peter's alienation is, however, adumbrated in a couplet double-marked for emphasis:

> And as these wrongs to greater numbers rose,
> The more he look'd on all men as his foes. (XXII, 49-50)

Finally, there are a good many marked passages that have no ostensible connection with the opera. Some are purely descriptive, but others may signal short-listed individuals who never reached the final list of characters, or whose fates illustrate in some way the penalty of complying with the values of a hardened society – a theme that runs through the opera as Peter's chief dilemma.[13]

Whatever the relation of these marked passages throughout *The Borough* to the early drafts of the scenario of the opera, there can be no doubt that the cast of characters remained in flux for some time and that, even more important, the central figure of Grimes himself did not easily fall into focus. A very interesting document, a list of characters written on the back of a letter from Elizabeth Mayer dated 1 June 1942, emphasises the extent of these problems. Balstrode has finally entered the picture, presumably to replace the unspecified landlord, whose role in the pub devolves on 'Auntie Puttock', as she appears here (already with her two nieces). But in addition to the characters that remain in the opera are May Boles (soprano), Mrs Sanders (mezzo soprano) and Dick Sanders (bass); and as in Crabbe there are two Swallows, senior (tenor) and junior (baritone). The list also shows the Rector as a bass and Mrs Nabob (i.e. Mrs Sedley) as a soprano. Rather more devastating in its implications is the listing of Peter Grimes as a baritone. If this was more than a temporary aberration on the composer's part it can only mean that Pears was not initially envisioned as the creator of one of his most important roles. It must be remembered that at this early stage of his career the young tenor was unlikely to be engaged for a premiere in the United States or at Covent Garden (where Boosey & Hawkes, having leased the house, wanted to put on the work). It was the *Serenade* (1943) and above all *Peter Grimes* itself that established him as the chief interpreter of his friend's music.

The choice for Grimes of the ambivalent baritone, half-way between the villainous bass and the heroic tenor of operatic tradition, also reveals an underlying ambivalence about the very nature of the title figure. To a certain extent this ambivalence still exists in the finished work: it gives symbolic power to the character, endows the opera with universal appeal – and causes critical discomfort. But in order to be so effective it had first to be tuned and balanced; and the fundamental weakness of the Pears *Axel Johnson* outline in this respect is the distinct shift in tone between Act II scene 3 and Act III scene 1, from Peter's terrorising the boy so crudely to his protesting his innocence to Ellen through the landlord. Without the brilliant device of the illegal posse to implicate the Borough in the boy's death, Peter would perhaps have appeared a whining criminal whose case even Britten's music might not have succeeded in pleading.

The shift in tone between these two scenes reflects a shift in attitude which began in the very first draft and continued in the same direction, as we shall see, right up to the last-minute changes before the first performance. Peter Pears has spoken eloquently about it:

As one was working on this one realised that Grimes without his crimes, as it were, which Crabbe reported, was a misfit – he was in any case a misfit – either a misfit who is excusable or a misfit who is inexcusable; but we thought that in the light of the more liberal view of human nature which has emerged during the last, what, two generations, his behaviour was excusable and understandable. And one therefore approached the whole story from that point of view. And in fact by the time we came back to London, the whole story of Peter Grimes as set in the opera was already shaped, and it simply remained to call in a librettist to write the words.[14]

The choice of a librettist was complicated by Christopher Isherwood's having turned down the job, as Donald Mitchell shows in chapter 2. It eventually fell on Montagu Slater, whose previously shadowy presence in the Britten circle has also been illuminated by Dr Mitchell.[15] Britten had evidently been disconcerted in his collaboration with Auden on *Paul Bunyan* at being presented by the poet with a *fait accompli*; according to Pears, 'from this experience, Ben learnt that in future he must discuss every step of a work with his librettists and work in harness with them'.[16] His collaboration with Slater, though not satisfactory in all regards, was the first in which he set the pattern he followed in composing all the later operas.

The first products of Slater's collaboration appear to be the drafts of part of the libretto mentioned earlier.[17] These include two versions of the Prologue, two versions of Act I scene 1, one of Act I scene 2, and finally most of Act II scene 1. The first thing to catch one's eye in this rather jumbled sheaf of papers is the enlarged list of characters. As Peter Pears has said:

There were still a great many characters, more characters than there are now. And those characters persisted, not I think when the music started being written, but there are certain references to scrapped characters, one might say, in the libretto. For instance, in the pub scene, when Boles is told to keep his wife upstairs [actually Act I scene 1 around fig. 36], that is a reference to the recently destroyed Mrs Boles, who was considered to be a lady of easy virtue . . . but she disappeared along with others, mostly wives, I may say, of characters – I think there was a Mrs Keene, but she disappeared at an early date.[18]

We have seen evidence of Mrs Boles, who turned from May into Polly before her ultimate demise. More important in these early drafts than the superfluous wives, however, was Dick Sanders, the rather loud fisherman to whom the back-chat with Auntie and the Nieces at the beginning of the pub scene originally belonged – the tone has always seemed to me a little unlikely for Balstrode, who later took it on. Among other surprises in this draft are Ellen's references to Peter's drinking in the great quarrel of Act II scene 1, and the provision of lines (in Act II scene 1) for the ultimately silent young apprentice, whom Pears in his Amityville draft actually described as dumb; Peter and Ellen call him 'young stranger', a name that stuck for a long time, as we shall see.

A complete typescript libretto represents the next stage. The date of its completion is uncertain; it may have been as early as Christmas 1942, for Britten later admitted that he had delayed getting down to composition for over a year (until January 1944) while the work simmered at the back of his mind – a not unusual process for him. At any rate, Eric Crozier remembers being given two days to read the libretto in spring or early summer 1943; as a stage director of Sadler's Wells Opera, in which Peter Pears was already singing several leading roles, he had won Britten's respect, and he was called in to give his opinion as a man of the theatre. From this time on he, Britten and Slater would meet fairly regularly and subject the libretto to intense scrutiny (see above, p. 37). But revision of the words did not cease until the opera actually opened (and has continued in a mild way since), and it is necessary at this stage to list the remaining documents and explain something of the discrepancies between them.

La The typescript libretto: the top copy, with few alterations or annotations. The words 'earlier version' are pencilled on the cover.

Lb A carbon copy of *La*. Clearly the working copy used during composition, it is heavily marked with revisions, drafts of new passages and so on, and therefore represents a later stage than *La*. On the last two pages there are some pencilled stage sketches.

Lc Another carbon copy of *La*, used by the stage director Eric Crozier, whose name and address appear on the cover. The Prologue and Act I are carefully marked up with corrections, many of them later than those in *Lb*. Acts II and III, on the other hand, are not so fully corrected as in *Lb*. The two parts of this libretto, then, represent very different stages of the overall textual evolution. Inside the cover there is a handwritten list of orchestral forces. This libretto is in the archives of the English National Opera; I have examined a copy belonging to the Britten–Pears Library.

C The composition sketch. As usual Britten composed in pencil and in short score, indicating the instrumentation as he went. The manuscript is inscribed 'to Reginald Goodall [conductor of the original production] – a souvenir of the splendid work, & great understanding over "the first performance" – June 7th 1945.' Mr Goodall presented this manuscript to the Britten–Pears Library in 1979.

VS The dye-line vocal score used for the first production. This agrees in the main with *C*, but further corrections have been made in one copy or another. The two copies I have consulted are British Library H.2472.c and Library of Congress M1503 B8608 P4 1945a.

FS The manuscript full score, Library of Congress ML30 3c2 B75 Case. It is dated at the end of volume 3 'Feb. 10th, 1945'. Presented by Britten to the commissioner, the Koussevitsky Music Foundation, Lenox, Massachussetts, it passed to the Library after Koussevitsky's death together with the warm and friendly correspondence between the composer and the conductor. To all intents and purposes it is identical to *VS*, also having had corrections made to it.

L1945 The libretto published by Boosey & Hawkes in 1945. The Prologue and Act I are so close to *Lc* that they may have been set up from it, with a few later readings incorporated at proof stage. Acts II and III regress in many instances to *La*; they must have been set up from a different copy and less carefully revised. The text was clearly not checked against a current vocal score – the heavily revised wording of the stage directions in *VS* is never followed, and the order of words as they eventually came out in the ensembles is rarely observed: see e.g., pp. 37 and 50. (A revised edition of 1961 corrected some but not all of the discrepancies with the score. A libretto corrected from the 1963 full score and the 1959 recording has been published by Boosey & Hawkes).

S The libretto as printed in Montagu Slater's *Peter Grimes and Other Poems* (London, 1946). In the words of his preface, 'as printed here *Peter Grimes* differs from the libretto as sung, inasmuch as I have omitted some of the repetitions and inversions required by the music – I believe it is a difference between the musical and the literary form that one welcomes, and the other [advantage is that it] avoids repetition. Thus the present text is to all intents and purposes the one to which the music was composed.' In fact, this libretto is closest to *La*, and incorporates only about half the revisions of *Lb/c* and almost none of those of *VS/FS*. Furthermore it includes two extensive passages at the beginning of Act II scene 2 (p. 42) that occur in no other source, and therefore appear to have been written expressly for this publication.

VS1945 The printed vocal score of 1945, which appeared in the autumn of that year; the first authoritative version, and the text used for musical quotations in this book.

FS1963 A few further revisions, all of the most minor nature, were incorporated into this full score published in 1963.

Quite early on during composition Britten played the Prologue and Act I to the directors of the Sadler's Wells Opera Company. As a result they chose to open Sadler's Wells Theatre with it when the European war ended, and this was eventually agreed with Boosey & Hawkes, who had wanted it to open Covent Garden. A production team was appointed by Tyrone Guthrie, general administrator of the Wells, consisting of Eric Crozier as stage director, Reginald Goodall as conductor, and as designer Kenneth Green, a friend of Britten's who was art master at Wellington College. It seems always to have been the composer's practice to involve every member of the production team of an opera as much as possible in the growth of the work – while guarding the conception fiercely, we may be sure – and *Grimes* was no exception. Indeed, discussions with Crozier appear to have been so valuable that he became from then on closely associated with Britten, as co-founder of the Aldeburgh Festival and of the English Opera Group, and as the librettist or co-librettist of three of the later operas and of the cantata *Saint Nicolas*.

Crozier has paid generous tribute to the originality and characterisation of Slater's text.[19] But it is clear that he shared Britten's reservations about many matters, and since Slater seems to have been both resistant to change and slow in delivering agreed revisions, the process must have been, as Peter Pears has said, 'hard work in one way or another'.[20] One of the things Crozier has said he found unfortunate was the influence of Auden. Such lines as 'Clocks have a moral sense, but tides have none' (originally conceived for the elder Swallow and later given to Keene in Act I scene 1 before fig. 22) have a clever abstract ring to them which he thought best avoided in a tale of simple fisherfolk. Perhaps it was he who persuaded Slater to change this to 'Man invented morals, but tides have none.' His practical influence may also have affected other moments where the original words were too high-flown or simply too metaphorical. Moreover, he now recalls that many of the most striking phrases were suggested by Peter Pears. Whoever was responsible, the minor process of tidying up the language can be traced all through the revisions, making the words more understandable as well as more singable. For example:

Lc, *C*	I'm provincial, rooted here	*VS1945*	I am native, rooted here
C	This unforgiving work	*VS1945*	This unrelenting work
La	Beer may be spiced as wine by clove, By like or dislike, hate or love.	*Lb/c*, *C*	We live and let live and look, We keep our hands to ourselves.

Even important moments were among those affected, for example:

La	Among the constellations . . .	*Lb/c*, *C*	Now the Great Bear and Pleiades . . .
La	Like a school-playground-full of noisy children	*VS1945*	Like a flashing turmoil of a shoal of herring

In looking for direct evidence of the working relationship of the librettist with the composer himself, we are lucky that there survives a letter from Slater to Britten (now in the Britten–Pears Library). It is dated merely '3 December', but it is clear that the year is 1944 from a reference to two passages in Act III scene 1 for which music had already been composed. The first concerns the stanzas sung by the two Nieces at the opening of the scene. We can see from *C* that Britten had already composed the present patter-like song to Slater's lines, repeating bits of them, to a greater or lesser extent, often in an ungainly way, in order to fill up the musical phrase:

Together we are safe, [x 2]
For safety in number lies
We find men are lighter [x 2] in the hand
When we're in threes.

Save us from lonely men [x 2]
And their intensity,
The saddest man is gay [x 3]
When one of three.

O pairing's all to blame [x 2]
to blame For all these sighs and tears
these tears Which would be saved [x 2] if people would
Keep threes and fours.

Slater proposes what is almost identical to the final version, gives alternatives for the last line, and comments 'Does this meet your need for patter in the last line? If you like it can be lengthened – for example: "Whene'er the tete a tete's in threes" for the first two stanzas, and "To have their tete a tetes in threes" in the third.' A similar adjustment is proposed for the 'Vengeance Song' (beginning two bars after fig. 36). This had not been in *La*, which ends the scene with Mrs Sedley's crazy ruminations. The three stanzas which Britten must have demanded for his climactic and most terrifying choral scene turn up in pencil in *Lb* (only two of them are printed in *S*). In the letter Slater proposes a revision for the third ('O we shall blind his bright, contemptuous eyes'):

> Our curse shall fall upon
> His work, his evil day
> He who despises us
> We destroy

It is hard to see from the music how this would have alleviated the problem. More words had to be written – one suspects not by Slater – in order to fill out the music. On the other hand, without the evidence of this letter it would be impossible to ascribe to Slater the important intensification of the last line, adopted in *L1945*, from the original 'We despise', retained in *S*. 'Destroy' is absolutely the right expression, musically and dramatically, and Britten must have seized on it. In approaching the many changes and differences between *S* and *VS1945*, then, one has to remember that Slater may indeed have allowed changes for the operatic text that he preferred not to incorporate into his own version.

The main substance of this remarkable letter, however, concerns the quartet at the end of Act II scene 1 and the role of Balstrode in the plot. As we have seen, Balstrode (who is not derived from Crabbe) was a latecomer to the cast who had already increased a good deal in importance, supplanting the landlord of Pears's early drafts and picking up the passage at the opening of the pub scene designed in the first instance for another character. Crozier must have felt uncomfortable about the quartet, and there must have been a scheme afoot to supplant it with a trio for Ellen, Balstrode and Auntie, as some notations in *Lc* show. Slater's defence of the *status quo* is eloquent, and worth quoting extensively. It argues well about the plot in general, and shows a modesty mixed with intense involvement that goes a long way towards explaining why Britten chose him as librettist in the first place (see also chapter 2). In this instance it is fortunate that his counsel prevailed.

Now I'm going to be a nuisance. This quartet. I've done a lot of thinking about it and still find a strong internal resistance to the fundamental change (which I must admit I agreed to at Yarner's[21]).

What I'm afraid of is that in building up Balstrode we may be endangering the main structure. The Yarner's scheme (let's call it that) must mean in practice, whatever else we think, that at this crucial moment the highlight is on Balstrode, or if you like on Ellen and Balstrode as a pair. Obviously we don't want the latter. Their conjunction is accidental and shouldn't be stressed. The other danger is that in high-lighting the fact that Balstrode is persuaded with difficulty to go up to Peter's hut we seem to be saying that his going to the hut and what he is going to see there is critical: whereas in fact it isn't. He's not going to find the clue of clues when he looks out of the cliff-side door. As things are there's a risk we may be underlining it too much though I don't think so . . .[22]

What I'm saying is that we've built Balstrode up enough and if we try and build him up further we may put the story out of joint . . . Essentially his function in the drama is a very ordinary traditional one. The old stock companies used to have a name for him. They called him Charles's friend. Read Peter–Ellen's. In Hamlet he's Horatio. His job is that he is the receiver of confidences, the giver of good advice, and the bloke who stands by at the climax. You'll find that it's quite normal for him to fade out in the second act (as Horatio does in the 2nd 3rd & 4th) . . .

However we finally work it out I'm convinced that the point of the curtain of Act II Sc i must be as it is now Ellen's feeling about it all. At Yarner's I said I regretted losing Ellen's quatrain but maybe one ought to lose one's purple patches. If it is a purple patch I agree one ought to lose it. But the more I think about it the more I'm convinced that it is simply the clue to Ellen's whole outlook and character and it should at all costs be the curtain line of that scene.

> Men are children when they strive
> We are mothers when they weep
> Schooling our own hearts to keep
> The bitter treasure of their love[23]

is Ellen's own summary of her own life and character. The crisis of the quarrel wrings it out of her. The whole point of the opera at that moment is to say this about Ellen, to have her see herself and her life with this sort of clarity . . . It should be led up to quite simply with no extraneous action by or about Balstrode or anybody else. The easy and natural way is to have her say it to other women. It isn't accidental that the quartet was of women. The other point I have made all along that there is some significance in the fact that Ellen opens her heart and gets comfort from the disreputable women of the Borough is useful but not all that weighty. Eric was objecting to this at Yarner's on the grounds that I don't develop it later on in the opera. At the moment I don't see why one should. All one is saying is that it's a common observation that when you're really in trouble you find sinners are often more sympathetic than saints. We don't need to go any farther than that.

If in this instance Slater was right, in many others, most notably Peter's mad scene, he certainly was not, his solutions serving neither Britten's conception nor the internal logic of his own dramatic argument. The fortunate survival of this letter prevents us, however, from oversimplifying Slater's role and contribution as we turn from a consideration of the libretto on its own to what one might call the musical assimilation of it.

The way *La/b* are set out first signals this musical assimilation. Many commentators have drawn attention to Britten's professing to adopt 'the classical practice of separate numbers' without being able to identify the numbers themselves, which are absent from both *VS1945* and *L1945*. But Pears had laid out his *Axel Johnson* summary scenario in this way, and *Lb* is similarly organised by number, with interesting marginal remarks inserted by the composer (in italic below). We may take Act II scene 1 as an example:

No. 1 Solo with chorus off (later) — *Bright, florid*
Ellen: Glitter of waves [The sun in his own morning *in La/b/c*]

No. 2 Duet (with chorus off)
Choir: O ye Light and Darkness [at Peter's entrance]

No. 3 Trio — *'gossipy', quick*
Auntie: Fool to let it come to this

No. 4 Recitative
Auntie: Doctor!
Ned: Leave him out of it
Mrs Sedley: What is it?

No. 5 Chorus — *Ostinato with interjections from soloists*
Chorus: What is it? What do you suppose
Grimes is at his exercise.

No. 6 Recitative with Chorus — *Quick passionate recitative*
Boles: People — . . . No! I will speak . . .

No. 7 Duet [deleted] — *Solo with ensemble (with chorus)*
Ellen: We planned that their lives should — *(Quiet & reassured)*
Have a new start,
Rector: You planned to be worldly-wise — *(Interruption)*

No. 8 Recit.
Rector: Swallow – shall we go and see Grimes in his hut? [home *in La/b/c*]

No. 9 Chorus (as they go)
Chorus: Now is gossip put on trial — *Chorus of Inspection*
Now the rumours either fail — *(march rhythm)*

No. 10 Quartet *(Meditative)*
Nieces: From the gutter, why should we
Trouble at their ribaldries?

At the end, Britten wrote '"Boy's suffering" fugato', crossed out 'fugato' and substituted 'passacaglia'. The remains of a fugato survive among the sketches, as we shall see.

Despite all these signs of an already fixed structure, the words 'typescript libretto' perhaps convey too formal an impression of the document they represent. My own sense is that those 'nearly eighteen months' of 'discussions, revisions, and corrections' (see chapter 7) had made Britten, never a slow worker, impatient to set notes to paper. The libretto as typed was perhaps regarded by him as a sort of compromise – something to hand with which to get on with the job. Moreover, during those eighteen months some of the music must surely have been conceived, if only in broad outline. When the composer set to work early in 1944, then, he had beside him a document he knew to be what he wanted in general but also incomplete and sometimes imperfect in detail. By comparing the composition sketch (*C*) carefully with the working copy of the libretto (*Lb*), one discovers that he adopted two attitudes to the libretto's remaining problems. Some of the most important revisions and additions he worked out during composition with the librettist. In other problematical passages he often simply took what was there, forcing it on to the music, in the knowledge that some other solution would later have to be found. Sometimes these two processes were linked: a passage not settled when composition began tended to need revision at several stages. In addition there were of course purely musical difficulties, though it is perhaps not surprising that these often arose as a result of problems in the libretto.

In approaching all these moments of difficulty for the composer, we need to take account of common assumptions about 'normal practice' in the matter of combining words and music. Broadly speaking, a composer is expected to follow his text sensitively and musically. Indeed, just such a sensitivity to poetry is vaunted as the strength of the British song-writers of the earlier part of this century. With composers of greater creative imagination, however, the musical idea is primary, and as a result the words are transformed, sometimes by means of an unconventional treatment that sounds far from 'sensitive'. Examples abound in vocal music with English words from Byrd to Stravinsky, and it is this unconventional treatment that Britten defends in his introduction to the opera (see chapter 7). We also tend to forget that setting text to music is as legitimate and venerable a practice as that of setting music to text. Rid of our assumptions, then, we will not be unnerved to see Britten forging ahead, as in the Act III passages already discussed, writing tunes whose relation to the words is a question less of perfect marriage than of shotgun wedding – or, more precisely, temporary cohabitation until such time as the librettist (or others) could find a more suitable arrangement to accommodate those dominant and demanding musical ideas.

Perhaps the most notable example of the problem occurs in Ellen's aria at the beginning of Act II, which Britten admitted to have caused him trouble for this very reason.[24] The version shown in Ex. 1 persisted

Ex. 1

[From *C*; the absence of G naturals in the last four bars indicates that Britten is still thinking in terms of the D major key-signature]

through to *VS* and *FS*, and must have been rectified during rehearsal (or even later – *L1945* has a slightly different, intermediate version, the complete revision first appearing in *VS1945*). As Donald Mitchell has pointed out to me, the image of the 'upward climb' of the sun had a useful and characteristic influence on Britten's shaping of the melody. But he must then have put the other verbal considerations on one side and worked out the theme in its first appearance in Interlude III (*Sunday Morning*), as can be seen from a separate sketch (see below, p. 74). The eventual rewriting of Ellen's words in fact extended throughout the whole of her scene up to Peter's entrance; *S* gives the original version much as it stands in *La/b/c* and *C*.

Other passages where the words were rewritten or considerably adjusted after composition (i.e. between *VS/FS* and *VS1945*) include:

(a) The end of Peter's and Ellen's duet in the Prologue.

(b) The middle section (figs. 44-6) of Peter's aria before Interlude II. The climactic line of the first stanza was wisely changed from 'I'll slip the painter' to 'I'll win them over'. The further statements of this 'set piece' in Act II scenes 1 and 2 also underwent considerable adjustment.

(c) Act II scene 2. The differences here are really extensive, as can be seen by comparing *S* with *L1945* and *VS1945*. A typical improvement occurs in the passage after Peter first hears the posse approaching, where the final version substitutes a moment of pure and dramatically potent paranoia for the weaker and more sadistic direction of Peter's anger at the boy in *Lb/c*, which have

> You sent them. You. O I'm not scared.
> I'll send them off with a flea in their ears.
> I want to know who is the spy.
> You sit there silently. Your eyes
> Are like Ellen's womanly.
> You sit there yearning like a girl
> Whose face has the wrong tale to tell.
> You sit there. Will you move
> If the cat starts making love?[25]

In view of what some commentators have attributed to Britten in terms of emphasising cruelty, both in this and other works, it is interesting to find him restraining the librettist here. Also, since by this time he had evidently decided against overt emotion between Grimes and the boy (see above, p. 52), he suppressed the sexual imagery here.

More important in their implications are those occasions when the libretto had to be changed or rewritten before or during composition, a procedure that affected some of the most important passages in the opera. Before entering into this topic, however, it is necessary to consider the nature of *C* in a little more detail since it holds so many clues to the nature and extent of the problematical passages, each of which tends to cause some hiatus in its otherwise orderly progress. It is made up of bifolios of 20-stave manuscript paper placed one after another (i.e. not grouped in fours as they tend to be when they come from the music shop). As economical in his working methods as in all aspects of composition, Britten appears not to have wasted a scrap of paper unnecessarily. If something went wrong he had a number of ways of dealing with it; the following most usual ones are listed in order of the extent of the 'blind alley', ranging from short to long:

(a) Erasure: the composer's lifetime habit of working in pencil has undoubtedly saved many of his premature thoughts from prying eyes.

(b) Deletion: this can extend for as much as a single side, but if the matter to be deleted extends much further then the usual practice was

(c) to remove a whole folio. The sheet was not wasted if it had any spare staves at all, but tended to be used up for further sketching. There are therefore a good number of 'sketches', almost all of which have an original place within *C* itself; apart from later entries, therefore, they consist for the most part not of what are usually thought of as sketches, in the Beethovenian sense, but of almost fully fledged but rejected passages.[26]

The implications for the would-be detective of Britten's compositional habits are that every disjunct folio signals a hiatus of some sort. For example, just into Act I scene 1, the composer came to a halt on the third side of a bifolio; but rather than waste paper and cause needless recopying, he detached the second leaf, which is now sketch B (see n. 27), cancelled the verso side of the remaining leaf, which was bound into *C* in reverse order with the torn edge outwards, and then started a new bifolio (pp. 21-4). The purpose of this was to insert in the passage between figs. 18 and 19 a repeat of the 'Good morning' exchanges followed by Auntie's reply to Ned Keene; this replaced some weaker lines in *La* which Britten had at first decided to cut, going straight from Ned's 'Had Auntie no nieces we'd never respect her!' into the following chorus. He must have changed his mind and asked Slater to revise so that the episode before the final stanza of the Borough's song would balance the previous one in length and importance; he must also have wanted to emphasise the Nieces' mocking participation in the respectable 'Good morning' ritual by repeating it, and give Auntie a musically inverted answer to Ned's jocular taunt (which is set differently in the deleted passage on p. 19 of *C*), as a further way of drawing attention to the Nieces' role in Borough life. The lines for Boles and Balstrode just before fig. 20 (also absent from *La*) were presumably added at the same time to sustain the emphasis – and possibly to relegate into decent obscurity the complementary lines at the end of the choral stanza:

> Yet only such contemptuous springtide can
> Tickle the virile impotence of man.

There are about sixteen places (not counting the Storm Interlude, which has a specially weather-beaten look for reasons that will become apparent) in a manuscript of 214 pages in which there appears to have been a moment of frustration or change leading to the removal of pages. Britten's fluency has been made sufficient occasion for unthinking criticism in the past for the present-day commentator with access to the manuscripts to be inclined to use them to show how great was his 'creative struggle'. But notwithstanding the composer's relative youth and the immensity of the project, the evidence simply does not warrant such an interpretation. There is no need to pretend otherwise: only the very naive will give extra credit to bookfuls of illegible scrawl as evidence of intensity of compositional thought over the stimulation offered by the click of billiard balls or the purr of a Rolls Royce negotiating Suffolk lanes with precision.

The first apparent moment of difficulty occurs right at the end of the Prologue. Strangely enough, the Peter–Ellen duet is not in *La*, though (as we have seen) it figured in the Pears *Axel Johnson* scenario. Indeed, *La* gives Ellen no lines at all in the Prologue; patches on p. 6 of *C* show that Swallow's questions and her 'I did what I could to help' were added later, not only for dramatic reasons, surely, but also to give the singer a moment to 'warm up' before the duet, a typical example of Britten's practical attitude in these matters. A pencil version of the duet occurs in *Lb*, in which Ellen concludes the bitonal section with

> You'll marry with children
> To make you proud,

and goes on to sing rather different words from Peter in the ensuing unison. Part of an early attempt to compose the duet is deleted at the bottom of p. 10 of *C*. The words, though almost satisfactory, give too little time for the phrase to unfold: there is too much musical tension too soon (see Ex. 2). This itself may be a second try, for there is an earlier erased version at the bottom of the page which seems to connect to a scrap found on one side of sketch A.[27] Now A began life as the original of p. 33 of *C* (Balstrode's announcement of the approaching storm towards the end of Act I scene 1), so it appears that the problem with the duet lingered on, or its composition was postponed owing to the lack of words. Indeed, another draft of the difficult bitonal section occurs on sketch D, originally the second page of Peter's 'Great Bear' aria. A complete solution was not found until rehearsal, because *VS* still preserves *C*'s final version (see Fig. 5) in which Peter and Ellen sing different words in their final unison stretch, Ellen's quatrain being ultimately abandoned in favour of Peter's.

Ex. 2

When we turn to Peter's scene with Balstrode at the end of Act I scene 1 we find no musical hesitation at all, but a continuing struggle to get the right words. In Slater's very first draft of the libretto, Peter addressed Swallow, and although Balstrode is firmly established in *La*, Peter's lines went through several stages. The section beginning 'Picture what that day was like' (fig. 41) began in *La* with a less convincing verse framed in questions:

> Have you ever been afraid of the fear
> Of a cringing child?
> Or known life being bound
> To a scared companion?
> Have you tried solitude
> Doubled by a shy one?
> When evening brings despair
> To your gaunt cabin
> And you launch your boat to find
> Comfort in fishing [etc.]

For composition, this was changed to something more specifically linked to the death of the first apprentice. This is what Britten set (and Slater printed in *S*):

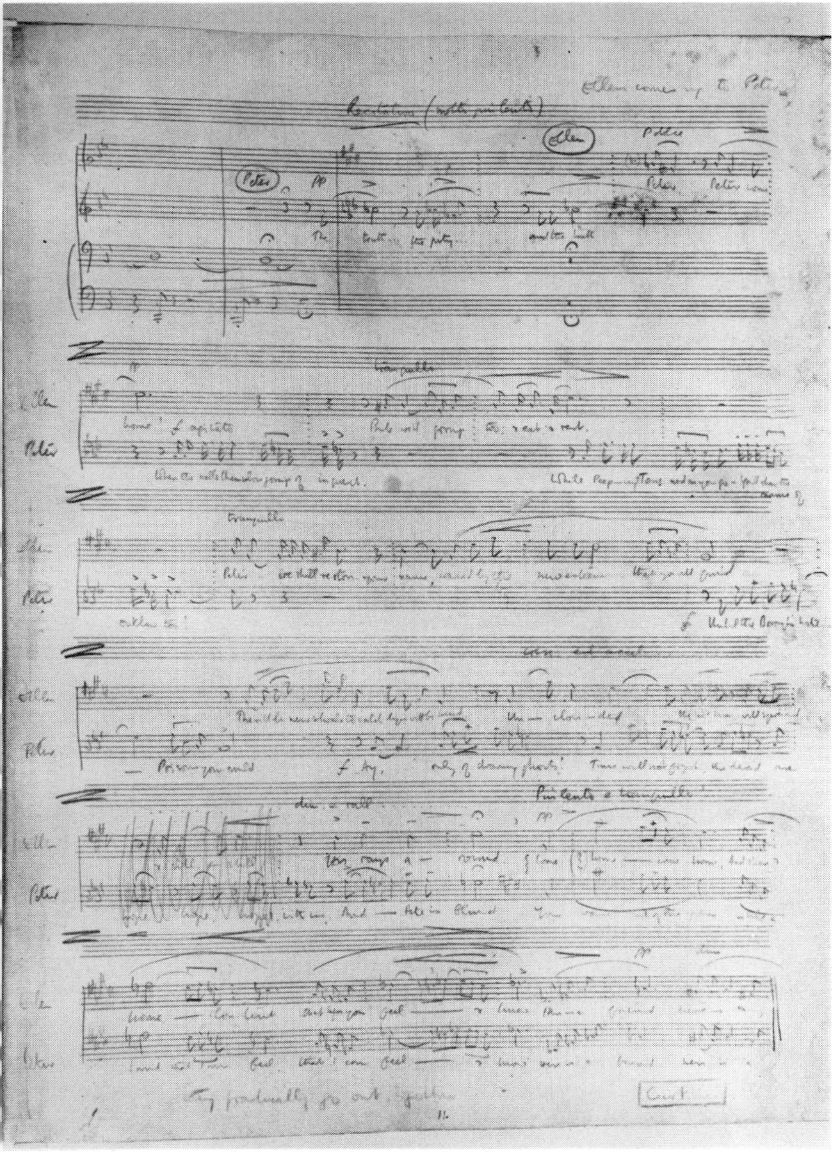

Fig. 5: The Peter–Ellen duet in the Prologue, as it appears in the composition sketch

Picture what my life was like
Tied to a child
Whose loneliness, despair
Flooded the cabin:
I launched the boat to find
Comfort in fishing [etc.]

In the final version, a description of the elements replaces this, validating Peter's anguish, diminishing his self-pity, and as elsewhere cancelling all trace of an emotional tie between fisherman and boy.

For the soliloquy before the storm, *La* sets out with a verse derived from Slater's first draft. Surprisingly, Peter addresses the young apprentice:

Young stranger shall we sail beyond
The borough streets, the timid land?
Is the way out to sail against the wind?
This time there'll be no quarrels, this
Time our wills not cross.
Stranger, we'll find out what the others missed.
Two other youngsters sailed with me.
We shared luck. It was all unlucky.
Young stranger, we shall sail – but they – but they . . .

This is crossed out in *Lb*, which suggests various alternatives. The one eventually settled on in *C* is close to *VS1945* except that the last line was indeed first set to those expressively semi-articulate but also dangerously incomprehensible words, 'but they', uttered three times.

No place in the whole score seems to have given the composer so much trouble as the Storm Interlude. Charting a course through this compositional maelstrom is complicated by the fact that Crozier needed an extra ninety seconds of music at a late stage to manage the scene change.[28] This accounts for the removal of the Interlude from *VS* and for a good deal of sticking and pasting in *FS*. To make sense of the conflicting patterns does not lie within the scope of this account; a few details must suffice. All goes well until fig. 57, the return of the initial motif with the descending horn counter-subject. The episode at 58 seems to have taken a variety of forms at various stages, and it looks as though Britten at some time had another episode, prominently figuring a triplet up-and-down wave-like motion, after the return of the main theme at 59 and before the return at 60 of the music of 'What harbour shelters peace' (58-60 is covered in a compressed manner in a separate sketch, C). But the part beginning twelve bars after 59 appears on an inserted bifolio of 16-stave paper in *C*, and this suggests that the episode was among Britten's attempts to expand the Interlude at a later date.

The larger expansion, however, probably occurred with the material after 60. There are sketches for the canonic version of the tune here on the reverse side of the page on which the finished version appears – an inserted single sheet. My tentative conclusion, then, is that in looking for places to enlarge, Britten tried to insert a new episode before 60, but then settled instead on the very beautiful canonic passage from 61 to 62. The whole matter is complicated because of the evident struggle with the piece in the first place; and since the different version of the episode at 58 got as far as *FS*, there is also the possibility that Britten took the opportunity to revise the whole Interlude during the rehearsal period.

Asked once what qualities he most desired in a libretto, Britten said 'What I require is memorable and thrilling phrases. I think the Pub Scene in *Grimes* was successful partly for this reason.'[29] Certainly Slater, who had a gift for humour and an ear for everyday speech, is at his best here, and *C* shows how smoothly work proceeded. In the early part of the scene, almost the only modification was the deletion of a third stanza of Auntie's short number, 'Loud man'; it is still perhaps a little too momentous for the occasion. There was, however, some unsureness over the crux of the scene, Peter's great aria and the ensuing skirmish, the moment when Peter and his adversaries come nearest to actual contact. Sketch D, the original p. 75 of *C*, shows the aria going wrong in the middle section ('But if the horoscope's bewildering'), where the metaphor was changed in *Lb* from the school playground to the herring shoal, as we have seen. After its removal, sketch D was set aside and used for a draft of the opening two bars of Act II (entitled here 'Summer morning') and, as already mentioned, the Peter–Ellen duet for the Prologue. But then the ensuing fugato came adrift. Britten originally began with an inversion of the subject, and with the Nieces' comment about sour beer set to a descending chromatic line. A second try kept the chromatic line but reached the present fugue subject and led on to what is now sketch E, which extends as far as 'Somebody start a song' at fig. 79.

It is possible that the doubt and trial here really hinged on what the passage was to leading up to. The round 'Old Joe has gone fishing' is one of the virtuoso moments of *Grimes*, a genre piece of which Verdi would have been envious. And yet the words, unlike the rest of those in this scene, were not determined until quite late in the day. Slater's first draft of the libretto has Balstrode (not Keene) starting off with a verse bemoaning the fisherman's lot. This is replaced in *La* by a more genial rhyme:

As I drank the home-brewed ale
Someone brought a likely tale.
That the hops that made the brew
Never in our hopfields grew,

with Peter singing

Never in our hopfields grew
What was in the wonder brew
For we know the devil's tail
Always stirs a home-brewed ale.

No setting of this has survived. At the end of E appear untexted sketches of the round – obviously to fit the present words, which are entered into *Lb/c* by hand. What began, then, as a purely diversionary idea was slowly transformed into the powerful musical confrontation between the crowd and Grimes in which two sides of his character are united – the scared fisherman looking back on the horror that haunts him and the visionary feeling intimations of his death. Since the present version also appears in *S* one can assume the librettist was pleased with the improvement. He did not, however, choose to print the last exchange of the act:

Ellen: Goodbye, my dear, God bless you. [be happy *in C*]
Peter will take you home.
Omnes: Home? Do you call that home?

One can think of few moments so quintessential to the opera as this tremendous curtain line.

The survival of a whole bifolio (sketch F) of abortive versions and sketches of the opening of Interlude III indicates another tough moment for the composer. In a first version (F1) there are only four bars' introduction before the melody, which is in D. (The two-bar draft on sketch D already mentioned was possibly an advance 'inspiration' for this opening.) F2 proceeds with Ellen's melody, F3 tinkers with a new idea for the opening accompaniment, and F4 goes back to Ellen's melody, whose rhythm and climactic moment come closer now to the final version. Perhaps the uncertainty here can be attributed, as already suggested, to Britten's having a clear idea for the lyrical moment but not being able either to make the words fit or to get a suitable revision out of the librettist. An even larger struggle in the sketches G, H and J concerns the conclusion of the Interlude (of which Ellen's first entry is part) and the opening of the hymn; the problem here arose from the composer's having initially conceived the hymn in four-part harmony, with Ellen's lines delivered over it in a more recitative-like manner.

A good deal of trial and error went into the rest of the scene. We may note a short deleted passage (bars 8 – 10 before fig. 6) giving a different harmonic twist to Ellen's linking passage here so that Peter's 'Buy us a home' would have come out a tone up. Was the change made to preserve the D major associations, which, despite the bitonal complication, connect the passage with its model in Act I scene 1 (at fig. 44)? Or was a much longer-range strategy at stake: to introduce the F which remains as a pedal from here to the climax, and is a potent musical symbol for the forces grinding Peter down (as David Matthews points out in chapter 6); and to allow that 'other note' of the ninth (or minor second) that denotes Grimes's loneliness to be foreshadowed here in its more optimistic guise as an F sharp before it becomes the G flat of 'Wrong to plan, wrong to try' later on? The F major chord on Ellen's 'peace' is as a result a slightly forced moment; but then Britten, like most major composers, always had a sense of when to sacrifice detail to the larger design, and the F major chord in its awkward simplicity is not inappropriate for Ellen at this moment (see below, Ex. 24).

Another change of harmonic direction occurred later on in the 'Grimes is at his exercise' ensemble where, at fig. 23, the music originally went to D major and is indeed written out in that key as far as four bars before fig. 27 in *C*, with directions to transpose. Two further sketches (L and N) and a deletion and insert (p. 113) testify to further difficulties with the passage. It would be easy to point to a practical reason for this since Balstrode's 'When the Borough gossip starts' reaches very high in D. But the real reason was surely to engineer a special tonal effect, namely not one but two very demonstrative – even crude – tonal shifts from B flat to C (at 23) and D (at 27): 'Popular feeling's rising', as the vulgar Swallow puts it, and the way Britten's tonal plan manifests this adds a graphic touch (as Peter Evans has pointed out).[30]

A difficulty of a more practical kind arose at fig. 37, where the composer's first attempt at 'Now is gossip put on trial' pitches the phrase a minor third lower each time it occurs (i.e. on F sharp as now, then E flat, C, A and finally F in place of the A flat two bars before 39). This version (on sketch O), for 'all the men (without Balstrode)', clearly goes too low, but it was not rejected until the composer got stuck over an extended repeat of the two bars after 39.

Undoubtedly the most important revisions in this scene concern the climax and the Peter–Ellen duet leading up to it (from fig. 16 to the sixth bar after 17). What is noteworthy about Slater's libretto, first of all, is that (as found in *La*) it provides no climax at all. Peter enters; there is the quarrel (slightly less sympathetic to Ellen, whose initial interrogatives 'Were we right . . . ? were we mistaken . . . ?' are the flatter statements 'We're wrong . . . we were mistaken'). Peter's response to Ellen's 'We've failed' is first to cry out and strike her as in the final version, but then rather oddly to address the apprentice:

> Now we'll see, young stranger come
> Where the road leads. Young stranger, home.

Two sketches of the whole section (K and M) give us some idea of the nature of Britten's indecisions. A first attempt (K) shows a minim rather than a quaver beat (which brings home to the observer just how expressive the notation is of the tension in the final version of this encounter), a shuffling of some phrases between Peter and Ellen, and an entry of the Chorus with the line 'He descended into Hell', which is certainly appropriate but perhaps a little too melodramatic and too suggestive of Don Giovannian associations. The other sketch (M), after beginning with an abortive two and a half bars at Ellen's 'Peter, you cannot buy your peace', goes on to what is possibly the most interesting draft of all (Ex. 3). The choral 'Amen' was to have underscored 'We've failed', and the words for Peter's crucial theme, the musical basis for so much of the rest of the opera, were not yet worked out. In *C* they are 'To Hell then, And God have mercy on me!', clearly referring to the deleted Chorus entry 'He descended into Hell' (see frontispiece). *VS* and *FS* have Ex. 4, with the final 'So be it, and' substituted for 'One' in *FS* without the precise notation of *VS1945* (see Ex. 26). In transferring the 'Amen' from Ellen's to Peter's entry, Britten appears to have realised the main thrust of the opera's underlying moral statement. Making the Borough endorse Ellen's view of the situation was a powerful idea. But to have Peter literally take his note and words from out of the mouths of his oppressors was to get at the root of the matter: Grimes at this moment not only succumbs to them but also in his own mind becomes the monster he perceives they think him to be. There could be no better illustration of how a real opera composer goes about making musical drama from the flat material of his libretto. This climax, the turning point of the drama, was purely Britten's creation, as these documents testify.

We have seen that Britten originally gave Interlude IV (the passacaglia) the title 'Boy's suffering' and that he intended it to be a fugato. This is borne out by sketches P and Q, which preserve various attempts to start it, the one at the beginning of P being worth quoting since it shows a combination of both fugato and ostinato (Ex. 5). It tails off expressively, like many of these abandoned passages. Sketch Q shows a next

Ex. 3

Ex. 4

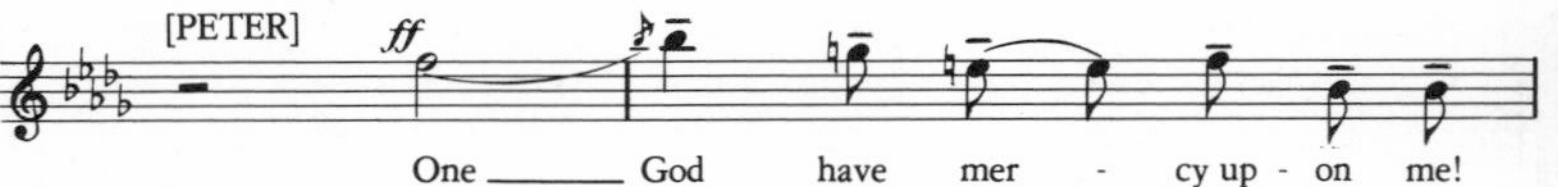

stage in which the fugue subject is incorporated in a violin–viola duet, which is then followed by the opening of a new variation for *tutti* strings. Perhaps more sketches existed which might have shown the interim stages between this and the completed version on pp. 139-44 of *C*, where there are signs of considerable erasure. Or perhaps, having worked so assiduously with these ideas on paper, Britten conceived the theme in its present form – dramatically and psychologically important on more than one level, as David Matthews points out (below pp. 142-6) – without much trouble. There is a limit, after all, to what we can know of the compositional process, however many sketches we possess.

After this hesitation, the whole of Act II scene 2 flowed easily. This is all the more surprising because of the adjustments to the libretto at a later stage, mentioned above. In other areas of the opera we have seen what amounts to a cumulative effect – a weakness or lack in the text of *La* leading to revisions before composition and sometimes to further revisions after. The opening words 'Go there' (not in *S*) are an example; they were needed for Grimes's coloratura gesture which makes both a dramatic point and a musical link. And some changes were made in the 6/8 section at fig. 58 ('They listen to money'), presumably – as in the corresponding section at figs. 44-6 of Act I – to help the musical flow and the enunciation of this difficult moment for the singer. Otherwise, in this scene it seems to have been decisions on certain dramatic points that caused change, not a basic lack in the libretto itself. For instance, at fig. 61 the Lydian–A major 6/8 aria ('And she will soon forget her schoolhouse ways') was originally addressed to the young apprentice: 'And you would soon forget your workhouse ways'. This beautiful moment, then, was first conceived as a fantasy about the life Grimes and the boy, not Grimes and Ellen, could share. And, as already mentioned, the arrival of the posse originally brought out Peter's wrath against the boy, whereas the paranoid reaction of the final version is more convincing. Moreover, the 'dead fingers' that stretch out to tear down Peter's fantasies were those not only of the dead apprentice but also of Grimes senior, who makes his ghostly appearance at fig. 64:

Ex. 5

Andante
pp
Db pizz.
(+Timp)
Vla Solo
pp
con 8va sempre
Vln Solo
p
Ob

Sometimes I see two devils in this hut.
They're here now by the cramp under my heart –
My father and the prentice boy before you came.
They sit here and their faces shine like flesh.

We can see how the changes here, taken along with others already discussed, amount to a significant reorientation of Peter's character, detaching him emotionally and dramatically not only from his father's ghost but also from the silent but palpable apprentice, and making him even more the captive of those dreams and fears for which Ellen serves as focus.

In the mad scene of Act III we shall see how Britten went on to detach Peter from Ellen, indeed from all his earthly surroundings, to become completely alone and self-involved. Compared with that crucial scene, the rest of Act III went smoothly.

Lb has a list of dances scrawled in its marginal notes which include 'Barn dance, Waltz, Country dance, Gallop, Lancers, Valeta, Sir Roger de Coverly, Washington Post (Galop), Paul Jones, Hornpipe' – many more than the four finally chosen. An interesting sketch (R, the original of p. 163 of *C*) shows that scene 1 was to have opened with the dance band playing the tune of the nieces' 'Together we are safe'; on the reverse side is a sketch for the fugue subject of *The Young Person's Guide to the Orchestra*, op. 34, written for a documentary film with text by Montagu Slater and first performed in October 1946. Another sketch (S, the original of p. 181 of *C*) shows an attempt to set several extra bars of dialogue between Ellen and Balstrode before the Embroidery aria (fig. 23), which originally took a slightly different form (Ex. 6). This failing, the composer sketched a bit more on the reverse side before arriving at the present melody. The sequel to the aria terminated in *La* with Balstrode's 'We have the power'; it was presumably for musical reasons that Britten asked for the elaboration (added in pencil in *Lb*) and for the key line 'We shall be there with him', which

Ex. 6

rounds out the scene, effects a B major resolution and gives yet another twist to the 'God have mercy upon me' motif.

Anyone who compares the published scores with *S*, or reads Slater's account of the plot,[31] will be struck by the dissimilarity of Act III scene 2 in the two versions. And if one goes further and examines *C*, one cannot help being moved on arriving at p. 204 to see at the conclusion of Interlude VI the beginning of an attempt on Britten's part to set Slater's version. What survives of this attempt is worth quoting in full because it shows once again and with some emphasis that for Britten the musical idea was inextricably bound up with the dramatic situation as he conceived it, and took precedence over the librettist's actual words, which could be sacrificed without hesitation if they did not fit. Slater's text actually contained some of the 'right' ideas and in *VS1945* one can see Britten going along in parallel, borrowing moments from it here and there. But Slater makes Peter too articulate to be 'weary and demented' (Britten's stage direction in *C*), and his dialogue remains strangely unfocused. Furthermore, given the subsequent corrections to Act II scene 2, the references to Grimes senior had to be deleted, as did the final plea 'Stranger forgive . . . Young stranger come. Young stranger home', which echoes Slater's original climactic (or rather, non-climactic) line for the crux of the drama in Act II scene 1, and was replaced by 'What harbour shelters peace' in the last scene.[32] In addition, the private encounter of Peter and Ellen which Slater arranges is falsely suggestive of a continuing bond between them, when in fact the musical truth is that Peter is far beyond responding to her actual presence in any terms whatsoever. So much more essential to Britten's purpose was his own eventual solution, arrived at with the help of among others, Ronald Duncan, the librettist of the composer's next opera, *The Rape of Lucretia.*[33] This entailed the utter and complete isolation of Grimes, his evocation of Ellen as a memory along with other memories in a musical recapitulation of his past experiences, and also that extraordinary effusion of sound on his own name when he comes to the point at which he 'roars back at the shouters'. The existing version is entered on a separate bifolio of the special 27-stave paper used for *FS* cut down to fourteen staves; it is placed between the two deleted passages printed here as Exx. 7 and 8. Ex. 7 begins on the second system of p. 204 of *C* (two bars after fig. 47); it has Slater's words on top and beneath them those of a version also found in the annotations of *Lb* – the first step towards a final solution. There must then have been a page or more that was subsequently detached and is now missing, leading into the second deleted passage (Ex. 8), on pp. 205-6 of *C*.

Yet these attempts to set the Slater text find exact parallels in *VS1945*, which preserves the two-stanza shape and chromatic line indicated in Ex. 7. Even in the more radically altered version of Ex. 8 one can discern the present form of the passage from four bars after fig. 49 to six after 50. The encounter with Ellen has been replaced by Peter's vision of her in what amounts to a flashback to the crisis of the opera, emphasising Peter's loneliness much more effectively than Slater's reiterated words could do. Also dropped are the references to drinking,

Ex. 7

[p. 204 of *C*]

PETER

p *sempre ad libitum*

Qui - et - ly There you are There you are This
Steady Nearly

break - wa - ter with splin - ters torn by winds is where your
home in - to har - bour Home into

dim.

fa - ther took you by the hand to this same
har - bour It will be calm

boat Leav - ing your home for the same sea Where he
there Deep wa - ter Wa - ter to drink my

died and you're go - ing to die
sorrows dry and the tide

più f

Quiet - ly There you are
Steady

CHORUS *pp*

Grimes

foghorn

pp

Ex. 8
[p. 205 of C]

ELLEN
Pe - ter! Pe - ter!
PETER
fa ther . . .
Was it
SA
pp
Grimes!
Ch
TB
pp
pp
ppp
Grimes! Peter Grimes
foghorn
ppp
[ELLEN]
più f
Pe - ter! Pe - ter!
you who called?
[PETER]
was it
f vivace
The ar - gu-ment's finished money all spent, The drin - king's

più f ancora
Pe - ter!
over wild oats sown
I'm a - lone now as you fore -
[CHORUS]
Pe - ter Grimes

Pe - ter!
Pe - ter
The
told
you hear
my name
I'm a - lone
as you fore -
Peter Grimes!
Peter Grimes!
Grimes!

cries you hear _ are in your mind. Hallucina - tion
told.
you hear it
pp cresc.
Peter Grimes
Peter
Peter Grimes
Peter Grimes
pp
[p. 206]
No!
[This is seven bars after fig. 50, the end of the deleted passage]
Grimes
Peter Grimes Peter
Grimes
Peter Grimes
Peter
fz
Grimes

money and wild oats, but with characteristic economy Britten retains 'The argument's finished' together with the line that follows it (transposed up in the final version). That there were other ideas for the scene we can tell from one last, very thinly identified sketch (T), which must represent some point in the abortive Peter–Ellen encounter (it lacks words, but incorporates the foghorn with chorus and two solo lines). This sketch finds fewer musical parallels in the scene as it now stands, and reminds us that the version crossed out on pp. 204-5 was a 'finished' effort, one that would be part of the opera now if the composer's natural dramatic instinct had not rebelled just at the moment when he came to the great climax of the scene – Peter's roaring back at his tormentors.

From the material the documents present, certain patterns of change emerge and are highlighted by the conflict of ideas between composer and librettist. The main issues of that conflict, moreover, are concentrated in the last scene, with the scene in Grimes's hut acting as a secondary point of focus. Slater was keen enough to go along with Britten in making Grimes (in Peter Pears's words) 'a misfit whose behaviour is excusable . . . and understandable'. But he would not go so far as the composer ultimately required in cutting him off from ordinary human conditions. For whatever reason (and it may have been faithfulness to the original conception as found in Pears's scenarios), Slater could not forebear to raise the spectre of Grimes's father and the two apprentices (with all their psychological implications), to drop hints of loose living, to engineer that final encounter with Ellen, and even to make the apprentice the focus of Peter's last moment. In removing the father, eradicating ordinary human weaknesses, playing down Ellen's role in the last scene, and intensifying Peter's lonely fantasy in his last moments, Britten first of all strengthened what was for him the major theme – the individual against the crowd – by emphasising more consistently the isolation of Grimes implicit in Act I, where it is symbolised musically by the rising minor ninth of his first aria. The breakdown of Grimes's connection to his fellow human beings, both friend and foe, begins with his very first appearance in the Prologue; after Act I his only encounters are with Ellen and the boy, but the boy's silence renders that connection one-sided to say the least, and one cannot avoid feeling that the value of Ellen's friendship, from the point of view of its function in the plot, lies chiefly in the inevitable rupture that precipitates the crisis. Indeed, the roles of Ellen and the prentice in Peter's downfall were more clearly delineated as the revisions proceeded: she became the focus of the fantasies connected with the inward-turning nature of Peter's anger, he the catalyst for the brutal and irrational compensating outward flashes. But to develop the work along these lines was to set the central character quite apart from the realism of his surroundings. Alienation was not enough; dissociation took over. It is hard not to conclude that Britten allowed it to do so, consciously or unconsciously, in order to enlarge the opera's significance. Grimes with a father figure; with common or garden weaknesses; with a woman friend to whom he is accountable even when deranged; with an attachment (of whatever sort) to his apprentice: this Grimes is much less clear a symbol than Grimes the lone oppressed visionary whose one notable moral flaw, his cruelty to his apprentices, makes him ambivalent enough to be humanly interesting and not simply a hollow idea. In excising the rounding-out of Slater's Grimes so ruthlessly, Britten perhaps precipitated the critical debate which occupies the last section of this book; but at the same time he ensured that, though more ambiguous in meaning, the work would gain in universal appeal by focusing on a central character drawn in the clearer, bolder strokes congenial to musical drama, and by depending more on the music than the words to convey its message.

With hindsight it is all too easy to see the problems of a libretto. And it is also evident that in the main this particular libretto was soundly constructed and written with painstaking care. But clearly, Montagu Slater cannot have been prepared for the consequences of writing for such a strong-willed composer. For what this story shows is that despite the comments, helpful or otherwise, of his team of supporters – Pears, Slater, Crozier, Duncan and perhaps others – and all the discussions, fruitful or unfruitful, it was Britten himself who made all the decisions, whether at his composing desk or later between rehearsals. Opera is ultimately a musical form. The composing history of *Peter Grimes* illustrates that fact, throws light on the historically difficult relationship of composer and poet, and demonstrates in a very telling way how an opera composer must take charge of his text.

4 *Breaking the ice for British opera: 'Peter Grimes' on stage*

PHILIP BRETT

It is a measure of the acceptance of *Peter Grimes* into the operatic repertory that it has gathered any 'stage history' at all in less than forty years. But undoubtedly the most important event in that history is the premiere, which coincided with the reopening of the Sadler's Wells Theatre and the return of its resident opera company shortly after the end of the war in Europe. This was the cast as it appeared in the original programme on that momentous first night of 7 June 1945:[1]

Peter Grimes (a Fisherman)	Peter Pears
Ellen Orford (the Borough Schoolmistress)	Joan Cross
Auntie (Landlady of 'The Boar')	Edith Coates
Her 'Nieces'	Blanche Turner, Minnia Bower
Balstrode (a retired Sea-Captain)	Roderick Jones
Mrs Sedley (a Widow)	Valleta Iacopi
Swallow (Lawyer and Magistrate)	Owen Brannigan
Ned Keene (Apothecary)	Edmund Donlevy
Bob Boles (a Methodist Fisherman)	Morgan Jones
The Rector	Tom Culbert
Hobson (The Village Carrier)	Frank Vaughan
Doctor Thorp[2]	Sasa Machov
A Boy (Grimes' new apprentice)	Leonard Thompson

The People of the Borough
Conductor – Reginald Goodall
Produced by Eric Crozier
Scenery and Costumes by Kenneth Green

In his production, Crozier aimed for a deliberately realistic style at the composer's behest, and in this he was aided by Kenneth Green's very full and detailed sets (see Fig. 6).

My aim as producer – and in 1945, it should be recalled, Aldeburgh and the Suffolk coast were familiar to far fewer people than today – was to evoke those ordinary streets, the curiously distinctive shapes and textures and juxtapositions of Aldeburgh buildings and the particular quality of light that bathes them, and also to recreate something of the life that had filled the town in the early years of the nineteenth century. Kenneth Green and I attempted, by what might be called selective realism, to express the truth of that particular place and its people.[3]

Fig. 6: The Borough preparing to visit Grimes's hut in Act II scene 1 of the first production (Sadler's Wells, 1945). Kenneth Green's set was modelled on his native Southwold, which has a lighthouse, rather than Aldeburgh (12 miles south), which has none

No doubt, as Crozier recalls, some critics felt at the time that the visual idiom did not match that of the music: it could not then be known that this was to be Britten's most realistic opera,[4] nor could everyone sense that his musical language was not 'experimental' in the least. Several eye-witnesses have told me that one of the most powerful effects of the production was the almost claustrophobic atmosphere engendered by the small and crowded stage – a quality they missed in the Covent Garden production two years later. Indeed, few of those who saw the Sadler's Wells production refrain from asserting its superiority, though of course they cannot help linking the production with its broader significance. Eric Walter White makes the connection clear:

> The orchestra might be too small to do full justice to the Interludes, the stage space too cramped for the full sweep of the action, the idiom of the music unfamiliar, the principals and chorus under-rehearsed, yet the impact of the work was so powerful that when the final chorus reached its climax and the curtain began to fall slowly, signifying not only the end of the opera but also the beginning of another day in the life of the Borough, all who were present realized that *Peter Grimes*, as well as being a masterpiece of its kind, marked the beginning of an operatic career of great promise and perhaps also the dawn of a new period when English opera would flourish in its own right.[5]

The new dawn did not rise without some stormy off-stage effects. Under the directorship of Joan Cross the Sadler's Wells Opera Company had not only done well artistically against all odds in the war, but had achieved what many would deem the impossible in opera by making a profit. Debts had been paid and salaries raised. But as Tyrone Guthrie later wrote, staking the future of the company on a new work by a young man barely thirty years of age was to the singers both unintelligible and outrageous. Even the more musically enlightened who thought it was a marvellous score were positive it would never 'take'.[6] According to Eric Crozier, even meaner causes lay behind the singers' revolt against the artistic management: 'they complained bitterly because the composer, leading tenor and producer of *Grimes* were conscientious objectors: they declared that it was a waste of time and money to stage such "a piece of cacophony" as the new work: and they stated that it was only being produced because Joan Cross wanted to sing a leading part in it'.[7] Some of these singers eventually demanded to be appointed as an executive committee in charge of the company and they attempted to obstruct the recording of the work. The opera was shortly afterwards withdrawn from the repertory at the composer's request and Joan Cross, Crozier and Pears resigned from the company.

This operatic squabble might also be seen as a symptom of a larger crisis affecting the Vic-Wells company as a whole. This period saw the breaking up of Lilian Baylis's triple empire – something that Tyrone Guthrie, under whose administration it happened, considered the most serious failure of his professional life. The ballet company was tempted away to Covent Garden, and the announcement of plans to found a new opera company there led to rumours that the best of the Wells singers were to move to Covent Garden and the ensemble was to be broken up. Guthrie was not consulted, and according to his biographer it was over this issue that he resigned.[8] Whatever the truth of the matter, it is hardly surprising that in this atmosphere of uncertainty and bad feeling the singers, who had worked hard to keep things going in the war, should become difficult and resentful.

At the same time, the young composer himself was scarcely sanguine about the opera's prospects:

> It never occurred to me that the opera would work. My only other operatic experience until then had been in America with *Paul Bunyan*. This had proved disastrous – the wrong piece in the wrong place – and so I had no confidence about *Grimes*. Besides, at that time such an off-beat story was hardly thought right for opera. This, and the quarrels going on in the company, were not very good auguries. At the dress rehearsal I thought the whole thing would be a disaster. But, of course, once the tension of the first night was over and people flocked to hear the opera, it *was* very exciting.[9]

This excitement is the one thing that comes across clearly in the reviews of the time, even when they are negative. Evidently it was difficult for the critics not to be impressed, and they almost all convey a sense of the importance of the occasion. Ernest Newman, for example, took three weekly columns to express his view of the work in *The Sunday Times* (10, 17 and 24 June 1945); and he returned to the subject as the opening of *The Rape of Lucretia* approached some months later (24 and 31 March 1946). In the first set of articles he is nearly all praise – for the title role ('the character is wholly consistent and excellent material for music'), for the silent boy, and for the music, especially the Interludes. And in one of the later articles (24 March), although he finds that it 'strains the sense of credulity' to hear Grimes singing the 'Great Bear' aria, he waxes even more eloquent:

> For the first time in English opera, we have a mind both rich in musical invention and at home on the stage . . . The really great things in *Peter Grimes*, the things that make us feel that this is he who should come, are the moments in which Mr Britten conceives the drama so entirely in

terms of music, and the music so entirely in terms of the drama, that there is no drawing a dividing line between the two.

This was just and generous praise from one who did not grant it lightly. Others were equally enthusiastic. William Glock in *The Observer* (10 June) wrote of the Prologue, 'could Verdi have been there he would have sat back in admiration if not always in comfort'. He concluded, 'it is in keeping with Britten's creative "innocence" that he should grasp at every kind of resource, and give us . . . every level from the most elementary operatic manoeuvre to the purest poetry'. Ferruccio Bonavia of *The Daily Telegraph* (8 June) also gave a favourable account, but by mishearing the music managed to raise what became a critical issue: 'Peter is played by the tenor, the protagonist in most operas. But he does not and is not meant to engage very deeply our sympathies.'

The responses of the anonymous critics of *The Times* illustrate what seems to have been a trend. The first account (8 June 1945) is almost rapturous: 'expectations ran high and were not disappointed' is the opening sentence of a panegyric with few qualifying remarks.[10] In 'Second Thoughts' (15 June) – how many reviewers of the time seem to have had these – there was a little rap on the knuckles for the spoken words in the last scene, 'a dangerous intrusion of an alien element'; and by 26 October the critic (probably Frank Howes) was asking 'was the principal character a strong enough central pillar for an international opera?', with the explanation that 'an opera with a chorus for protagonist might do for choral-minded England, but how would it go in the more tenor-minded countries of operatic tradition?'. If the aim of this comment was chiefly to claim the work for the English 'renaissance', there was clearly very little else of Britten's dramatic work that the reviewer wanted to claim on any account at all by the time of the Covent Garden production of *Grimes* two years later: 'its successors from the same pen are by comparison progressive aberrations after mistaken ideals' (7 November 1947).

Not all the press was generous even at the first performance. The aging W. McNaught of *The Manchester Guardian* remained as cool to this as to other works of Britten.[11] McNaught was perhaps the most persistent source of the common complaint of the old guard of British musicians against their brash young Benjamin: what they considered heartless facility and called 'cleverness'. An account along these lines is the one by Geoffrey Sharp, editor of the *Music Review*, who called *Grimes* 'opera virtually without melody', and deemed the music 'poverty-stricken' and 'devilish smart'.[12] Neville Cardus, McNaught's successor on *The Manchester Guardian*, reviewing the Covent Garden production

(12 November 1947), felt he had to assure his readers that *Peter Grimes* 'left [Britten] no time, for once, for fussy cleverness'. He also made the astute remark that '*Peter Grimes* is English through and through without trustful resort to folklore', but then concluded that 'Grimes is not a strong enough character, not psychologically realised. For this reason the opera cannot strike the authentic tragic note.'

Not the least of the merits of Michael Kennedy's book on the composer is that it demonstrates by ample quotation why Britten's so-called 'morbid sensitivity to criticism' was not entirely neurotic or irrational. The rather appalling schoolmasterly tone of so many of the reviews of *Peter Grimes* bears out the observation in a long anonymous article in *Time* magazine (16 February 1948) that 'English critics, having adopted Benjy Britten as a national hero, now insist on talking like Dutch uncles to him'. It is easy to gain an impression of the reviewers, even during this greatest of successes, as a chorus of Dutch uncles pursuing the composer with something of the obsessive intensity that the Chorus pursues Grimes in the opera. Take, for instance, the account in *The Spectator* (15 June 1945) – the reviewer was Dyneley Hussey: 'The weakest instrument in the composer's equipment is the solo voice. His writing for it is always apt to be less interesting than the accompaniment which supports it.' Much the same had, after all, been said of Mozart. But if this strikes a genuine note as the cry of a disappointed canary fancier, what follows is pure parrot-talk: 'There is no limit to what such a talent may accomplish, if the composer will aim at bold and simple effects, avoid excess of clever devices and subtle points that fail to make their effect in the theatre, and above all, concentrate on the broad vocal melody as the central feature of his music.' Hussey also had his 'second thoughts' (22 June 1945) in which he marvelled that Britten 'should yet have failed to perceive that the central figure in his scheme was completely lacking in those qualities that arouse the tragic emotions, and especially the emotion of pity'.

These 'second thoughts' that are mostly less favourable than the first are an interesting phenomenon of the critical response to *Peter Grimes*. We have perhaps all had the experience of being faced with normally judicious men carried away by enthusiasm who rein in their feelings as their control is successfully re-exerted. This process seems to have happened on something of a collective scale among the London critics after the initial triumph of *Grimes*, leading to one of those recurrent periods in the composer's life when no one in the swim dared be extravagant in his praise. Of course, there were those who re-entered battle on his behalf; in his second thoughts in *The Observer* (24 June),

William Glock berated those who called the opera a fierce and challenging work: 'What spoiled babies we have become! I should have thought the most noticeable thing about Britten was his gift for making statements of undoubted originality in terms which everyone could understand.'

What these accounts reveal, of course, is the insufficiency of most of the daily and weekly critics of the time. Their reviews served a useful purpose in publicising the event, but not even a practised hand like Newman can be said to have shown any real penetration into the music. Even those who had time to absorb the work rarely did it justice. There is a promising opening to the article entitled 'The significance of *Peter Grimes*' by R. L. Jacobs in *The Listener* (7 March 1946) that accompanied the first broadcast performance, but after raising some interesting issues it goes on to deal with the question about 'mere cleverness' that haunted Britten. A noble exception is the two-part article in *The New Statesman* by Desmond Shawe-Taylor, reprinted here as chapter 9. Not the least of its achievements was to turn the 'cleverness' question into a firm and authoritative demonstration of Britten's 'competence'.

Another considered and thoughtful statement was that of Philip Hope-Wallace in *Time and Tide* (14 June 1945). He begins by calling the premiere the 'most important operatic event since Hindemith's *Mathis der Maler* at Zurich', and goes on to point out a connection, which he must have been the first to notice, between Britten's work and Shostakovich's *Lady Macbeth of Mtsensk*.[13] Hope-Wallace recognises and applauds the significance of Britten's work but like Shawe-Taylor, though in different terms, he argues that there is a flaw in the conception of the title role:

> Powerfully though [the opera] evokes the atmosphere of a harsh way of life in an East Anglian fishing village, it just fails to make explicit enough either in music or drama its essential and difficult 'hidden' theme of its hero's divided nature . . . Montagu Slater's libretto would seem to have extracted from Crabbe's curious poem not merely the crowded surface picture (inevitably overcrowded, for the real hero of the *poem* is the *Borough*), but also some of the essence of a tragic conflict in a man's soul. Yet in the collaboration not enough light falls on this central theme, which is finally the sole claim on dramatic interest. [Describes the plot.] These tragic external events make the 'story' of the opera as we have it, but the inner nature of the man and his motives – a wonderful subject for music – have very largely to be accepted on trust. In short, this hero remains curiously negative and the conflict of his divided heart is not disclosed.

As he admits, Hope-Wallace was writing after only one performance 'in which the role was diffidently sung, and in which the words were often fatally inaudible' (this last was a common complaint at the time). But his lengthy exploratory article, together with that of Shawe-Taylor, brought immediately to the surface the two issues – the moral ambivalence of the work and the unexplicit nature of the conflict within Grimes himself – that have constantly worried serious critics, especially British critics, of the work. We might now wonder why so few looked beneath the surface of the plot. For Edmund Wilson, pausing to express his admiration of the opera (see chapter 10) at a time when he found little else to like about Britain, it was natural to think in terms of allegory. Why were the music critics unable to do so? Can it have been fear (conscious or unconscious) of what they might find there? Or is it to be explained more conventionally by the fact that *Grimes* so clearly belonged not to the Wagnerian but to the grand opera tradition, in which the symbolic or allegorical had little place?

The obtuseness of the critics about 'such an off-beat story', however, could not cloud the brightness of this moment of Britten's first real triumph. The war had ended a month earlier; Britain was beginning to undergo an immense social and cultural change, marked immediately by the election of a Labour government a month later. The appearance of *Peter Grimes*, not unconnected to these other matters, as Edmund Wilson suggests, was for the musical world no less momentous an event. Not since the time of Purcell and Handel had the country heard such a brilliant new work in the theatre from one of its own composers. After two dull centuries, it signalled a turn of events in which music, in particular opera, would flourish as never before in the land. As Britten himself said later, 'I think it broke the ice for British opera.'[14]

When the Aldeburgh Festival opened in 1948 its programme book contained a list of the productions of *Peter Grimes* compiled by Eric Crozier – as if to assure those who braved the journey to Crabbe's Borough in the difficult conditions of post-war England that the 'native, rooted here' had also gained an international reputation to equal, if not better, that of any other British musician. It is an impressive list by any accounts: Sadler's Wells, 1945-6; Covent Garden, 1947-8; Antwerp, 1946; Brussels, 1948; Rome (radio), 1946; La Scala, Milan, 1947; Stockholm, 1946; Copenhagen, 1947; Hamburg, 1947; Mannheim, 1947; Berlin, 1947; Tanglewood, 1946; Metropolitan, New York, 1948; Los Angeles, 1948; Graz, 1947; Basle, 1946; Zurich, 1946; Brno, 1947; Budapest, 1947; Paris, 1948; Sydney (radio), 1947.[15]

The Covent Garden production which opened on 6 November 1947 perhaps raises more important issues about the work than any other after the opening at Sadler's Wells. Though it was an entirely new production, it took over six of the twelve main singers from the original cast – among them Pears, Cross, Coates and Brannigan – and the composer himself was still involved. This time Tyrone Guthrie himself, now free of his Vic-Wells administrative duties, directed the work, and the design was by his closest associate, Tanya Moiseiwitsch, daughter of the concert pianist. Guthrie had admired Eric Crozier's production, but he had different ideas about the opera:

> I felt that in the vast dimensions of Covent Garden intimacy was out of all question and that the majestic sweep of the score, the evocation of the sea and its ineluctable influence on the destiny of the characters, could be better interpreted by a simpler, more spacious setting. Tanya Moiseiwitsch designed a superb set using the entire width and depth of the Covent Garden stage. A horizon cloth surrounded a single enormous set piece suggesting a jetty [see Fig. 7]. This worked splendidly for the scenes of storm and stress; but I must admit that it was rather implausible and overwhelming to the moments of intimate and would-be humorous conversation.[16]

Fig. 7: The 'sea-scape' set by Tanya Moiseiwitsch for Covent Garden, 1947

From the defensive tone Guthrie adopts it is clear that these ideas did not go over very well with the composer:

Immensely as I admire Britten and respect his taste and intelligence, I have never been able to sympathize with his desire for a naturalistic staging of his operas, and for the inclusion in his scores of conversational scenes as are entirely appropriate in Puccini, who aimed consistently at *verismo*. But Britten, so I feel, is not consistent: snatches of *verismo* are interpolated with the boldly abstract expression of atmosphere and emotion.[17]

The result, according to Guthrie, was that a year or two later, at the composer's request, the setting and his 'choreography' (as he calls it) were scrapped, and more naturalistic ideas prevailed.

This view of Britten's attitude to staging has been brought up to date, so to speak, by those who argue that he 'lost touch with theatrical life' as a result of his 'retreat' to Aldeburgh.[18] It is surely more reasonable to assume that as a real operatic composer he had notions about staging that throw some light on the nature of his works. Support for this idea comes unexpectedly from an interview about *Billy Budd* by the director Ande Anderson, who joined the Covent Garden staff in the late 1940s. He talks about Britten's not liking the accent thrown on the ship by its too realistic representation on stage in the first production of that opera. 'He said the opera was nothing to do with the ship; it was about the people on the ship.' And, Anderson continues,

Britten did the same thing with *Grimes*. We had a brilliant production by Tony Guthrie, but Ben didn't like it at all because the accent was thrown on the sea. Ben said, 'No, it's got nothing to do with the sea. It has to do with the people in the village.' Tony said, 'But Ben, the sea made the people what they were', and Ben replied, 'No, these people would be the same wherever they were.'[19]

There is no need to put Anderson's memory on trial: the gist of what he says is all too clear from the scores. Britten rarely allowed himself to interpret his music in words, wisely trusting it to speak for itself. In breaking that rule in his introduction to *Peter Grimes* (see chapter 7), he misled many into a windy world of abstraction about the nature of the sea imagery, when the real dramatic values lie elsewhere and can only be brought to life by the human interactions on stage. The issue for Britten in both *Grimes* and *Budd* was one not of realism, naturalism or abstraction in production, but of the interplay of character. The sea is graphically enough portrayed in the music of *Grimes*, as is the ship-on-the-sea in *Budd*, to need no further emphasis from anyone. What is needed from a stage director is adequate support for – or no distraction from – the presentation of the drama in human terms. This need would take different directions – in *Budd* the elimination of the too overpowering presence of a lifelike man-of-war, and on the other hand in *Grimes* the naturalistic presentation of an oppressive society, 'each one at his exercise' in a believable manner.

Although the history of the opera in the land to which it belongs and which it reflects is of prime importance, the way it fared in the country where it was conceived and commissioned is in some ways equally revealing. As it was the first important commission of the foundation he had endowed in 1942 in memory of his wife, the conductor Serge Koussevitsky had every reason to be pleased, and his proclaiming it the greatest opera since *Carmen*, while it upset a few, reflects his pleasure. His idea had been to hold the premiere at his Berkshire Music Festival at Tanglewood, where the Boston Symphony Orchestra had been playing its famous summer series since 1937. The war had made this temporarily unfeasible, and Koussevitsky generously relinquished his claim to the first performance, saying that the opera belonged not to him but to the world. In 1946, however, plans to stage the work went ahead and, perhaps inspired by the composer's youthfulness, Koussevitsky assigned the musical direction to the young Leonard Bernstein, who had studied with him at the Tanglewood summer school in 1940 and 1941 and had become his assistant at the festival in 1942. The production was not blessed, and indeed came close to disaster. Eric Crozier, who was rushed in at the last minute to rescue it, later wrote to say he was glad that Koussevitsky had been undismayed by his prophecies of doom and had insisted that the work be given.[20] 'The most unimpressed member of the Tanglewood audience', reported *Time* magazine (19 August 1946), 'was Composer Britten himself. Said he stiffly: "There's no use pretending it was professional . . . It was a very lively student performance."'

The opera was nevertheless well received, and in a few well-chosen words, Jacob Avshalomoff made a far-reaching claim for it:

> Perhaps a flaw in the libretto is that it never gives the cause for Grimes's original isolation from the community. But beyond that the piece has the quality of a Greek tragedy, wherein misfortune comes not from direct malfeasance on the part of the protagonist, but as a result of some failing in his character, in this case the arrogance which brings about his destruction.[21]

A Broadway producer, Eddie Dowling, planned to bring the work to New York, but to everyone's surprise it was taken up by the Metropolitan

Opera, then and for some time afterwards one of the most hidebound of the world's great opera houses, where the cards were stacked from the very start against any contemporary work it dared foist upon its subscribers. As Virgil Thomson put it in *The New York Herald Tribune* the morning after the opening on 12 February 1948,

> the steamroller processing that our beloved Met, geared to Wagner, puts any new work through is one of the severest known tests for the strength of theatrical materials. If Mr Britten's work came out scarcely in English, vocally loud from beginning to end, and decorated in a manner both ugly and hopelessly anachronistic, it also came through the ordeal with its music still alive and its human drama still touching.

Thomson is not particularly sympathetic to Britten, whom he once dubbed 'a local Shostakovich'. But in characterising *Peter Grimes* as a 'rattling good repertory melodrama' with a simple and efficient musical structure 'calculated for easy effect' he overstated his case to make a valid point. Compared with the later operas, *Grimes* does indeed have a larger share of purely theatrical effects, what Thomson calls 'wow' material: it is after all a second opera not a sixteenth, a *Rigoletto* not an *Otello* – and with the *Paul Bunyan* flop behind him, Britten was working overtime for a success. And despite the poor quality of the Met performances, which Irving Kolodin attributes largely to Emil Cooper's musical direction,[22] the work attracted great attention. The composer even appeared on the cover of *Time* magazine, against a background of fishing nets, with the caption 'Britain's Britten' (see above, p. 93).

Another critic to see the opera as 'pure melodrama' was Joseph Kerman, who in *The Hudson Review* put *Grimes* and *Lucretia* to the test in the stringent manner he was later to develop in *Opera as Drama*. *Lucretia* fails miserably, and *Grimes* hardly gets off scot free – it is judged 'a fairly weak piece of dramatic action' in which 'Grimes's break with Ellen . . . is bungled in book and score alike'. But Kerman also acknowledges Britten's gifts ('above all he has a God-given sense of pace'), and writes well about the last scene 'in which music is reduced successively to absolute zero on a grand scale . . . Its expressive decrescendo, ending in non-musical speech, is a powerful evocation of the dead hopelessness, past tragedy, of Grimes's ultimate predicament'.

After the enormous international attention it attracted in the 1940s, *Peter Grimes* lay comparatively fallow in the following decade. Covent Garden revived its production with new directors (John Cranko and Ande Anderson) and much-altered sets, but the other major European capitals did not see the work, nor was it put on in America. The interesting development of these years was its appearance in the Far East

(Tokyo, 1956) and its further penetration of the Soviet bloc (Zagreb, 1955; Warsaw, 1958). An amusing report in *The Sunday Times* (6 January 1952) noted that theatres and dramatic societies in East Germany had been ordered to perform the work as often as possible for propaganda purposes, the object being 'to present a harrowing but authentic picture of the degeneracy of life in Britain as portrayed by and for Englishmen'. The East German critics were reported to have said that Britten had derived most of his musical ideas from Musorgsky.

Interest in the work picked up again in the 1960s, undoubtedly stimulated by Britten's complete recording of 1959. A review of the Covent Garden performance of 17 November 1960 in *Opera* (January 1961) points out that two years earlier average paying attendance for the work had been 1,114, whereas now it was 2,129, just short of Joan Sutherland's *Traviata* (2,166). Since it had no 'star' attraction, the reviewer concluded that *Grimes* filled Covent Garden 'simply and solely on the merits of the score'. In 1963, Sadler's Wells at last reintroduced the opera to its repertory, and in that year and 1965 toured several important European cities with it. In the same decade the work reached Cincinnati (1960), Rome and Montevideo (1961), Wuppertal (1962), Riga and Sofia (1964), Leningrad and Oslo (1965), Rio de Janeiro (1967), the Edinburgh Festival (Scottish Opera production) and Turin (1968), and Pretoria and (in the same production) Johannesburg (1969); and there were new productions at Basle in 1965 and at Strasbourg (where the work had first been produced in 1949) in 1962. Two notable events came towards the end of the decade. In 1967, the Metropolitan Opera engaged Guthrie and Moiseiwitsch to mount a new production, which also marked the debut of Jon Vickers in the title role, the first appearance of Colin Davis as a conductor of the work, and Geraint Evans's resumption of the role of Balstrode (which he had not sung since the Covent Garden season of 1953-4). In 1969, the year this trio appeared together in the revived Covent Garden production, John Culshaw persuaded Britten to record the work at the Maltings, Snape, for presentation on BBC TV.[23]

The last decade has seen no falling off, rather a continued growth of interest in the work. In the United States it made its impact more widely felt through productions at San Francisco (1973, 1976) and Chicago (1974); these made a great impression, owing largely to Jon Vickers's powerful advocacy of Grimes and Heather Harper's sympathetic portrayal of Ellen, combined with Geraint Evans's straightforward stage direction.[24] Undoubtedly the success of *Grimes* helped to provide a suitable climate for the simultaneous, and very fine, productions of *Billy Budd* at the Met and at San Francisco in the autumn of 1978.

In 1975 Covent Garden staged a new production, the work of the Australian stage director Elijah Moshinsky and the designers Timothy O'Brien and Tazeena Firth. With its lack of realistic scenery it seemed to mark a further break from Britten's notion of a naturalistic presentation. Harold Rosenthal in *Opera* (September 1975) called it an 'almost Brechtian conception', and its stark, spare and tough nature excited a good deal of debate. Most interesting, perhaps, was the reinterpretation of the chief secondary characters that Rodney Milnes discerned in his review for *The Spectator* (19 July 1975):

> Particularly equivocal are Ellen and Balstrode, who emerge less as Grimes's only friends in the Borough, more his most implacable enemies. In the Sunday scene, Ellen is prying from the start, keeping the apprentice out of church so that she can interrogate him, knitting furiously as she peers at him, and exposing the tell-tale bruise with a violence akin to that which caused it. Only then can she smile and enfold him in a maternal embrace: the trap is sprung. This is a chilling moment. Similarly Balstrode, having knocked away Grimes's few remaining defences in the first act, purposefully stands aside during the man-hunt in the second; he conducts his own investigation once they have gone, as if claiming the victim for himself.[25]

It is interesting also to find British critics at this stage beginning to adopt Virgil Thomson's slightly condescending tone of thirty years before. For instance, Bayan Northcott in *The New Statesman* (18 July 1975) begins by asking if the work is 'after all no more than a brilliantly revamped hearty old provincial British romp?' before going on to admit that by the second act he was 'as hooked as ever' and concluding that '*Grimes* will live because on balance it has dated in the right way'.

Peter Grimes strode into the 1980s with a production at the Komische Oper in Berlin (January 1981), and the Covent Garden production was presented the same year at the Paris Opera, where the work had not appeared since the 1940s, but returned belatedly with great celebration, accompanied by a fine exhibition mounted in the vestibule of the opera house by the British Council. A production that apparently brought out new and plausible glosses on the text was one by Nicholas Hytner, given at the Brighton Festival in May 1981. Meanwhile the BBC recorded the Covent Garden performance of 30 June 1981 (according to Stanley Sadie in *Musical Times*, CXXII, August 1981) for eventual release on video cassette. There seems every reason to conclude that the opera has won a safe place in the repertory and no company can now properly ignore it.

Of the various interpretations of the title role in recent years, it is the one by Jon Vickers that has attracted most attention and won over the greatest number of new admirers for the work. The recording conducted by Colin Davis has moreover brought this *Peter Grimes* to many

Fig. 8: Ellen (Heather Harper), flanked by Auntie and Balstrode, with the other principals behind, begins 'We planned that their lives should have a new start' (Act II scene 1, Covent Garden, 1975, producer Elijah Moshinsky). Compare

Fig. 9: Jon Vickers (right) as Peter Grimes with Geraint Evans as Balstrode (Act I scene 1, Covent Garden, 1975)

who have not seen it in the theatre. The impression Vickers creates on stage is unforgettably powerful and tragic, and Davis's conducting, full of whipped-up excitement, goes well with the intensity of the portrayal. Its conviction appears to owe a good deal to the singer's identification with the role. Indeed, as Andrew Porter – to whose judicious account of Vickers in *The New Yorker* (21 July 1980) there is little to add – has observed, 'there have been moments when I've wondered whether I was watching and hearing Jon Vickers as Peter Grimes or Peter Grimes as Jon Vickers'.

The trouble with this heavy-voiced, monumental Grimes for many people is that it comes too close to Crabbe for comfort. The composer himself is reported to have disliked it. His views on the singing of the role were expressed in an account, written long before Vickers came to prominence, of a CBC broadcast performance in Toronto in which Grimes was sung by William Morton: 'This young singer has a voice of just the right timbre. It was not too heavy, which makes the character simply a sadist, nor was it too lyric, which makes it a boring opera about a sentimental poet-manqué; but it had, as it should, the elements of both'.[26]

Many critics have taken the perfectly justifiable line that the composer's is not the only valid interpretation of a work, and some are pleased to hear a Grimes dissociated from the distinctive mark of Pears's vocal personality. Yet few have at the same time admitted the corollary that it is the composer's conception, not interpretation, that must command absolute respect, or noted in this regard Vickers's omission of phrases and alteration of words in the crucial scene in the hut (Act II scene 2), or the extremes of tempo change that Davis adopts to accommodate Vickers's unwieldy enunciation of the phrases in the Prologue, to mention but two instances.[27] Yet the existence of another contrasted and powerful interpretation, whatever its shortcomings, must surely be good for the future of the piece, which can only grow in stature by being explored for new meanings. To leave the last word to the composer:

> If a work is to survive at all, it must be strong enough to stand on its own legs. Good operas are surprisingly tough and can somehow survive all kinds of treatment.[28]

SYNOPSIS AND ANALYSIS

5 *'Peter Grimes': the story, the music not excluded*

HANS KELLER (1952)

Derived from George Crabbe's poem, *The Borough*, the scenario of *Peter Grimes* was sketched by Benjamin Britten and Peter Pears; Montagu Slater undertook the libretto. 'In writing *Peter Grimes*,' says the composer, 'I wanted to express my awareness of the perpetual struggle of men and women whose livelihood depends on the sea . . .' [see chapter 7]. This, together with the light thrown by the story on the early 19th century practice of buying apprentices from the workhouse, pertains to the sociological aspect of the work. Psychologically, however, the significance of the story transcends its time and place. Peter Pears once wrote: 'There are plenty of Grimeses around still, I think!' [see chapter 8].

Peter Grimes is the living conflict. His pride, ambition, and urge for independence fight with his need for love; his self-love battles against his self-hate. Others too, he can (sometimes) love as intensely as he can despise them, but he cannot show, let alone prove his tenderness as easily as his wrath – except through the music which, alas, the people on the stage don't hear. Thus he is destined to seem worse than he is, and not to be as good as he feels. *Peter Grimes* is the story of the man who couldn't fit in.

I should indeed go further than Pears and say that in each of us there is something of a Grimes, though most of us have outgrown or at least outwitted him sufficiently not to recognize him too consciously. But we do identify him, and ourselves with him, unconsciously, which is one reason for the universal appeal of this work.

Another reason is the composer's ability to satisfy both the 'connoisseurs' and the 'less learned' – I put these words in inverted commas because Mozart used them with reference to his first three Vienna piano Concertos. It is in fact the outer perfection of Britten's music that prevents some listeners from realizing its depths.

Prologue

The time is 1830, the place a court-room in the Moot Hall of The Borough, a small Suffolk fishing town [see Fig. 10]. An inquest is held on Peter's first boy apprentice who died of thirst at sea when Peter made the imprudent attempt to sail to the London market with 'a huge catch – too big to sell here'. Though the verdict is accidental death, the coroner-lawyer Swallow is nowise convinced of Peter's innocence. He advises Peter not to get another boy apprentice, or else to 'get a woman help you look after him'. Peter: 'That's what I want, but not yet!' 'Why not?' 'Not till I've stopp'd people's mouths!' Indeed the townspeople are just as unconvinced of Peter's innocence as Swallow. But he has a friend among them, Ellen Orford, the widowed schoolmistress, who had helped him to carry the dead boy home. Now, after the court has been cleared, she comforts him. The inquest has, incidentally, shown that he has another friend: the music (including the orchestration).

The music of the *Dawn* Interlude which follows now continues during the first part of, and later reappears in,

Act I scene 1

which opens, a few days later, on a cold grey morning on the Borough beach and street. The fisherfolk work and sing quietly to themselves (Ex. 9). Here and at the end of the opera the librettist quotes directly from Crabbe. This first episode comes to a sudden end as Peter is heard off stage: 'Hi! Give us a hand!' There is silence. Again he shouts: 'Haul the boat!', and again nobody moves; Bob Boles, fisherman and Methodist

Ex. 9

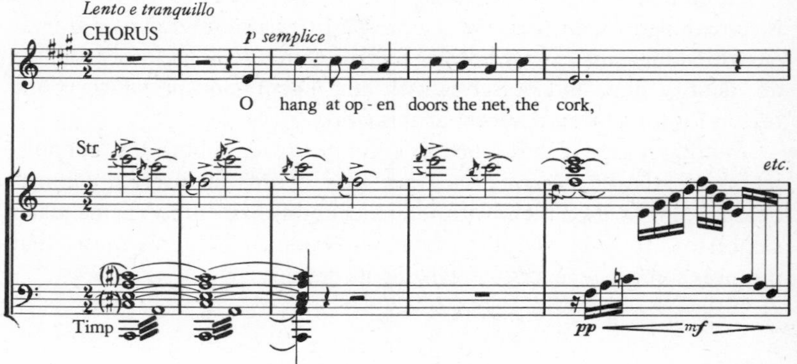

Fig. 10: The Prologue in the first production (Sadler's Wells, 1945). Peter is in the witness-box above the others, facing Swallow, who has Hobson on his right. On the extreme left are Boles and the two Nieces; on the extreme right, the Rector and Mrs Sedley

preacher, shouts back: 'Haul it yourself, Grimes!' It is certainly no easy matter for Peter to work without an apprentice. But at last the local apothecary and quack, and Captain Balstrode, a retired merchant skipper, come forward to help him. Balstrode's attitude towards Peter is in fact benevolent. As for the quack –

> Grimes, you won't need help from now,
> I've got a prentice for you . . .
> I called at the workhouse yesterday.
> All you do now is fetch the boy.
> We'll send the carter with a note.
> He'll bring your bargain on his cart!

The quack's bargain, rather.

Carter Hobson, however, who is also the town constable, wants to keep out of this business. He is supported by the townspeople: 'He's right! Dirty jobs!' But at this point Ellen Orford steps in: 'Carter! I'll mind your passenger.' The people: 'What! and be Grimes' messenger?' Ellen: 'Whatever you say, I'm not ashamed. Somebody must do the job.' She offers to accompany the carter to the workhouse at Ipswich and to welcome and comfort the boy on the way back.

The crowd protests: 'Ellen, you're leading us a dance, fetching boys for Peter Grimes . . .' The bass here develops from the tune of the carter's refusal to fetch the boy, a tune that has also been used in the crowd's 'Dirty jobs!' as well as in Ellen's subsequent intervention. Ellen now again interrupts the people, first with her previous words: 'Whatever you say . . .' But she leaves the sentence unfinished, using the phrase as introduction to her D minor aria (Ex. 10). The two musical phrases of

Ex. 10

these words are the thematic material of the piece, an arioso that is overpowering in its simultaneous ardour and dignity. The listener may like to observe how Britten turns toward his characteristic C major at the end of the last-quoted words and at the corresponding place in the restatement ('Will have no trouble to find out how a poor teacher . . .'), as well as at the end of the number: 'Mr Hobson, where's your cart?'

Small wonder, after this music, that Hobson is willing to fetch the boy with Ellen's assistance.

Earlier in the scene Balstrode has forecast a storm; he now announces its approach by way of the subject of a stormy fugue in which everybody below and on the stage participates, except of course Peter. We find him still working at his boat after the approaching storm has driven the crowd into the local pub, 'The Boar'. Balstrode stays with him: 'Grimes, since you're a lonely soul . . . why not try the wider sea, with merchant-man, or privateer?' 'I am native, rooted here.' They talk about the inquest and the hostility of the townspeople. 'Your boy was workhouse starved,' says Balstrode, 'maybe you're not to blame he died.' This rouses Peter to 'picture what that day was like, that evil day' when the boy died. (Here follows Ex. 11, a minor version of Ex. 13a.) Involuntarily,

Ex. 11

he also pictures his own character:

> They listen to money
> These Borough gossips.
> I have my visions . . .
> I'll win them over . . .
> I'll fish the sea dry,
> Sell the good catches . . .
> I'll marry Ellen!

Marry her now, without your booty, says Balstrode. 'No, not for pity!' 'Then,' Balstrode warns him,

> the old tragedy
> Is in store.
> New start with new 'prentice
> Just as before!

Inevitably, Peter abuses even Balstrode – 'Take your advice, put it where your money is!' – who finally leaves him for the more pleasant atmosphere of 'The Boar'. Alone, gazing intently into the sea and the approaching storm, Peter shows what lies beneath the storm in his own mind (see Ex. 13a):

What harbour shelters peace,
Away from tidal waves, away from storm.
What harbour can embrace
Terrors and tragedies?
With her there'll be no quarrels,
With her the mood will stay,
Her breast is harbour too,
Where night is turned to day.

The turbulent and the yearning aspect (Ex. 13a) of Peter's mind are further contrasted in the following *Storm* Interlude in which the gale breaks out in all its strength. This music develops out of the latter part of the above scene and breaks into

Act I scene 2

(inside 'The Boar', the same evening) whenever somebody opens and struggles with the door. In fact the storm music plays here the paradoxical and therefore fascinating role of intruding into the scene which, structurally, it unifies. (Britten employs the same device in the last act of *Albert Herring*, where the rhythm from the preceding 'Manhunt' Interlude is the unifying intruder.)

The first part of the present scene offers not so much essential story as characterization and a strained atmosphere which is never really relieved, not even by Balstrode's number, 'We live and let live, and look – we keep our hands to ourselves', in which refrain everybody joins (Ex. 12).

Ex. 12

Suddenly the door opens and Peter enters, accompanied by a wild version of Ex. 13a. Indeed, by recurring at vital junctures, this theme contributes a great deal to the cyclic structure of the opera. At the same time its characteristic ninth, associated with loneliness and yearning, has also 'super-cyclic' significance in Britten's work. That is to say, we have met it before in the *Michelangelo Sonnets* (Ex. 13b)[1] and we shall meet it again in *The Rape of Lucretia* (Ex. 13c).

Ex. 13a

Ex. 13b

Ex. 13c

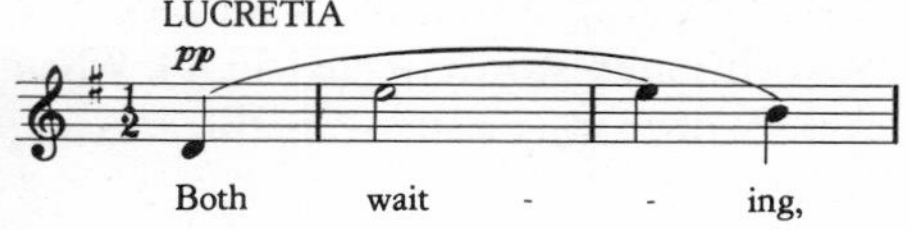

The theme recedes, though not the tension it has created. Peter's E major arioso, however, poises above the excited atmosphere. He looks to heaven –

> Now the great Bear and Pleiades
>   where earth moves
> Are drawing up the clouds
>   of human grief
> Breathing solemnity in the deep night

– and so does the music. But in the last stanza –

> But if the horoscope's
>   bewildering
> Like a flashing turmoil
>   of a shoal of herring
> Who can turn skies back and begin again?

– he seems to divine the inescapable tragedy of his character.

This sublime piece of music falls into four parts, though the verse consists of three stanzas. The first two musical strophes, that is, coincide with the first two stanzas, while the third (last-quoted) stanza is at first taken up by a contrasting *molto animato* middle section, and then returns, in the last line, to the music of the first two strophes. These are constructed (with the help of the strings) as a repeated canon which proceeds from the double basses upwards. But when the canon returns in the last line, it starts upstairs and proceeds downwards, and the entries are drawn closely together. The uncanny, expressive stillness of the canon is in part due to the fact that the melody proceeds in conjunct motion. The vocal line, moreover, is motionless for more than four lines of the first and second stanzas respectively, and again for more than two bars at the end.

It remains to be added that at the end of the second stanza we observe again a turn into Britten's own C major.

Peter's arioso creates understandable bewilderment – 'He's mad or drunk!' – and when in the course of events Boles is about to throw a bottle at him, Balstrode knocks it out of his hand and shouts: 'For peace sake, someone start a song!' An elaborate round is now sung by all (except, at first, Peter) which is thematically connected with Exx. 13a and 14 as well as with the above-mentioned storm fugue (Sc. 1). When Peter enters the piece he disturbs it by distorting each of its three tunes, but eventually the round overwhelms him.

A dramatic return of the storm music accompanies the entry into 'The Boar' of Ellen, Hobson, and Peter's new boy apprentice. 'Peter takes the boy out of the door into the howling storm' whose music ends the act with more than one bang.

Act II scene 1

Again the Interlude (*Sunday Morning*) is the basis of what follows it. In point of fact, the Interlude and the first part of Scene 1 are really one and the same piece of music and, as such, go to form the concert version of the Interlude.

The curtain rises again on the village street and beach. It is a Sunday morning, weeks after Act I. While the townspeople are going to church – we hear the church bell – Ellen and the boy (who doesn't speak or sing a word throughout the opera) enter, and Ellen sings what we know already from the Interlude: 'Glitter of waves and glitter of sunlight . . .' As the organ sounds from the church they sit down on a breakwater and Ellen tries, still by way of the Interlude music, to make the boy talk. But the only reply she gets is her own previous tune, given by the strings in (fairly) canonic imitation.

'Nothing to tell me, nothing to say?' she asks as a new section begins with the church chorus singing off stage; here her notes are no longer those of the Interlude, yet derive from it.

The listener will easily note how impressively the successive phases of the church service (including the organ) on the one hand, and Ellen's and the orchestra's (and later Peter's) part on the other hand, are integrated and together build up what is to become a dramatic and musical climax.

As the boy does not want to talk, Ellen tries to guess what his life at the workhouse was like, and also tells him about her own experiences with children. Then –

> John, you may have heard the story
> Of the 'prentice Peter had before;
> But when you came I
> Said, Now this is where we
> Make a new start. Ev'ry day
> I pray it may be so.

Here the Hymn in church ends. So does, of course, this section as a whole, though Ellen uses the notes of her last-quoted words in the following *recitativo agitato*: 'There's a tear in your coat. Was that done before you came? Badly torn' [Ex. 21].

This recitative proceeds together with the responses in church: '. . . and we have done those things we ought not to have done . . .' Here Ellen sings: 'That was done recently. Take your hand away. Your neck, is it?' The recitative closes with her cry, 'A bruise – well, it's begun!'

Then follows, after the Gloria has started in church, her moving piece – 'Child you're not too young to know where roots of sorrow are'. The accompaniment, and later also her own part, take over from the Gloria. When, after she has finished, she rises and fastens the boy's shirt, the oboe reminds us of her discovery of the bruise.

At the beginning of the Benedicite, Peter enters excitedly: 'Come boy!' He has seen a shoal. Ellen objects: 'This is a Sunday, his day of rest.' Peter: 'This is whatever day I say it is! Come boy!' Ellen reproaches him [Ex. 24]:

> This unrelenting work,
> This grey unresting industry,
> What aim, what future,
> What peace will your hard profits buy?

Peter's reply derives, musically and otherwise, from his excited vision near the end of Act I scene 1 ('They listen to money . . . I'll marry Ellen!'):

> Buy us a home, buy us respect,
> And buy us freedom from pain

Of grinning at gossip's tales
Believe in me, we shall be free!

The Credo starts in church, and Ellen asks Peter to tell her 'one thing, where the youngster got that ugly bruise?' 'Out of the hurly burly!' (A minor ninth here which does not readily betray its kinship with the minor version of Ex. 13a, though it also goes on to the octave.) 'Take away your hand!' (same minor ninth) he shouts when she asks him whether they were right in what they planned to do. Suddenly he grows tender: 'My only hope depends on you, if you take it away – what's left?' But when Ellen suggests again, 'Were we mistaken when we schemed to solve your life by lonely toil?' he bursts out: 'Wrong to plan! Wrong to try! Wrong to live! Right to die!' [Ex. 25]. This forceful passage is again based on the previous minor ninth motif (which interval is now inverted) and shows a striking rhythm which has gone unrecognized in the last Interlude.[2]

Peter repeats this angry shout to other words, and into Ellen's insistent 'Were we mistaken . . .' And when at last she says, 'Peter! We've failed, we've failed!' he cries out in despair and strikes her, the orchestra accompanying him with his own previous shouts. From the church we hear an 'Amen', and from Peter Ex. 14, which is four times imitated in the orchestra while he 'drives the boy fiercely out in front of him'.

Ex. 14

Here we have reached the turning point of the opera. As far as the action is concerned, Peter has now shown that he is even unable to keep peace with, indeed capable of hurting, the woman he loves, his only friend. There is only one future for him, namely, none. And musically, Ex. 14 is the last chief theme to be stated for the first time. In fact it, together with the other Grimes-theme whose first phrase is quoted in Ex. 13a (and to which it is related), are the two most important tunes of the work.

Via Ex. 14, the now following part of the scene looks forward into the next Interlude, i.e. a Passacaglia on Ex. 14 [cf. Exx. 27, 28, 33].

The tragic scene between Ellen, the boy and Peter has not gone unobserved, and the rumour that 'Grimes is at his exercise' (cf. Ex. 14) spreads among the departing churchgoers who collect outside the church door. They develop a savage hatred against Peter – surely the man is going to murder the boy. Eventually the Rector and Swallow, with a crowd of men behind them, go to see Peter in his hut. [Left behind, Ellen expresses her predicament in a lyrical quartet in which she is joined by Auntie and the Nieces – the disreputable women of the Borough.]

The Passacaglia follows, and once again this Interlude anticipates the subsequent

Act II scene 2

which takes place inside Peter's hut (an upturned boat). Peter arrives with the boy to prepare for the fishing. He blames the child for the quarrel with Ellen. His mood alternates between fury, tenderness – 'There's the jersey that she knitted, with the anchor that she patterned' – and ambition (a quotation here from Act I; see Ex. 15).

Ex. 15

With deep and tender passion he dreams aloud of an illusory happiness with Ellen: 'In dreams I've built myself some kindlier home . . .' (Here we get yet another moving turn to C major.) A lyrical *Adagio* of great beauty develops its accompaniment out of the preceding vocal line. 'But dreaming builds what dreaming can disown. Dead fingers stretch themselves to tear it down.' With these words the music reverts to the beginning (complete with C major turn), despite its opposite emotional content. We observe that even the last-quoted sentence is sung to the same notes and note-values as the initial phrase, '. . . warm in my heart and in a golden calm', though the character of this passage is, of course, altered in the restatement in order to reveal the contrast in mood and meaning. Britten shows himself often able, in fact, to express contrary feelings by similar means, and we always find a point in this procedure. Psychoanalysis has taught us that in the unconscious mind opposite emotions are intimately connected; in the case of a man like Peter, whose mind is really swayed by his unconscious, the togetherness of contradicting impulses will inevitably show on the surface.

From afar Hobson's drum is heard: the Borough procession approaches, unnoticed, for the moment, by Peter, who is overcome by a hallucination of 'that evil day' when his first apprentice died. This section is still based, in voice and orchestra, on the preceding *Adagio*, whose music is, however, distorted, and alternates with Hobson's drum. This is heard coming nearer and nearer, until Peter finally hears it. He turns on the boy: 'You've been talking! You and that bitch were gossiping! . . . The Borough's climbing up the hill. To get me . . .' He 'isn't scared', but all the same it seems best to go fishing before they arrive. The boy goes out of the door that opens to the cliff. 'Careful or you'll break your neck! Down the cliff side to the deck . . . Now shut your eyes and down you go!' We hear a scream – the boy has fallen to his death.

The Rector and Swallow enter, but all they find 'is a neat and empty hut'. The act ends with Ex. 14.

Act III

The searching, yet simple *Moonlight* Interlude prepares us for

Scene 1

– once again the village street and beach, three nights later. There is a dance in the Moot Hall, and people pass to and fro between the Hall and 'The Boar'. Thus we gather that Peter has not been seen since Sunday, nor has his boat. Mrs Sedley, a widow who is Peter's chief antagonist besides Boles, suspects, for a change, murder.

The street empties for a while, and Ellen and Balstrode appear from the beach. They believe themselves alone, but Mrs Sedley eavesdrops.

Balstrode has discovered that Peter's boat has been in for more than an hour. Peter himself, however, seems to have disappeared. Ellen has found, down by the tide-mark, the boy's jersey (which, as we remember from the last act, she had knitted and embroidered). Upon identifying it with the help of Balstrode's lantern, she sings two verses of meditation, and full of restrained sorrow. Here is the first:

Embroidery in childhood was
A luxury of idleness,
A coil of silken thread giving
Dreams of a silk and satin life.
[Refrain] Now my broidery affords
The clue whose meaning we avoid!

Before the second strophe there is a short *parlando* middle section of one and a half bars: 'My hand remembered its old skill. These stitches tell a curious tale.' This beautiful B minor aria is the most independent number of the opera.

Balstrode reminds Ellen that 'in the black moment when your friend suffers unearthly torment, we cannot turn our backs . . .' They walk out together, with the pledge: 'We shall be there with him' (Ex. 14 in counterpoint, straight and inverted).

Mrs Sedley informs Swallow that Peter's boat is back. Swallow summons Hobson, and soon a Ländler from the previous dance music (Ex. 16) is uncannily transformed to serve a brutal manhunt after poor Peter, who by now is more dead than alive, anyway.

For about his condition the Interlude which follows here does not leave us in any doubt. Mental pain and physical stress have driven Peter

Ex. 16

all but insane. His madness and Britten's method combine to make this short piece an immensely gripping fantasy, which integrates Peter's disintegrated mind with the help and against the background of a constant dominant seventh on D, sustained by three muted horns. Throughout, too, we hear disjointed, fragmentary reminiscences of Peter's own music. First the flute recalls his 'They listen to money . . . I'll marry Ellen!' from the latter part of Act I scene 1 (see Ex. 15). Next the harp introduces, downstairs, a reminiscence of his dream in the hut (Act II scene 2). This is the only quotation of a theme that has made its first appearance later than Ex. 14. Now Ex. 13a is heard on three solo violins; it is, however, disturbed by the oboe's excerpt from Peter's E major arioso in Act I scene 2, which in its turn is followed by two clarinets' version of what was once his outburst, 'Wrong to plan! Wrong to try! . . .' (Act II scene 1). Into this, double basses and double bassoon enter with another distortion of Ex. 13a which is imitated by the clarinets. This theme then renders its hidden help to the building up of a climax, where it leads into its brother theme, Ex. 14 (inverted and straight). The latter finally disrupts and ends on a repeated minor second which comes both from Ex. 14's minor second and from the minor version of Ex. 13a.

Every second Interlude in the opera, we realize now, is a Grimes Interlude. Or to put it another way, those Interludes which are really Preludes to the three acts are Sea Interludes, while the Interludes between the scenes are Grimes Interludes. The *Storm* Interlude, however, is both.

Act III scene 2

The same scene, a few hours later. Fog. We hear the distant fog-horn (tuba) continuing the minor second with which the previous Interlude has ended. But it has not really ended; its dominant seventh, too, is now continued in the far-off cries of the townspeople: 'Grimes! Grimes!'

Peter stumbles in, demented. 'Steady! There you are! Nearly home!' This again to the same minor second. In fact this fateful interval will be heard to remain faithful to Peter right to the end.

The preceding Interlude has of course once again foreshadowed the scene: Peter's mad recitative consists of reminiscences (Britten's title figures – Lucretia, Albert Herring, Billy Budd – are always given reminiscences in the end). But now we do not hear solely his own music. Thus, in Ex. 17, he quotes Swallow's verdict from the *Prologue*, though Swallow sang other (if rhythmically related) notes to these words. At

Ex. 17

Ex. 18

the same time the tune of Ex. 17 (with which the opera actually opened) is not only Swallow's own characteristic theme, but was sung by him in his initial warning (Ex. 18).

A quotation easily recognized is 'Turn the skies back and begin again!' from Peter's arioso in Act I scene 2. 'There now my hope is held by you' will also be well remembered (Act II scene 1: 'My only hope depends on you . . .'). But Peter interrupts his own tenderness: 'Take away your hand!' These words and this motif previously (Act II scene 1) preceded the tender passage which they now interrupt; it is as if we were given a concrete example of Peter's mental retrogression.

'The argument's finished, friendship lost . . .' – again the 'I'll marry Ellen!' tune from the latter part of Act I scene 1, whose derivatives we have previously heard at 'Buy us a home, buy us respect' (Act II scene 1) and at the beginning of the last Interlude. Here, incidentally, we are offered a further instance of the expression of opposite emotions by similar means.

'To hell with all your mercy! To hell with your revenge, and God have mercy upon you!' This, of course, is Ex. 14.

The voices of the townspeople have now come very near, and Peter roars back at them. Just as he calms down, Ellen and Balstrode appear. Ellen sings, 'Peter, we've come to take you home. O come home out of this dreadful night!' She, too, uses her previous music, i.e. 'Peter, tell me one thing, where the youngster got that ugly bruise?' from Act II scene 1.

Peter, however, does not hear her. Nor is he now disturbed by the shouters who seem to have lost the track and are again heard from far away. He sings his last notes – Ex. 13a. The words, too, are the same as in Act I scene 1 (see their quotation above), though two lines are omitted, namely: 'With her there'll be no quarrels, with her the mood will stay . . .' And the end of the theme, once so yearningly insistent, now dies down in pairs of semitones. An unworldly desire for death and rebirth has taken the place of his worldly (though unrealistic) struggle for a new life.

The fog-horn has the last word, or rather the last minor second.

Balstrode tells Peter to sail out and sink the boat. Peter does so.

Dawn begins and the music reverts, slowly but unperturbedly, to the first Interlude and the opening chorus of Act I. Crabbe's own words, too, appear once more:[3]

> To those who pass the Boro' sounds betray
> The cold beginning of another day . . .

Peter's was a lonely tragedy.

6 *Act II scene 1: an examination of the music*

DAVID MATTHEWS

In the lucidity of its design and the economy of its means, *Peter Grimes* set an example for all Britten's subsequent operas. Each of its three acts is divided into two scenes, and each scene is prefaced by an orchestral interlude; in addition, the first act has a Prologue in which almost all the characters are introduced. Each of the scenes has its own distinct and well-rounded dramatic shape. I have chosen to examine the first scene of Act II because, standing at the centre of the opera, it contains the hub of the drama, while its music is of remarkably high quality throughout and exhibits a wide variety of contrasts. In my examination of the music I have concentrated on three major areas, which are interrelated. First, the precise relation of music and text, and Britten's choice of particular musical phrases for particular lines. (Here I have occasionally made use of the theory advanced by Deryck Cooke in *The Language of Music*: that music is a language capable of expressing very definite emotions, and that certain musical phrases have intrinsic emotional meanings. This theory, in my own experience, 'works' for romantic music at least; and *Peter Grimes* is undoubtedly a romantic work.) Second, the way in which Britten builds his musical structures out of a limited number of short motifs. Although he rejected the Wagnerian method of opera construction, with its leitmotif technique, in favour of, as he put it, 'the classical practice of separate numbers that crystallize and hold together the emotion of a dramatic situation at chosen moments' (see chapter 7), Britten in fact provides as closely knit a musical structure as one finds in Wagner or Strauss. Third, the use of tonality, in particular to heighten the dramatic action. Anthony Payne has drawn attention to a basic key conflict in *Peter Grimes* between A and E flat (an augmented fourth apart, the furthest distance in the tonal order), symbolising, as he says, 'the impossibility of co-existence between Grimes and the Borough' (p. 22). A secondary conflict between two other keys an augmented fourth apart, E and B flat, may also be deduced; in fact it is perhaps more useful to think in general terms of a polarity of sharp keys and flat keys, as Philip Brett does when he writes of 'the conflict between [Peter's] fantasy-life (generally expressed in D, E or A major) and the outside reality represented by, say, the E flat of the storm and pub scene, or the B flat of the courtroom and the final manhunt' (see chapter 13). B flat is probably the key most closely associated with the Borough, and it is the move into B flat at Peter's climactic 'And God have mercy upon me', in the middle of Act II Scene 1, that gives tonal expression to his capitulation to the judgment of society. It may be added that the association of sharp keys with the world of fantasy and the imagination persists in other Britten works: for example *Death in Venice*, where E major is associated with Aschenbach as an artist and A major with Tadzio.

My examination of the music, which assumes a fairly detailed knowledge of the remainder of the opera, should be read in conjunction with Hans Keller's excellent account of the story (see chapter 5). Strictly speaking, Act II Scene 1 ends with the quartet for women's voices; but I have included the passacaglia (Interlude IV), which forms both an epilogue to the first scene and the prelude to the second.

Act II opens *allegro spiritoso* with the well-known Interlude III (*Sunday Morning*): its bright D major with sharpened fourth[1] makes a bold contrast with the E flat minor of the storm that ended Act I. It is 'a fine sunny morning, with church bells ringing'. The horns' ostinato thirds, which overlap to make pungent diatonic dissonances, suggest the pealing of the bells; over them the woodwind play a sprightly tune built out of, at first, only A, E, D and G sharp (Ex. 19a). There is an obvious resemblance between this music and the coronation scene from *Boris Godunov* (see Ex. 19c), especially at the recapitulation where Britten adds a deep bell to his texture (see Ex. 19b); but Bayan Northcott has pointed out to me another, less-known source, which provides a still closer correspondence. This is the Balinese music transcribed by Colin McPhee for piano duet, which McPhee and Britten recorded in the USA and which Britten also played at the Wigmore Hall in London with Clifford Curzon at the very time he was composing *Peter Grimes*.[2] Britten's marked copy of these pieces shows that he took Piano II, which means he would have played the deep gong sound that makes a harmonic clash almost identical to that of the *Peter Grimes* bell (see Ex. 19d: to make the comparison clearer, I have transposed the music down a semitone). Once this Balinese influence is recognised, it can be observed also in the contour of Ex. 19's tune, whose four melodic notes form a Balinese scale.

Ex. 19a

Ex. 19b

Ex. 19c

Ex. 19d

The flat seventh at bar 14 and the E flats a little later add to the harmonic piquancy of this opening. The woodwind tune peters out on a descending chromatic scale and at fig. 2 the violas and cellos enter with a broad lyrical theme in A major, again with sharpened fourth (Ex. 20a). This is a diatonic transformation of the chromatic second subject of Interlude II (*Storm*) (Ex. 20b), which itself derived from the final brass passage of Interlude I (*Dawn*) (Ex. 20c). Ex. 20b's sinister power was always latent in Ex. 20c, but Ex. 20a, with its major 6-5 pendant to the rising scale, is a much more positively joyful theme: as Deryck Cooke has shown (pp. 153-5), the phrase has been used by countless composers to express innocent, unclouded happiness.

At fig. 3 D major returns with the repeat of Ex. 19a, *fortissimo* on trumpets and trombones, and the curtain rises on the entry of the bell nine bars later (Ex. 19b). Ellen appears with John, Peter's new apprentice, as other villagers head towards the church. At fig. 4 brilliant D major flourishes for strings and trumpet herald the return of Ex. 20a, in D, which, as Peter Evans has noted, completes a sonata form without development. At this second appearance the theme is sung by Ellen, her opening words 'Glitter of waves and glitter of sunlight' emphasising its association with the sea in beneficent mood. The bell continues to sound, and at fig. 6, as Ellen ends her phrase 'And goes to church to worship

Ex. 20a

Ex. 20b

Ex. 20c

on a Sunday', the church organ is heard from behind the scene playing the horns' ostinato, while a tenor bell in E flat replaces the B flat one. Ellen's invitation to John to stay behind and talk, sung to the woodwind tune from Ex. 19a, produces no response from him; he goes on playing while Ex. 20a surges up in E major on the strings, in canon. The warmth of its lyricism makes this a poignant moment: there is still hope for the future, symbolised by the bright morning. But the E flat bell continues to toll against the aspiring string lines, bringing them down to earth: E flat is one of the Borough's keys, and the one most strongly asserted in this scene. The strings end on a D sharp and the music moves into E flat major as the service begins.

Now follows a *scena* in five sections, each corresponding to a different part of the service of matins, which is heard going on in the background and which from time to time provides an ironic commentary on the foreground action between Ellen, John and Peter. Ellen's appeal to John produces no response – the boy's silence throughout the opera is a striking device in itself and makes his dying scream doubly effective. Here it prompts Ellen to guess at his feelings about his workhouse upbringing and at the same time to reveal something about herself – exposing her own vulnerability as she does so – while the congregation sings the opening hymn, 'Now that the daylight fills the sky'. The hymn is an English version of the Latin hymn 'Iam lucis orto sidere' from the office of prime, and Britten has used the simplification of the plainsong setting given as Hymn 1 in *Hymns Ancient and Modern*.[3] (Britten's opening line, alternating E flat and F, brings to mind Peter's E – F sharp 'Where night is turned to day' from the end of his first soliloquy.) The original plainsong provided Britten with the notes of Ellen's first phrase, 'Nothing to tell me, nothing to say', from which the rest of her arioso derives: this link between hymn and arioso emphasises their complementary nature, both being concerned, in their different ways, with 'making a new start'. Ellen's vocal line flows in even crotchets, in similar manner, as Peter Evans has pointed out, to the third of the *Michelangelo Sonnets*. Evans draws attention (pp. 106-7) to the special function of this type of word-setting in Britten's operas: to enable crucially important lines to be enunciated clearly and with emphasis on the expressive significance of each interval. Much of Ellen's part in this scene is written in this style, and it is she who has the most important lines to deliver, until Peter's great outburst – the turning point of the scene, and of the opera.

The hymn reaches its final Amen as Ellen ends '. . . now this is where we make a new start. / Ev'ry day I pray it may be so'. The strings sustain

Ex. 21

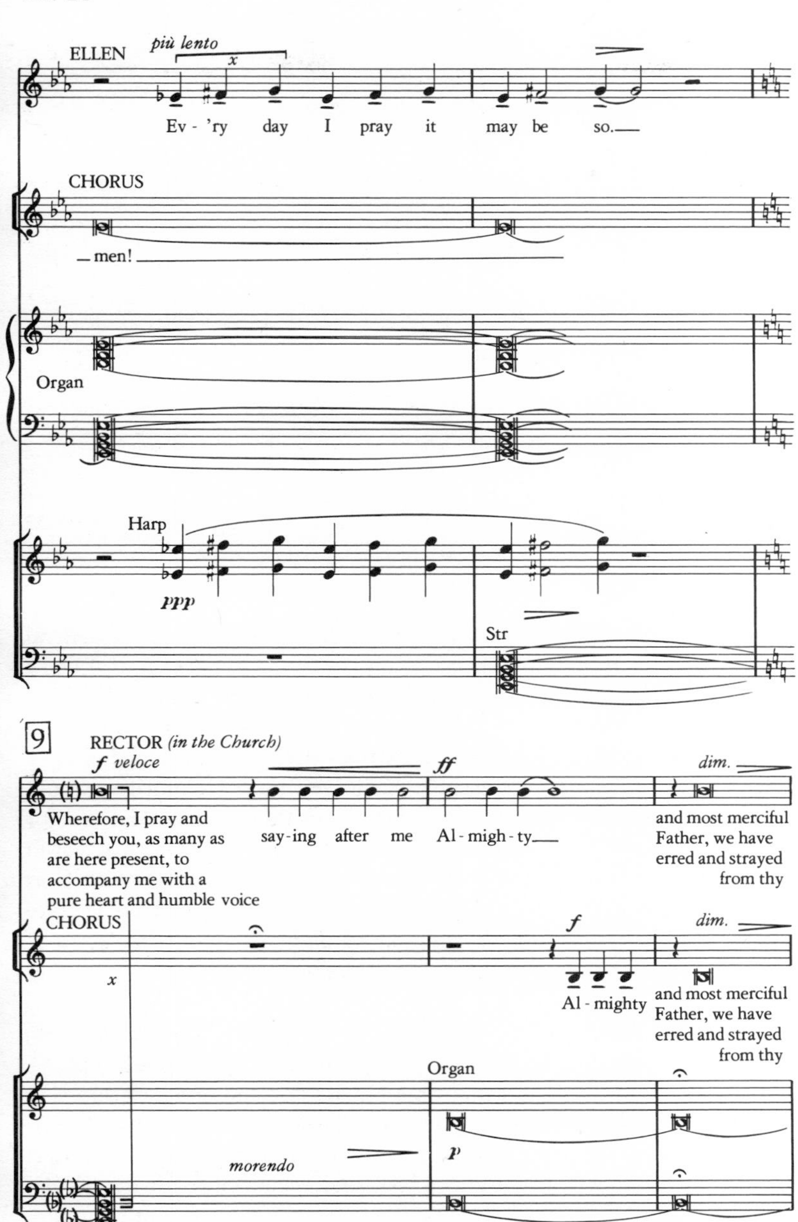
ELLEN
più lento
x
Ev - 'ry day I pray it may be so.
CHORUS
men!
Organ
Harp
ppp
Str
9
RECTOR (in the Church)
f veloce
ff
dim.
Wherefore, I pray and beseech you, as many as are here present, to accompany me with a pure heart and humble voice
say-ing after me Al-migh-ty
and most merciful Father, we have erred and strayed from thy
CHORUS
x
f
dim.
Al - mighty
and most merciful Father, we have erred and strayed from thy
Organ
morendo
p

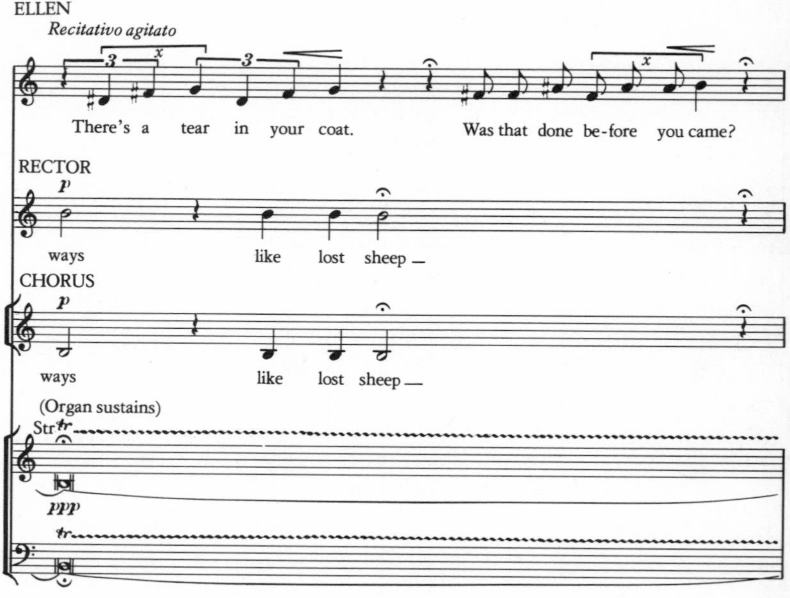

an E flat triad while, from the church, the Rector begins the general confession on B natural, immediately breaking the spell of Ellen's private prayer. This is soon overlaid with an uneasy string trill which signals Ellen's anxiety as she notices a tear in John's coat: no sooner has she uttered her hopes for a new start than they are threatened. Ex. 21 shows this transitional passage: the pervasive three-note motif *x* (whose origin was Ellen's 'nothing to say') provides all the musical material for the new section. 'Ev'ry day I pray it may be so' and 'There's a tear in your coat' are sung to the same notes; but the first phrase, with G as the secure major third of E flat resolving the unstable F sharp, is quite different in its effect to the second, in which G is the flattened sixth of B (major) and the semitonal tension between F sharp and G is acutely felt.

The string trill cadences into B major; the cadence is twice repeated, leading to Ellen's decisive B major proclamation at fig. 10: 'A bruise . . . well, it's begun!'. At the same time the Rector and congregation sing the responses, the initial E flat becoming the third of C minor and shifting to D major. What we hear is, in fact, motif *x* in retrograde: E flat, D, B. The C minor/D major chord progression continues for the Gloria, sung to the notes E flat, F and D – the same notes that began the opening hymn. The orchestra takes up these notes, enharmonically changed to D sharp, E sharp and C double sharp, as a B major ostinato over a steady *andante* march rhythm, and Ellen sings to the boy. Her first phrase, in tender arioso, still expresses some of the hope felt at the beginning of the scene, especially when in the repeat the initial major third expands to a rising fifth for 'Let this be a holiday'. But the second phrase, as she sings of 'how near life is to torture', is a minor key transformation of the hopeful Ex. 20a, with the crucial major 6–5 now become a painful minor second and underpinned with dissonance, turning her hopes sour. Her new sense of hopelessness is still more acutely expressed in the repeat: she sings ironically (Ex. 22) of how the treasonable sea 'Glitters like love', repeating the phrase an augmented fourth higher to stress the contrast with Ex. 20a and her previous, innocent use of the word 'glitter'.

Ex. 22

Ellen's repeated Fs and G flats in the following four bars are prophetic of the final section of the *scena*; the music subsides on a dominant ninth of G minor in the strings, over which she sings 'After the storm will come a sleep' in E flat minor, the key of the storm, her rising major seventh (G flat to F) descending to a low B flat, her lowest note in the opera. The Balinese ostinato recommences as Ellen ends her lament, her alternating low A sharps and B naturals anticipating the mournful minor seconds of the foghorn and of Peter's last sung words. The strings take up the B trill again as Ellen fastens the boy's shirt and the oboe recalls the moment when she first found the tear (motif *x* from Ex. 21).

At fig. 12 a new section begins, *allegro agitato*, a thoroughly uneasy setting of the most exuberant of the canticles, the Benedicite: with each successive section Britten gradually builds up the tension that will finally explode at the climactic moment of Peter's break with Ellen. The chorus, again in unison, sing in a scurrying 15/8; their notes are the alternating semitones of the string trill, B and C, plus motif *x* in its original ('nothing to say') form, all of which is inverted for 'Praise him and magnify him for ever' (Ex. 23: the melody as a whole has the flavour again of Balinese music). The scene is well prepared for Peter's entrance. The G major of his opening words, 'Come boy . . . I've seen a shoal', immediately cuts across the Chorus (as Ellen's vocal line has never done). The hectic recitation of the Benedicite continues in what is in effect the dominant of E minor, staying rooted to this key while Peter and Ellen, disputing about the boy – Peter wants him to come fishing, Ellen pleads that Sunday is his day of rest – pursue an upward spiral of keys in their argument, until its climax in Ellen's entry on a high B flat. She adopts the Chorus's 'Praise him and magnify him for ever' for her own repeated 'Hush, Peter!' and descends nearly two octaves to begin 'This unrelenting work' with the notes of Ex. 23, now in E minor proper (Ex. 24). But what sounds like a resolution of the dominant implications of the Benedicite is immediately wrenched, at Ellen's 'What peace will your hard profits buy' with its dramatic *ppp* F major triad, on to what becomes yet another dominant. It has been foreshadowed a few bars earlier in the 'Hush, Peter!' section, where chords of F alternate with ones in B major, but here it sounds quite new. Ellen, having made her first protest, is to put Peter on the spot yet again in even more threatening terms. His response, 'Buy us a house, buy us respect . . .', centred on F, derives musically from his 'They listen to money . . .' in Act I. 'Believe in me, we shall be free', he sings; but his melody in D major (the hopeful *Sunday Morning* key) clashes painfully with the relentless F minor bass line, insisting that they will not. As Peter reaches high F sharp, the congregation begins the Creed on F natural. The note F is

Ex. 23

CHORUS
12 Allegro agitato (♩. = 126)
mf
O all ye Works of the Lord, bless ye the Lord;
Organ
O ye Sun and Moon, bless ye the Lord;
Peter Grimes comes in
O ye Winds of God, bless ye the Lord.
excitedly from the harbour.
f
Praise Him and mag - ni - fy Him for e - ver.

Ex. 24

sustained throughout this fifth and culminating section of the *scena* as obsessively as is the note B in the murder scene in *Wozzeck*, though Britten's masterly use of the dramatic resources of tonality (which Berg reserved for his final orchestral interlude) produces a more dynamic kind of tension than the doggedly static pedal does in *Wozzeck*.

The chorus fades after three bars, but the horns continue to suggest the recitation of the Creed with their incessant, stuttering Fs. Ellen and Peter now sing together for the last time. Staccato G flat major triads on trombones accompany Ellen's G flat Lydian first phrase – which incorporates the 6–5 progression and derives from her first response to Peter in the previous section. She asks how the boy got his bruise. 'Out of the hurly burly', Peter replies with a lunging minor ninth familiar from Act I. The minor ninth softens to an octave leap as he sings *his* creed, in F major, *dolce semplice*: 'My only hope depends on you, if you take it away what's left?' Ellen's reply, in her sweetest even-note arioso manner, softly accompanied by harp and lower strings, side-slips into B flat for 'mistaken', gently suggesting the key which will soon devastatingly confirm their failure. Peter's violent response, with vain fragments of D major in the bass, only underlines the truth of her suggestion (Ex. 25).

Ex. 25

Ellen repeats her question, Peter cutting in over her: the music shows they are now worlds apart. The G flat triads in the brass rise to their highest pitch of drama. Ellen repeats her arioso phrase for the third time, now no longer in the form of a question, but as a plain statement: 'We were mistaken'. A solo violin – that most overworked of emotive devices, and exactly right here – echoes her voice. Peter cries out 'as if in agony' and strikes Ellen; the violent, jagged *tutti* incorporates his minor-ninth-imbued response 'Wrong to plan' over a double-time version of her 'We were mistaken' (both Ex. 25), ironically united now that catastrophe has fallen. The terrible confusion it creates is dispelled by the Chorus, singing Amen to their Creed on the pivotal F. Peter echoes them: 'So be it'; and, with an overwhelmingly powerful cadence into B flat, sings, to the decisive motif of the opera, 'And God have mercy upon me' (Ex. 26). The motif's curt, emphatically cadential quality seems graphically to seal Peter's fate, and the resolution into B flat indicates his submission to the Borough.

This has been a tremendous scene, with a dramatic tension reminiscent of Verdi at his best. The succession of pedal points – which persist throughout each of the sections – is a simple but wonderfully effective generator of tension; while the much-used device of a long-held dominant pedal cadencing on to the tonic, which Britten had exploited with great skill in earlier works,[4] was never to be more powerfully used by him, nor, to my knowledge, by any other composer born this century, with the possible exception of Walton in the passage (also on the dominant

Ex. 26

of B flat, though minor not major) leading up to the recapitulation in the first movement of his First Symphony.

The next thirty-five pages of the full score, up to fig. 31, are built almost entirely out of the Ex. 26 motif (*y*), which is immediately punched out by the brass in canon as Ellen and Peter leave the stage in opposite directions, Ellen in tears, Peter driving the boy in front of him. Trombones, tuba and the other bass instruments, reinforced by timpani and bass drum, hammer out low B flats in a similar rhythm to the solo bass drum at the parallel climax in *Wozzeck* (Act III, bars 114-15). And just as in *Wozzeck* the pub piano takes up the bass drum's rhythm and turns it into a banal popular tune, so here Auntie, Keene and Boles, emerging from the background where they have been eavesdropping, begin a jaunty B flat major trio based on motif *y* (Ex. 27). This is Britten's light-music style: the music is very similar to the Christmas party scene

Ex. 27

in *Paul Bunyan* (the ultimate source for both is probably Gershwin's *Porgy and Bess*, which had considerable influence on *Grimes*, notably the Act I storm music; see Northcott, 'Search'). But its effect is in complete contrast to the uninhibited jollity of *Paul Bunyan*; the music's hollow jauntiness only emphasises the Borough's total incomprehension of Peter's tragedy. 'Grimes is at his exercise', the trio proclaim with gleeful malice (the line is Crabbe's own). In the fourth bar of fig. 21 the organ voluntary (on motif *y*) announces the end of the service. Mrs Sedley emerges from church, asks what has happened, and adds her spiteful comment, to a *con forza* version of *y*. Balstrode, with a sturdy A major arioso phrase (derived from the entry of the Chorus in Act I scene 1), pleads that Peter should be left alone: 'Let us forget what slander can invent', he sings to a rising A major scale, reminding us of Ex. 20a and of the key of Peter's highest aspirations. But the A minor entries of the Chorus sweep his protest aside, and at fig. 23, as the organ finishes its voluntary on *y* with a cadence into C major, they start a *Presto* 6/8 ensemble, with a pattering ostinato accompaniment based on *y*. The device of one half of the Chorus asking 'What is it, what do you suppose?' and the other half answering 'Grimes is at his exercise' most likely derived from the opening chorus of the St Matthew Passion (of which we are more directly reminded with the shout of 'where' in the bar after fig. 28: see Ex. 28). Over the Chorus's ostinato a succession of villagers, including Swallow with his customary rising sixths and the nieces in staccato thirds, offer their individual moralising comments. Balstrode ends this section with another rising scale phrase: 'When the Borough gossip starts / Somebody will suffer!', and his comment seems to trigger the sudden rise of the Chorus's cries of 'Grimes!' from C through C sharp to D (fig. 27): Evans notes (p. 114) 'the blatant crudity of the harmonic shift . . . as the crowd begins to scent the hunt'.

Motif *y* and its inversion are played simultaneously in the two-bar *tutti* introduction to this new D major *allegro molto* section, as Keene tries in vain to prevent Boles, the most bigoted of the Borough's moralisers, from mounting the Moot Hall steps to address the crowd. Boles delivers his harangue in mock-heroic Handelian manner, with interspersed comments from Balstrode and the Chorus. The inversion of *y* provides the musical material, together with a new and forceful version of *y* in its original form with the final note raised an octave (Ex. 28).

Ellen reappears: Auntie speaks kindly to her, to a *cantabile* variant of the inversion of *y*,[5] but Boles and the Chorus turn on her; and to her 'What am I to do?', sung to Auntie's *cantabile* phrase, they reply: 'Speak out in the name of the Lord!' This is vehemently sung to Ex. 28,

Ex. 28

with *y* and its inversion forming an ostinato accompaniment, as at the beginning of the section, but now in A major instead of D. At fig. 31 Ellen gives her answer, for the last time attempting to win the Borough's sympathy; her new A minor theme, 'a tensely sorrowful plea of good intentions' as Deryck Cooke calls it (p. 140), is repeated in groups of three phrases, the first two always of three bars, the third varying from five to seven bars (Ex. 29). Cooke shows that the melodic shape exemplified by this passage is invariably expressive of an outburst of painful emotion which falls back into acceptance: Ellen's cause is lost even as she pleads it. As the other voices join in, the music modulates to D major and Britten builds up a superb Verdian ensemble texture, all the characters offering their separate comments, some sympathetic, others hostile, in a mixture of staccato and legato phrases. This ensemble is, in fact, similar to the one in Act III of *Otello*, begun by Desdemona over a four-note descending scale ostinato in the bass. Britten uses a

Ex. 29

Larghetto (♩=44)
31
semplice ma marcato
ELLEN
ten.
a
b
3
We planned that their lives should have a new start,
colla parte
Ob
Harp
pp
dolce ed espr.
Hns
Bsns
That I as a friend could make the plan work, By bring - ing
cresc.
com - fort where their lives were stark.
RECTOR f
You plann'd to be world - ly
pp
Vlas

similar four-note descending motif (*b* in Ex. 29) as a bass (from the tenth bar of fig. 31); the characteristic Verdian phrase construction of Desdemona's 'Quel Sol sereno e vivido', a repeated two-bar melody followed by a four-bar extension, is adopted in Ellen's opening 'We planned that their lives should have a new start', suggesting that Britten was using Verdi as a model here – which is confirmed by Ellen's soaring above the voices of the Borough at the climax in comparable manner to the unjustly accused Desdemona.

At fig. 33 the Chorus enter forcefully in A major with the Ex. 28 version of *y*, confirming their rejections of Ellen's pleas; at fig. 34 they mock her cruelly, turning the three-note motif *a* from Ex. 29 into a driving, dactylic ostinato. Auntie leads Ellen away to Chorus shouts of 'Murder!'. The ostinato figure is developed as the Rector and Swallow decide to form a party to go to Grimes's hut; Swallow's ubiquitous rising sixth is taken up by the whole ensemble. Hobson beats his tenor drum over an F sharp pedal on horns and timpani and the men line up behind him; the F sharp forms a dominant pedal to the unison B major of the final chorus of this scene, which bursts out with terrifying power (Ex. 30). As Peter Evans remarks (p. 114); 'this bare unison writing, with its ominous long notes at phrase ends, represents the sanctification of per-

Ex. 30

secution in ritual'. Against this unanimity of ill-will, Peter stands no chance. The phrases descend as the pedal moves down the B major scale as far as G sharp (notated as A flat), at which point the voices die away as the procession moves into the distance.

After this second cumulative build-up to an emotional climax, containing some of the most powerful choral writing in the opera, there is a desperate need for some relaxation of tension, and, after such a display of inhumanity, for compassion. In providing these the final ensemble of the first scene succeeds beyond all expectation. The four women – Ellen, Auntie and the two Nieces – are left behind on stage. 'Back to the gutter, you keep out of this', Boles has said to the Nieces, and they take up his insult as the starting point of the quartet: 'From the gutter / Why should we trouble at their ribaldries?'; but they go on to express their innate compassion for all men. 'They are children when they weep, / We are mothers when they strive, / Schooling our own hearts to keep the bitter treasure of their love', Ellen sings, to a phrase of heart-rending pathos. There are three verses, and a thrice-heard refrain. Each verse and each refrain is prefaced by a ritornello for the two flutes; they descend in parallel major seconds through a chain of thirds (Ex. 31a), which can be heard both as successive overlapping statements of the first three notes of *y* (compassion for Peter) and as a reference back to Interlude I (see Ex. 31b), which evoked the impersonal healing power of nature. The strangely beautiful sound of the flutes' seconds immediately begins the healing process, before the voices enter. As Evans points out (p. 111), Britten had used this same flute sound to similar effect in the finale of the *Sinfonia da Requiem* (see Ex. 31c); he was to do so again, for instance in the introduction to the last scene of *Death in Venice* (compassion for Aschenbach), where there is only one flute – the major seconds are in the bass – but the same descending chain of thirds (Ex. 31d).

The vocal lines in the verses are based on arpeggios (Auntie's first phrase uses the falling fifth of Ex. 30 with telling effect on the word 'comfort' – all she has to soften the men's brutality); the refrains are based on rising scales that once again remind us of Ex. 20a, though they are minor scales and express sorrow rather than joy. The sensuous interweaving of voices at the climax of each refrain, and especially in the final one where the first Niece reaches top D flat, suggests unlikely comparisons with *Der Rosenkavalier*; indeed this kind of writing was almost unprecedented for Britten, though he was later to exploit it in *The Rape of Lucretia*, in the 'Linen' ensemble, for instance. I say 'almost' since there was a model for this quartet in Britten's first setting

Ex. 31b

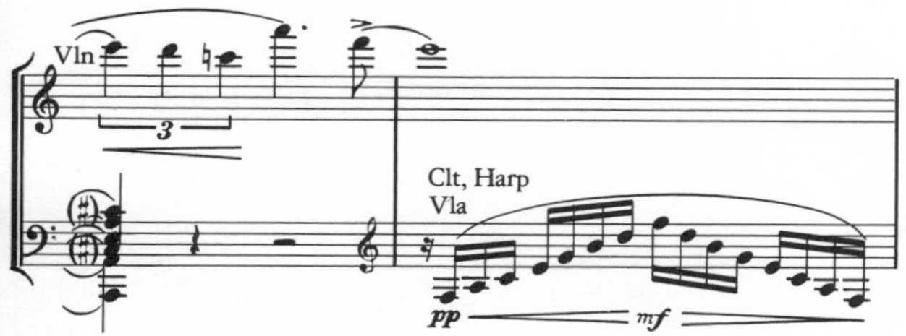

Ex. 31c

Ex. 31d

The HOTEL MANAGER watches ASCHENBACH go out to the deserted beach. He goes to his usual chair.

Slow (as before) *Lento (come sopra)* (♩ = 72)

of words by Montagu Slater, 'Mother Comfort', the first of two ballads for two sopranos and piano which he composed in 1937. I am grateful to Donald Mitchell for drawing my attention to this little-known piece, which, with its verbal and musical similarities, almost seems like a

Ex. 32a

Ex. 32b

ELLEN
pp legato
Do we smile or do we weep or wait
TWO NIECES
unis. pp marcato
poco a poco cresc.
Do we smile or do we weep or wait
AUNTIE
pp legato
Do we smile or do we weep or wait
Muted Tpts with Ellen and Auntie
Obs with Nieces
Str
poco a poco cresc.
espr.
pp
qui - et - ly till they sleep?
espr.
pp
qui-et - ly till, till they sleep?
espr.
pp
qui - et - ly till they sleep?
Flt
pp
espr.
ppp

preliminary study for the *Peter Grimes* quartet. The textures in 'Mother Comfort' are understandably less rich, but the scheme of verse and refrain is the same, and there is a similar alternation of arpeggio writing in the verses and scalic refrains. Compare the refrain of 'Mother Comfort' (Ex. 32a) with that of the *Grimes* quartet (Ex. 32b). The cadential chord in both cases is a dominant seventh with added sixth, though in the quartet, instead of the expected resolution in E flat, Britten moves effortlessly into C major.

The quartet's passionate compassion is of a kind we associate more readily with Tippett than with Britten (compare *The Heart's Assurance*, which has many points of similarity). From a musical point of view, the quartet and the passacaglia that immediately follows it represent the high-point of Act II, and indeed of the whole opera. The quartet's climax, the final *pianissimo* D flat major chord, significantly on the word 'sleep', is the opera's still centre. (The quartet has progressed from its opening C minor to its D flat close through many subtle modulations, in contrast with the four-square tonality of the previous choral episode.) The calm is momentary; for the die has already been cast by Peter himself, and from here on events move inevitably towards their tragic denouement. The flutes' major seconds drift downwards from a high A flat/B flat chord, to be taken over by clarinets, and then as the curtain falls by horns, descending over four octaves to a low F and the beginning of the passacaglia.

With the passacaglia we return to motif *y* and to Peter's dark and obsessional world. Motif *y* becomes the ground bass, whose irregular length of eleven beats means that in the prevailing 4/4 metre it takes eleven bars to work itself back to the beginning of the bar, and the counter-subject is also derived from it (Ex. 33). All commentators have associated the first solo viola statement of the counter-subject with the apprentice (and see above, p. 65); this interpretation would appear to be confirmed at the end of the act when the theme, now in inverted form, is played as a requiem for his death. The boy, however, is hardly more than an expression of Grimes's will; and the theme, and the passacaglia as a whole, are concerned less with him than with the conflicts within Grimes's own personality. The relentless emphasis on F in the ground bass – which is repeated thirty-nine times without interruption – refers back to the F pedal in Peter's 'creed'. The bitonality there symbolised the gulf between Peter and Ellen; here the tension between the restlessly modulating counter-subject and the unyielding, unchanging bass mirrors the two conflicting sides of Peter's nature, his visionary aspirations constantly frustrated by his obsessive, self-destructive will.

The frustration of Peter's hopes is implicit in the shape of the counter-subject itself (see Ex. 33). It begins with a rising fifth which falls back to its starting point, F, via four repetitions of the three-note cell *z*. It then rises a major seventh, to E, and again falls back through repetitions of *z*, this time as far as A, from where it leaps up an octave. So far the rising interval has expanded, as if each time making a more determined effort to oppose the debilitating effect of *z*. Now it contracts: the next

Ex. 33

rising interval is a minor sixth, then a fifth. Another minor sixth is countered by a final augmented fourth, the smallest interval of the series, and classically the interval of negation. So this melodic line may be seen as encapsulating the internal drama of the opera: the initial growth of Peter's hopes and their gradual ebbing away into defeat. The overall rise in tessitura – from low F to a harmonic E almost three octaves higher – seems further to indicate the gap between Peter's aspirations and reality, represented by the ground bass. Moreover, it is *z*, derived from the ground bass, that is the agent of the continual undermining of the rising interval.

The viola's final E acts as a dominant to the A major woodwind chords that open Variation 1. This presents a more determined version of the counter-subject, advancing from A major to E major (two 'aspiring' keys) through E flat minor (the storm key); the successive leaps of a fifth, an octave and a tenth to the *forte* E major triads on trumpets and trombones at fig. 46 represent the most confident moment of the passacaglia. The first half of Variation 2 is superbly defiant, the strings energetically striving upwards with swift successions of *z*; but the forceful reiterations of *z* on the brass at the ends of the bars fall each time, and from the sixth bar of 46 to the end of the variation the string figures also fall, fading out on a quiet E major triad for muted horns and wind at 47.

The rising-interval idea, having attained its maximum impetus in the bar before 46, now disappears altogether; the remainder of the passacaglia is exclusively concerned with the ultimately self-defeating motif *z*. In Variation 3 the slow-moving muted horn statements of *z* cadence on to a *sforzando* chord of a superimposed perfect fourth and augmented fourth – the chord that is associated with the advent of the storm in Act I. This storm chord underlies the harmony of the next variation, in which *z* is played slowly and expressively by the strings over staccato quavers in the wind. There is a gradual build-up of tension from here until the end of the passacaglia. At fig. 52, the beginning of Variation 8, the perfect and augmented fourths are fused together into a more acute dissonance; a rising scale figure begins to invade the texture and *z* is inverted. The scales, together with *z* in its original form but with accelerating repetitions of the initial minor third until it becomes almost a tremolo, increasingly dominate: at fig. 54 they are savagely seized by the trumpets, and a climax is precipitately reached on a chord of D flat – complementing the end of the quartet. At this point the curtain rises on scene 2, but there is no sense of a conclusion to the passacaglia here; in fact it takes the whole of the second scene to work itself out and find its proper ending,[6] in the key of C, in the last bars of the act – by which time Peter's own drama is virtually over, and there is nothing left for him but madness and death.

CRITICISM

7 *Introduction*

BENJAMIN BRITTEN (1945)

During the summer of 1941, while working in California, I came across a copy of *The Listener* containing an article about George Crabbe by E. M. Forster. I did not know any of the poems of Crabbe at that time, but reading about him gave me such a feeling of nostalgia for Suffolk, where I had always lived, that I searched for a copy of his works, and made a beginning with *The Borough*. Mr Forster's article is reproduced in this book: it is easy to see how his excellent account of this 'entirely English poet' evoked a longing for the realities of that grim and exciting seacoast around Aldeburgh.

Earlier in the year, I had written the music of *Paul Bunyan*, an operetta to a text by W. H. Auden, which was performed for a week at Columbia University, New York. The critics damned it unmercifully, but the public seemed to find something enjoyable in the performances. Despite the criticisms, I wanted to write more works for the stage. *The Borough* – and particularly the story of 'Peter Grimes' – provided a subject and a background from which Peter Pears and I began trying to construct the scenario of an opera.

A few months later I was waiting on the East Coast for a passage back to England, when a performance of my *Sinfonia da Requiem* was given in Boston under Serge Koussevitsky. He asked why I had not written an opera. I explained that the construction of a scenario, discussions with a librettist, planning the musical architecture, composing preliminary sketches, and writing nearly a thousand pages of orchestral score, demanded a freedom from other work which was an economic impossibility for most young composers. Koussevitsky was interested in my project for an opera based on Crabbe, although I did not expect to have the opportunity of writing it for several years. Some weeks later we met again, when he told me that he had arranged for the commissioning of the opera, which was to be dedicated to the memory of his wife, who had recently died.

On arrival in this country in April 1942 I outlined the rough plan to

Montagu Slater, and asked him to undertake the libretto. Discussions, revisions, and corrections took nearly eighteen months. In January 1944 I began composing the music, and the score was completed in February 1945.

For most of my life I have lived closely in touch with the sea. My parents' house in Lowestoft directly faced the sea, and my life as a child was coloured by the fierce storms that sometimes drove ships on to our coast and ate away whole stretches of the neighbouring cliffs. In writing *Peter Grimes*, I wanted to express my awareness of the perpetual struggle of men and women whose livelihood depends on the sea – difficult though it is to treat such a universal subject in theatrical form.

I am especially interested in the general architectural and formal problems of opera, and decided to reject the Wagnerian theory of 'permanent melody' for the classical practice of separate numbers that crystallize and hold the emotion of a dramatic situation at chosen moments. One of my chief aims is to try and restore to the musical setting of the English language a brilliance, freedom, and vitality that have been curiously rare since the death of Purcell. In the past hundred years, English writing for the voice has been dominated by strict subservience to logical speech-rhythms, despite the fact that accentuation according to sense often contradicts the accentuation demanded by emotional content. Good recitative should transform the natural intonations and rhythms of everyday speech into memorable musical phrases (as with Purcell), but in more stylized music, the composer should not deliberately avoid unnatural stresses if the prosody of the poem and the emotional situation demand them, nor be afraid of a high-handed treatment of words, which may need prolongation far beyond their common speech-length, or a speed of delivery that would be impossible in conversation.

The scarcity of modern British operas is due to the limited opportunities that are offered for their performance. Theatre managers will not present original works without a reasonable hope of recovering their costs of production: composers and writers cannot thrive without the experience of seeing their operas adequately staged and sung: the conservatism of audiences hinders experimental departures from the accepted repertory.

In my own case, the existence of Sadler's Wells has been an incentive to complete *Peter Grimes*: the qualities of the Opera Company have considerably influenced both the shape and the characterization of the opera. Whatever its reception may be, it is to be hoped that the willingness of the Company to undertake the presentation of new operas will encourage other composers to write works in what is, in my opinion, the most exciting of musical forms.

8 *Neither a hero nor a villain*

PETER PEARS (1946)

In Crabbe's great poem *The Borough*, Peter Grimes is nothing more than a villainous fisherman who, having rebelled against his father's discipline, takes to poaching, smuggling, and hard liquor. He is not satisfied in his 'cruel soul' until he has 'some obedient boy to trouble and control'. Because of his abominable treatment of three successive apprentice boys he is outlawed by the Borough and dies wretched and insane in 'a parish-bed'. Not a very glamorous figure for the operatic stage! But Crabbe also gives us a picture, showing an amazing power of observation, of the whole life of a Suffolk fishing-port of a hundred and fifty years ago, including all the various layers of society, the local types, trades and recreations, as well as the individuals in the almshouses and prisons – in fact, every detail that went to make up the community. It was this extraordinarily strong background, with the sea behind it all, which suggested to the composer an opera based on the conflict between society and the individual – a conflict implicit in many of Crabbe's stories.

In the opera, the Borough is very much the same as Crabbe's Borough. Most of the characters are taken from Crabbe as they stand: Auntie, the landlady of 'The Boar', and her two nieces; Ned Keene, the quack; Swallow, the lawyer; the Rector, and so on. Peter Grimes himself, on the other hand, is a more complicated character and considerably removed from the desperado of the poem. In the prologue, when he tells before the Coroner the story of his apprentice's death at sea, it is clear that he is telling the truth, and from his hallucinations in the hut later, when he seems to see the dead boy's face staring at him, it is clear that he was no murderer. It is prejudice that sets the crowd against him, and the Coroner's words confirm it.

Grimes wants them to understand 'the truth and the pity' of his squalid life with the 'prentice, but the Borough is not interested. After all, it was the custom for children to be given away to men to look after, together with a lump sum for their keep. Life was squalid everywhere

'ig. 11: Peter Pears as Peter Grimes and Leonard Thompson as his apprentice in the irst production (Sadler's Wells, 1945)

for a poor man then, though not as squalid in agricultural Suffolk as in the growing young industrial cities of the North, where Trade Unions were still forbidden and a man could be thrown into prison if he left his job.

Grimes sees no way of escaping from his wretched hut other than by vindicating himself in the eyes of the Borough, making money, and becoming respectable. He despises the measures and complacency of the Borough, but passionately wants to make good in the Borough's way, by 'setting up household and shop'. Then he will marry Ellen. But to do that he must 'catch a record shoal', and so the wretched 'prentice must be overworked, and society must deal with Grimes in its own way, which is to lynch him.

If he had lived in a city, Grimes might have been a revolutionary or gone to join one of Robert Owen's settlements. But there were no politics in the Borough – only the many and the few, the conventional and those outside the pub. And Grimes, of course, is quite 'outside the pub'. He is not a 'nice person', certainly. He is rude and unkempt and exceedingly irritable. He snubs Balstrode, the friendly sea-captain, who is interested in him and tries to help, and he quarrels with Ellen, whom he loves and who is his only hope, and all about a bruise on the wretched apprentice's neck which the lad may have received in the hurly-burly of a storm at sea. Grimes considers it quite unimportant, but it is the beginning of the end, and the temper of the Borough is up! Grimes was undoubtedly a harsh master, but his fits of rage would very probably have passed unnoticed if he had put a conventional face on them. But he had no truck with the Borough and it would not tolerate him.

Grimes is not a hero nor is he an operatic villain. He is not a sadist nor a demonic character, and the music quite clearly shows that. He is very much of an ordinary weak person who, being at odds with the society in which he finds himself, tries to overcome it and, in doing so, offends against the conventional code, is classed by society as a criminal, and destroyed as such. There are plenty of Grimeses around still, I think!

9 'Peter Grimes': a review of the first performance

DESMOND SHAWE-TAYLOR (1945)

I

By the time these words are printed an important musical event will have occurred – or, rather, two simultaneous events. The return of the Sadler's Wells Opera Company, after six years of exile, to their home in Rosebery Avenue, would have been welcome enough in any case, even if the occasion had been celebrated by nothing fresher than *Madame Butterfly*. But the Wells have done the thing in style. Nothing would content them but a world premiere, namely that of Benjamin Britten's first full-length opera, *Peter Grimes*. Of this work and its performance I hope to give a full account next week. What follows is a prefatory note based on a glimpse of the score, on the preliminary lecture-concert arranged by its publishers at the Wigmore Hall, and on a study of libretto, sources, and certain expository material which has appeared.

The most useful preparation one can make before hearing an opera is to read its libretto; and this holds good whatever its literary quality may be, for the listener is thereby relieved of the distracting effort to follow the *logical* course of the stage action and can surrender wholly to the emotional and atmospheric impact of music and drama. The book of *Peter Grimes*, by Montagu Slater, has been published by Messrs. Boosey & Hawkes; and another publication, by the firm of John Lane [Crozier (ed.), *Peter Grimes*], contains essays by composer and librettist, a reprint of the broadcast talk on Crabbe by E. M. Forster which set the idea stirring in the composer's mind, and a long and quite admirable musical analysis (with plenty of music-type) by Edward Sackville West. Both these pamphlets cost half a crown, and both are illustrated by the designer of the stage sets, Kenneth Green. To complete a utilitarian paragraph, I would add that the opera is to be repeated to-night (June 9th) and on June 12th, 15th, 20th, 25th and 29th. The B.B.C., having failed to broadcast even a part of the first performance, shows as yet no indication of repairing this unfortunate lapse.

Crabbe published his poem *The Borough* in 1810. It is a series of twenty-four 'letters' which paint a minute and realistic picture of a place which he knew inside out, the poor fishing-town of Aldeburgh in Suffolk. His account of its customs and inhabitants is neither flattering nor romantic, but it is honest, it possesses great social and historical interest, and it is written in rhyming couplets which rise at moments to a grey, sober beauty of their own. To Britten, working in 1941 in the brilliant sunlight of California, the homespun, truthful words seem to have brought a rush of nostalgic affection; this was the county and this the weather-torn coastline which he had known all his life. The notion of building an opera around Crabbe's poem began to attract him, and the generosity of Koussevitsky allowed him to realise his dream.

To write good operas it is not enough to be a good composer; it is not even enough to have dramatic sense. Unless the composer is to be his own librettist, he must possess the knack of first choosing the right one and then bullying him unmercifully. In the book of *Grimes* I do not know the precise proportions of Britten and Slater, but, broadly speaking, the result is a success: a rapid and dramatic action, full of atmosphere, of vivid country characters, and of genre pictures of a kind ideally suited to musical treatment. There is a pub scene with the storm growling outside and bursting in whenever the door is opened; a sunny Sunday morning on the beach with matins drifting through the open church door as a background to dialogue; a dance at the Moot Hall, with an unseen stage-band; a dreadful interlude of sea-fog and terror before the final scene. With all these racy qualities it is of minor importance that the text shows no particular literary distinction. What is perhaps a more serious defect resides in the conception of the principal character.

Who is Peter Grimes? In Crabbe he is a mere brute, guilty of the manslaughter (if not the murder) of his father and of no less than three poor workhouse boys whom he has bought as his apprentices with the deliberate intention of ill-treating them; 'untouched by pity, unstung by remorse, and uncorrected by shame . . . a mind depraved and flinty': in fact, the perfect S.S. Camp Commandant. In the opera nothing is heard of the father, and the number of unfortunate boys is reduced to two, an inquest on one of whom is in progress as the curtain rises, while the other is bumped off during the action – unintentionally, it is true, but as the result of callous treatment. Grimes himself wears a very different aura. He is not presented as a worthy character (that would be too much), but as an outcast: romantic, Byronic and misunderstood. There is supposed to be something poetic and elemental about him which sets him apart from the bickering and petty gossip of the township. 'They listen to money, these Borough gossips. I listen to dreams and fiery visions.' I cannot, however, feel that the librettist has made much of a case for this view of Grimes. For what precisely are these dreams and visions of his? Why, of making his pile, rehabilitating himself in the eyes of his fellows, and settling down in matrimony with his only champion, a forty-year-old widow schoolmistress. A laudable ambition, of course – but surely the last word in bourgeois respectability! Meanwhile, no opportunity is missed of maligning Mrs Sedley, described by the librettist as a 'rentier', who suspects Peter's cruelties and arouses the townspeople against him; but what neither composer nor librettist seems to realise is that, after all, the sympathetic schoolmarm was wrong (and therefore, in effect, an accessory in the second boy's death), whereas poor Mrs Sedley was dead right.

I know that operas are not ethical treatises, and that I shall be accused of taking too literal a view of a poetic creation. Maybe. But is there not something shocking in the attempt to win our sympathies for a character *simply because* he is an outlaw and an enemy of society – and no more questions asked? What I am quite prepared (especially after the Wigmore Hall concert) to believe is that the richness and dramatic power of Britten's music will enable us to ignore (for the time being) an adolescent conception of man and society which is in sober truth indefensible. In the theatre we may well be lulled into acquiescence; but at home, shall we not begin to wonder?

II

After hearing several performances of *Peter Grimes* one can scarcely avoid seeing in Benjamin Britten a fresh hope, not only for English, but for European opera. Constantly, during this past week, audiences at Sadler's Wells have been saying to themselves: 'At last! After so many amateurs, a professional composer of operas!' If they are right, it is none too soon. With the death of Puccini and the long *decrescendo* of Strauss, the species looked like becoming extinct. *Turandot*, says the encyclopædic Loewenberg, was 'the last world success in the history of opera'; and that was nearly twenty years ago. Even were it another *Turandot*, there would be much to prevent *Peter Grimes* from enjoying now the international success which it might have had in the Twenties; not least, the fact that the old world of 'international' opera does not, at the moment, effectively exist. But of one thing I am convinced: if the world returns to sanity, and if Britten chooses to remain in the theatre, he has it in him to write an all-conquering work of the order of, say, *Der Rosenkavalier*. As for ourselves, *Grimes* should acquire for us something of the significance which *A Life for the Czar* has for the Russians or *The Bartered Bride* for the Czechs: it should lay at last the foundation-stone of a national school of opera. Its vigour, audacity and mastery of dramatic movement place it in a different category from the tentative affairs which we have hitherto known; indeed, in a first opera, they are remarkable judged by any standards. We are apt to forget how long an apprenticeship is generally served by even the greatest masters of the form: Verdi began with *Oberto, Conte di San Bonifacio*, Wagner with *Die Feen*, Strauss with *Guntram*, Puccini with *Le Villi*; all forgotten now, even in their native lands. But all these works were written in their composers' twenties, while Britten has waited until his third decade to produce his firstling. Those additional years of study and experience he has turned to excellent account.

The moment the curtain rises (there is no overture) the spectator is seized by a powerful impression of competence. Everything happens rapidly, clearly and inevitably. The business before the Borough Court is transacted with despatch – as though music were quite the simplest and most natural of mediums in which a Coroner's Inquest could be conducted. Different though the mood is, one thinks of the opening of Verdi's *Falstaff*; there is the same effect of speed and precision. A bustling, pompous little tune gives us the self-important magistrate; a shrill figure in the wood-wind the bickering, gesticulating crowd. And Grimes? His romantic, larger-than-life personality is immediately established in purely musical terms by the remote modulations and soft string chords which underpin his slow answers and repetition of the Oath. Thus, in the first ten minutes, before any set pieces bring up the question of 'inspiration', we are convinced that the composer is a born opera-writer. In the light of all that follows, this impression of naturalness, ease and sheer competence may seem a slight virtue to insist on, but it is not. It is the pre-condition which makes all the later flights of imagination possible; it is that quality, the lack of which has strewn the history of English opera with so many distinguished corpses.

Competence assured, poetry steals in with an unaccompanied duet between Grimes and the school-mistress Ellen Orford. The curtain drops, and the flat, salty, windy coast is magically evoked in an orchestral interlude: bare grace-noted minims on the higher strings, clean arpeggios on the harp, soft chords on the brass. It looks so simple, that innate pictorialism of Britten's, which we have already admired in the *Serenade*, and now it serves so well the broader need of opera: when the curtain rises we see only what we have already heard. These preludes and interludes, of which there are six in all, form a major item in the musical design: they are about equally divided between the pictorial and the psychological. Here, almost alone, the composer unleashes the full power of the orchestra, elsewhere subduing it most carefully to allow the voices to dominate and the words to be heard; also, they are the only respect in which he departs from the generally late Verdian lay-out of the score. I am not referring to the musical idiom, but to the division of the score into set-pieces; arias, ensembles and choruses, linked by recitatives which slip insensibly into *arioso*. He shows great mastery too of a kind of operatic writing known as the *scena*, of which a notable example, containing perhaps the most expressive and touching music in the whole opera, occurs in the first scene of the second act. Here Ellen and the new apprentice sit down in the Sunday morning sunshine, while the hymns and responses of matins float out through the open church door; she talks to the boy (who won't answer) and falls into a reverie. Musically, the idea of a soprano occupied with her own troubles against a liturgical background is as old as Gounod's *Faust*; but with what freshness and skill Britten has treated it! There is the device, borrowed from broadcasting, of 'fading up' and 'fading down' the two component parts of the scene, and there is a subtle musical interrelation between them; as when a theme is picked up from the church service and adapted, in a most affecting manner, to form the substance of Ellen's lament. Such things are 'tricks'; but, like a poet's skill in versification, they are the necessary foundation for the noblest ideas.

At a first hearing the first two acts may seem a trifle episodic. Later, the realisation that the chorus is as much the protagonist as Grimes himself partly removes this impression: we begin to see the big choral scenes, not as so much 'atmosphere' or 'colour', but, like those of *Boris Godunov* or *Turandot* (both of which they often recall), as one of the mainsprings of the action. The last act, however, immediately makes an impression of intense and concentrated dramatic power. There is a steady rise in the temperature of the first scene, from the rough, burlesque gaiety of the Moot Hall dances, a moment of almost Schubertian charm when the Rector goes off to water his roses, Ellen's lovely 'embroidery' aria, up to the electrifying climax of that tremendous series of cries which herald the man-hunt: 'Peter Grimes! Peter Grimes!' This call resounds, distant and mysterious now in the sea-mist, through the final scene, which is also punctuated by the boom of the fog-horn. This is the background of another *scena*, for the distraught Grimes, in which snatches of remembered melody, almost in the manner of the *cadenza* in Elgar's *Violin Concerto*, flicker by out of the past. As we reach the last hours before dawn, all colour and sound drain out of the world: the chorus is silent, the orchestra is silent, at last Grimes himself is silent. In the intense stillness, and with profoundly dramatic effect, occur the only lines of spoken dialogue in the work. They are spoken by the honest sea captain Balstrode: 'Sail out of sight of the land, and sink your boat'. Wordlessly, Grimes obeys. After a long pause, life returns: dawn breaks, the mist disperses, the music on the high strings which began Act I comes back again, the townsfolk begin to go about their daily business; we reach 'the cold beginning of another day'. It is a wonderful conception, which needs perhaps another two or three minutes of music for full realisation.

The performance was a triumph for Sadler's Wells. Seldom are composers so well served as was Britten by the conductor, Mr Reginald Goodall, and the entire cast. Joan Cross has never sung of acted with so touching a gravity as in the part of Ellen Orford. There are moments in the role of Grimes which demand a sort of tenor Chaliapin; Peter Pears is not that, but he was in every other way worthy of the composer's intentions. All the singers clearly felt the unusual happiness of singing a text that did not sound (as so many English operas do) like a translation. The chorus, though on the first night the public-house 'round' went badly, rose to their great moments, and, like the soloists, were wonderfully free of that depressing one-eye-on-the-conductor tradition. Eric Crozier's production was imaginative and effective, though it was a mistake not to make the fog visible, and there were times when I could have done with a little more light, and a more specifically early morning *kind* of light at the beginning and end of the main action. Kenneth Green's sets and costumes are more than beautiful: they are right. It is not his fault that the principal scene looks a bit cramped; it will look wonderful one day at Covent Garden when there is enough space between and above the necessary buildings for the great East Anglian sky.

A last word of advice to the intending spectator. Neglect Crabbe. If you have not just been reading 'Ellen Orford' and 'Peter Grimes', you will find it much easier to see these characters from the composer's standpoint; and you will be able to appreciate the libretto for the very skilful piece of work it is.

10 *An account of 'Peter Grimes' from 'London in Midsummer'*

EDMUND WILSON (1947)

I was a little taken aback one evening for which I had had vague other plans to find that I was going with G.[1] to a new opera by Benjamin Britten which was being done at Sadler's Wells. She had bought the tickets herself and said nothing about it in advance. The only thing I had heard by Britten had been a *Requiem*[2] that had not much impressed me, and I did not feel particularly eager to sit through an English opera called *Peter Grimes*, based on an episode from Crabbe. G. did try, with her usual lack of emphasis, to get me to read the libretto, of which she had procured a copy, but she did not explain that this work had been something of a sensation in London, where the critics, who, like me, had not at first expected anything extraordinary, had been roused from their neat routine to the point of hearing it several times and writing two or three articles about it. But she knew that I ought to hear it, and it is one of my debts to G. that she made me go to *Peter Grimes*, which I should unquestionably otherwise have missed.

For, almost from the moment when the curtain went up on the bare room in the provincial Moot Hall – which no overture had introduced – where the fisherman Peter Grimes was being examined at a coroner's inquest in connection with the death of his apprentice, I felt the power of a musical gift and a dramatic imagination that woke my interest and commanded my attention. There have been relatively few composers of the first rank who had a natural gift for the theater: Mozart, Musorgsky, Verdi, Wagner, the Bizet of *Carmen*. To be confronted, without preparation, with an unmistakable new talent of this kind is an astonishing, even an electrifying, experience. The difficulty of describing *Peter Grimes* to someone who has not heard it is the difficulty of convincing people whose expectations are likely to be limited by having listened to too much modern music that was synthetic, arid, effortful and inadequate, that a new master has really arrived; of conveying to them the special qualities of a full-grown original artist. In my own case, I am particularly handicapped by lack of technical knowledge and training, so that I can only give an account of the opera's spell without being able to analyze it intelligently. The best I can do, then, is to report my impression – subject to expert correction – that Britten's score shows no signs of any of the dominant influences – Wagner, Debussy, Stravinsky, Schoenberg or Prokofiev – but has been phrased in an idiom that is personal and built with a definiteness and solidity that are as English as Gilbert and Sullivan (one can find, for an English opera, no other comparison in the immediate past). And the result of this is very different from anything we have been used to. The ordinary composer of opera finds his conventions there with the stage; but, when you are watching *Peter Grimes*, you are almost completely unaware of anything that is artificial, anything 'operatic'. The composer here seems quite free from the self-consciousness of contemporary musicians. You do not feel you are watching an experiment; you are living a work of art. The opera seizes upon you, possesses you, keeps you riveted to your seat during the action and keyed up during the intermissions, and drops you, purged and exhausted, at the end.

The orchestra, in *Peter Grimes*, plays a mainly subordinate role, and the first effect on the hearer, during the opening scene in the Moot Hall, is of a drastic simplification of opera to something essential and naked, which immediately wakes one up. There is no Wagnerian web of motifs that tells you about the characters: the characters express themselves directly, either conversing or soliloquizing in song, while the orchestra, for the most part, but comments. The music is a close continuity, though articulated rather than fluid, of vivid utterances on the part of the personages and – except in the more elaborate interludes – sharp and terse descriptive strokes, in which from time to time take shape arias, duets, trios and choruses. These – almost never regular in pattern and never losing the effect of naturalness – have their full or fragmentary developments, and give way to the next urgent pulse of the blood-stream that runs through the whole piece. In the same way, the words of the libretto, by the poet Montagu Slater, which are admirably suited to the music and which the music exactly fits, shift sometimes into the imagery of poetry but never depart far from the colloquial and are sometimes – with no loss of dignity – left perfectly bald and flat. But we soon come to recognize in the music the extraordinary flexibility, the subtlety and the variety, which are combined with a stout British craftsmanship that has a sure hand with mortise and tenon and that knows how to plant and mass a chorus, and with a compelling theatrical sense, an instinct for tempo and point. And – what is most uncommon with opera – we find ourselves touched and stirred at listening to an eloquence of voices that does not merely charm or impress us as the performance of well-trained singers but that seems sometimes to reach us directly with the emotions of actual people. Nor do these voices find their expression exclusively through the singers' roles: one of the most effective devices of *Peter Grimes* is the use of the orchestral interludes that take place between the scenes while the curtain is down. Thus at the end of the first scene in the Moot Hall, where you have just been seeing Peter Grimes consoled by Ellen Orford, the school-teacher, the only being in the town who cares for him, the orchestra develops a theme which seems to well up out of Ellen's heart, and then rises and falls with a plangency that, sustained through the long passage with marvellous art, conveys, as if her spirit were speaking, her sympathy and pain for Peter. And at the end of the scene that follows, when a storm has been heard coming up as Balstrode, the retired captain, has been trying to remonstrate with Peter over his plan to take another apprentice and prove to the town that he is not a monster, the winds and the waves break loose the moment the curtain falls, fiendishly yelping and slapping in a way that represents with realism – Britten was born on the Suffolk coast – the worrying raving crescendo of an equinoctial gale but that howls at the same time with the fierceness of Peter's rebellious pride and of the latent sadistic impulse of which he is half unconscious but to which the new situation will eventually give free rein. The sea's restive and pressing movement has been all through the scene that preceded, and in the next, in the local tavern to which the people have resorted for warmth and cheer, the hurricane wildly intrudes whenever the door is opened and at last, with the entrance of Grimes, rushes into the room to stay. This long act, which is brought to its climax by the silence that greets Peter's appearance and that concentrates the hostility of the town, and by the arrival of the orphan whom, the carrier refusing, Ellen has herself gone to fetch and for whose welfare she hopes to make herself responsible – this act has an intensity and an impetus that carries one through, without a moment's let-down, from the opening to the end. Nor is what follows much less effective. The whole drama is a stretching of tension between the inquest and the inevitable crisis when Grimes will, if not deliberately kill, at least cause the death of, the second apprentice; and I do not remember ever to have seen, at any performance of opera, an audience so steadily intent, so petrified and held in suspense, as the audience of *Peter Grimes*. This is due partly to the dramatic skill of Britten, but is due also to his having succeeded in harmonizing, through *Peter Grimes*, the harsh helpless emotions of wartime. This opera could have been written in no other age, and it is one of the very few works of art that have seemed to me, so far, to have spoken for the blind anguish, the hateful rancors and the will to destruction of these horrible years. Its grip on its London audiences is clearly of the same special kind as the grip of the recent productions of *Richard III* and *The Duchess of Malfi*.[3] Like them, it is the chronicle of an impulse to persecute and to kill which has become an obsessive compulsion, which drags the malefactor on – under a fatality which he does not understand, from which he can never get free, and which never leaves him even the lucidity for repentance or reparation – through a series of uncontrollable cruelties which will lead, in the long run, to his being annihilated himself. At first you think that Peter Grimes is Germany. He is always under the impression, poor fellow, that what he really wants for himself is to marry Ellen Orford and to live in a nice little cottage with children and fruit in the garden 'and whitened doorstep and a woman's care'. Above all, he wants to prove to his neighbors that he is not the scoundrel they think him, that he really means no harm to his apprentices and that he will make a good family man. But he cannot help flying into a fury when the boy does not respond to his will, and when he gets angry, he beats him; and his townsmen become more and more indignant. At last, shouting, 'Peter Grimes!', they go on the march against him, determined to capture him and make him pay, just at the moment when he has paused and relented, and when their approach will precipitate, in his dash to escape, his pushing the boy so that he falls over the cliff, which is finally to settle his fate. (A comparison of the text of the opera with the story as told by Crabbe in *The Borough* shows that Britten and Montagu Slater – though they have used here and there a few lines from Crabbe – have put Peter in a different situation and invented for him a new significance. The outlaw fisherman in Crabbe is married, though his wife does not figure in the story, and he has no connection with Ellen Orford, who is the heroine of a separate episode. The mainspring of the original version is Peter's rebellion against his father: he is in Crabbe completely antisocial and has no hankering for middle-class decency.) But, by the time you are done with the opera – or by the time it is done with you – you have decided that Peter Grimes is the whole of bombing, machine-gunning, mining, torpedoing, ambushing humanity, which talks about a guaranteed standard of living yet does nothing but wreck its own works, degrade or pervert its own moral life and reduce itself to starvation. You feel, during the final scenes, that the indignant shouting trampling mob which comes to punish Peter Grimes is just as sadistic as he. And when Balstrode gets to him first and sends him out to sink himself in his boat, you feel that you are in the same boat as Grimes.

11 *Music and motive in 'Peter Grimes'*

J. W. GARBUTT (1963)

Is there such a 'person' as Peter Grimes? Is there such a dramatic, poetic or musical entity? We cannot help noting the tendency of critics and commentators to build him up off-stage, as it were, to project a more complete Peter than the contradictions and ambiguities in Britten's opera should allow. His conduct oscillates between the extremes of blind violence and self-absorption in a near-visionary state. How can we account for such instability? According to Hans Keller,

> Peter Grimes is the living conflict. His pride, ambition, and urge for independence fight with his need for love; his self-love battles against his self-hate. Others too, he can (sometimes) love as intensely as he can despise them, but he cannot show, let alone prove his tenderness as easily as his wrath – except through the music which, alas, the people on the stage don't hear. Thus he is destined to seem worse than he is, and not to be as good as he feels. *Peter Grimes* is the story of the man who couldn't fit in.
>
> I should indeed go further than Pears and say that in each of us there is something of a Grimes, though most of us have outgrown or at least outwitted him sufficiently not to recognize him too consciously. But we do identify him, and ourselves with him, unconsciously, which is one reason for the universal appeal of this work [see chapter 5].

One must say, not unkindly, that however much the above writer identifies himself with Peter Grimes, identification is not essential to an appreciation of the work. These supposed conflicts are in fact discrepancies, which Montagu Slater's libretto has juxtaposed without integrating. They have stimulated Britten's inventive genius into composing so immediately rich a score that the listener lives in almost total suspension of disbelief. With most operas the quality of the music is far more important than the quality of the plot: the libretto provides merely the pretext and if the libretto is credible the listener is pleased and surprised. If the libretto is incredible it hardly calls for discussion. But Britten's instinct is towards psychological fidelity, and his approach to realism calls up questions of verisimilitude, because his music claims from us an alertness to the work of art as a whole. We can never say: 'The words don't count; it's only the music that matters'. Hence the reconstructions of Peter outside the opera house, in articles and printed programmes. Most operatic heroes obey the synopses of their actions. Peter defies synopsis.

The two main discrepancies lie in the nature of Peter's guilt, and in the motives of his ambition. In an article for the *Radio Times* Peter Pears wrote: 'In the prologue, when he tells before the Coroner the story of his apprentice's death at sea, it is clear that he is telling the truth, and from his hallucinations in the hut later, when he sees the dead boy's face staring at him, it is clear that he was no murderer' [see chapter 8]. Peter is no murderer – and we should expect to add 'not guilty'. As Balstrode points out to Peter,

> Your boy was workhouse starved –
> Maybe you're not to blame he died.

Balstrode declares that Grimes, by speaking at the inquest, has 'set his conscience free'. But the exigencies of the libretto make us deduce a guilt where there was no murder – and then make us pity a mental torment which contains no remorse. To be blamed for the death of the first apprentice produces effects in Peter that only true guilt should do.

If we seek the causes or motives leading to the death of the second apprentice, we must not miss a word or a note of the remarkable scene in the hut. We know that the cliff is down, and the path is dangerous. We know that Peter has been ill-treating the boy John; and now he orders John out of the cliff door for another fishing expedition:

> Be careful, or you'll break your neck
> Down the cliff-side to the deck . . .
> Now shut your eyes and down you go!

The boy goes; he screams and falls out of sight. Peter runs to the cliff door, feels for his grip, and then swings after him. When the Rector and Swallow enter by the other door, they observe that there has been a recent landslide making 'almost a precipice' fifty feet deep. What was Peter's intention? The audience is understandably bewildered, and its bewilderment is never resolved. The audience is diverted by the next interlude and Barn Dance, and is allowed little time to think; but those who have followed Peter's progress so far may run through the possibilities. Accident pure and simple? Permitted accident? Encouraged accident? Contrived accident? Impulsive murder? Deliberate murder? Reluctantly one comes to the conclusion that this was either a permitted accident, arising from Peter's blank, amoral, isolated state of mind, or that it was an impulsive murder, a retaliation upon the boy for allegedly 'talking' and being 'the cause of everything' – and also for reminding him of the first apprentice, who died watching Peter with a similar expression on his face.

Peter, always unpredictable, has now become inexplicable. If we wish to understand why, we must turn back to Crabbe's great poem, *The Borough* (1810), Letter XXII, which contains the source of Peter Grimes, one of the 'Poor of the Borough'. As Montagu Slater found him, Peter was a juvenile delinquent who grew up to be a thief, poacher, callous liar and sadist, and was directly or indirectly responsible for the deaths of three apprentices. His only redeeming feature was a blush of guilt at the inquest. He died unredeemed, tormented by delirious visions of his father and the three boys, and his spirit was consigned to a 'place of horrors'. It is a highly 'moral' tale, well in advance of its time in its intention to edify and instruct. Clearly such a villain does not appeal as the central figure of a modern operatic libretto. And so he must be rendered more sympathetic. Montagu Slater takes an opportunity which Crabbe provides in his narrative of the death of the second apprentice:

> One day such draughts the cruel fisher made
> He could not vend them in his borough-trade
> But sail'd for London-mart; the boy was ill . . .
> Rough was the passage and the time was long;
> His liquor fail'd, and Peter's wrath arose –
> No more is known – the rest we must suppose,
> Or learn of Peter; – Peter says, he 'spied
> The stripling's danger and for harbour tried;
> Meantime the fish, and then th' apprentice died'.
>
> [XXII, 138-40, 148-52]

'No more is known': Crabbe's Peter is guilty at the very least of cruelty and neglect. His boy apprentice was little more to him than a mechanical aid. Crabbe's Peter shows little sign of caring.

'No more is known'. Montagu Slater's libretto reverses the meaning of the incident, and supports Peter's character by a string of new suggestions. Peter had been accidentally blown off course by a strong wind. When the drinking water ran out the boy died. Peter threw the fish overboard, returned home, called the apothecary for help. We learn that Peter had previously saved the boy from drowning in the March storms. So far this looks like an entirely different Peter, innocent, and misjudged both by the Coroner (who calls him 'callous, brutal, coarse') and by the

Borough gossips, who maliciously suspect murder. The new Peter has shown pity, as we learn in Act II scene 2 where he obsessively re-enacts the incident in his mind:

> Stop moaning, boy. What's that? Water?
> There's no water. You had the last yesterday.
> We'll soon be home.

So far, consistent. But a discrepancy lies in the fact that he cannot forget how the boy's eyes had been fixed on him, cursing him with a guilt comparable to the guilt of Coleridge's Ancient Mariner. He is cursed with a guilt he does not deserve. And we find him rough-handling his second apprentice. He has already struck Ellen in return for her befriending him, and for her honest admission that their plan had failed. He allows the second apprentice to risk and lose his life on the treacherous cliff face. He appears to have been sacrificing lives as well as affection in order to become successful. The slanderous persecution of the gossips, added to his guilt, and conflicting with his ambition, drives him out of his mind.

There is no way of accounting for this pattern of behaviour, other than by saying that the librettist whitewashed the Peter of Crabbe's poem, to gain him sympathy, but then was forced back point by point into something nearer Crabbe's original conception. The blackening which follows the Prologue works retrospectively, with the result that we can believe by the end that Peter did not, in fact, care about the death of his first apprentice, and sacrificed him – as in Crabbe's poem – to his trade. Hence we do not know, and cannot know, whether the Peter of the opera is guilty or not guilty: and we cannot resolve the contradictions and ambiguities. Crabbe's Peter is struggling with Slater's Peter. One rough-handles his apprentices: the other stands in the dock. One has hallucinations of guilt: the other has visions and dreams of peace. Nor can we account for Peter's treatment of his second apprentice except by referring to Crabbe's poem: the more thefts he committed,

> The more he look'd on all men as his foes.
> He built a mud wall'd hovel, where he kept
> His various wealth, and there he oft-times slept;
> But no success could please his cruel soul,
> He wish'd for one to trouble and control;
> He wanted some obedient boy to stand
> And bear the blow of his outrageous hand;
> And hoped to find in some propitious hour
> A feeling creature subject to his power. [XXII, 50-8]

In the opera, on the other hand, Peter shows compassion for the first apprentice, and asks for a replacement because he needs help like every other fisherman. One could perhaps see the rough way he treats the second apprentice as one element in a truthful portrait of a many-sided personality (just as David has to take some knocks from Hans Sachs in *Die Meistersinger von Nürnberg*): but rough treatment is given another dimension when lives are lost. In Crabbe the loss of life serves to emphasize Peter's unredeemable and pagan character. In the libretto the loss of life endangers the portrait of a compassionate semi-religious visionary who is to replace Crabbe's Peter. Suppose, however, that tolerant of the fictions and necessary illusions inherent in the theatre, we ignore this dramatic and moral ambiguity. Let us look more closely at Peter's attitude to the Borough gossips. It is disturbing to realize that Peter suffers from their scandalous talk without appreciating his responsibility for any acts he has committed. Can we pity his suffering in this way if he continues in his cruelty? We have the feeling that he does not suffer as a free, responsible protagonist, but is doomed to suffer, from the moment we hear the agitated musical rhythm behind the lines:[1]

> The Borough gossips
> Listen to rumour,
> Listen to money.
> One buys the other,
> I shall buy rumour.

The hurrying music indicates obsession and neurotic anxiety. The quick shift from his story of the death at sea to the subject of his social ambition is disquieting, and suggests callousness.

We are driven back to a reassessment of Swallow's words at the inquest. Swallow's verdict has been too often quoted for the same purpose – to show how brilliantly Britten's vocal line, with its strutting melodic shape and pompous rhythm, conveys the lawyer's provincial attitude of self-importance. What seems to have escaped notice is that Swallow's warning is perfectly justified and that Peter is reprehensible for ignoring it. It is true, of course, that the Borough gossips are busily engaged in purveying malicious rumour, like a tribe seeking some scapegoat for its own sins; but our sympathy for Peter is limited by his obstinacy. His disregard of the warning, with Ellen's well-intentioned but misguided complicity in fetching a new apprentice, results in another death and his own doom. Once again the doomed Peter is in reality the Peter from Crabbe's poem: while the Peter who aims ultimately to marry Ellen and who is unjustly slandered is the new fiction of the libretto.

The second major discrepancy in Peter, which lies in the motives of his ambition, is equally strange. A fisherman who is clear-sighted enough to see that the Borough gossips listen only to money is at the same time blind enough to desire their respect. He defers to their hollow standards. Their hypocrisy is plain to him, yet he seeks to belong. This ambition is surprisingly short of his imaginative potential as a visionary who knows he is 'different'; the most vivid illustration here is provided in the 'Great Bear and Pleiades' aria, sung in 'The Boar' to an unappreciative audience of Auntie, her nieces and customers. Grimes, we are to understand, is in the tragic grip of the scandalmongers whom he condemns, because their effect on him is to exert pressure to conform. Unhappily, his love for Ellen, and hers in return, is the basis of an unpromising plan to settle down. Neither he nor she envisages marriage first. Ellen defends herself before the Borough and its spokesmen in Act II scene 1, speaking of Peter and his apprentice:

> We planned that their lives should have a new start,
> That I as a friend could make the plan work,
> By bringing comfort where their lives were stark.
> . . . We planned this time to care for the boy,
> . . . Mending his clothes and giving him regular meals.

The unfeasibility of this plan has been clear since Act I scene 1, just after the Borough gossips' outburst, when Balstrode gives Peter good advice. He tells Peter to ask Ellen to marry him at once, without waiting for financial success and improved social status. At this point Balstrode proves himself to be the wisest and most acute observer of the Borough, an impression to be reinforced by his satirical attack on conversation in 'The Boar' during the storm. But Peter postpones thought of marriage, showing how ill-founded are his schemes for self-salvation, since he vainly seeks spiritual peace through accumulating material things. Perhaps Ellen's 'schoolhouse ways' act as a deterrent. This hint could have been made less oblique.

This discrepancy, like the first, arose when the librettist was developing for the opera a more subtle Peter than the central figure of the poem. The operatic Peter has to bear an artist-and-society symbolic weight, as well as to endure the burden of guilt without evidence of a crime. The rampant Borough Philistines eject the man of imagination, because his life is indirectly a criticism of theirs. The artist, whether in nineteenth or twentieth century, fails to find roots. But can the structure of the story bear such extra weight? One is left in doubt. Peter's explicit ambition is so futile that one hopes he will *not* succeed in settling down on the Borough's terms. It is too naïve an ambition to represent the artist's task. Is it the product of a febrile brain? How could it be the product of an outstandingly independent mind?

The two compass-points by which Peter steers his erratic course are his love-hate relationship with Ellen, and his love-hate relationship with the Borough way of life. We may learn more about the problem of motives if we look at each in turn.

Ellen has a separate portrait in Crabbe's composite poem, and it is the ingenious librettist who brings her into the story of Peter Grimes. She has helped Peter carry the body of the first apprentice home, as we learn in the Prologue; she has sided with Peter in public. And later in 'The Boar' we see how she dares the hostility of the customers when she undertakes Peter's errand for him.[2] Her sympathy extends to acts which mean devotion. And yet this second gesture is curiously misguided. Not only does she endanger the boy's life by placing him in Grimes's power, she simultaneously implicates herself in the social evil of the workhouse labour system. Even Boles, the lapsed Methodist preacher, can demand:

> Is this a Christian country? Are
> Workhouse children so enslaved
> That their bodies sell for cash?

Furthermore, the 'new start' which Ellen and Peter 'planned' is so flimsily based (extending only to domestic help) that it could not possibly stabilize Peter, even if it does make the hut neat. Ellen, like Peter, does not deserve the Borough's cruel gossip, but their criticism has a shadow of truth in it. Her intention is to redeem Peter by work-therapy rather than by love. Thus she never seems to *share* Peter's problem, and never could reach the centre of the opera where she could be interesting. Her music leaves us in no doubt of her likeable qualities: her actions suggest her limited judgment. The ironically grouped ensemble at the end of Act II scene 1, where Auntie, the nieces and Ellen dwell upon their power to give peace and comfort to men, does act, by association, in reducing Ellen's scale, and in reducing the pity of her loneliness at the end. If she has never really known Peter, her loss is diminished.

The relationship between Peter and the Borough is plain. Although Crabbe makes the 'gentle females' sympathetic to Peter's torment, the gossips of the opera are consistent in their calumny: and since Peter cannot beat them, he decides to join them. The Prologue presents the situation almost in tableau form, where Peter is arraigned before the people and officials, who chiefly enjoy their sense of power and are not primarily concerned with justice. The Borough's hypocrisy is obvious, except to the gossips and officials themselves. The words which Balstrode puts into their mouths, later, are laden with blind self-righteousness:

We live, and let live, and look
We keep our hands to ourselves.

As in Sheridan's *The School for Scandal*, the scandalmongers cannot see their own acts of interference. Strong social comment is conveyed to the audience through this, and through the later, equally bracing irony of hearing the same people singing the Morning Service off-stage. Ned, Robert and Auntie comment when the congregation emerges:

Now the church parade begins
Fresh beginning for fresh sins.
Ogling with a pious gaze
Each one's at his exercise.

Respectability thinly covers pseudo-Christianity, drunkenness, loose sexual morals, exploitation of child labour . . . It is ironical that such a community should in the name of justice persecute one of their number; but of course justice is not the issue. The real issue is conformity. We feel overwhelmed in the final scene by the enormous irony that the Borough may pursue its trade and routine activities in apparent innocence, while the Borough's victim drowns himself out at sea. The power of music to convey implicit comment was never demonstrated so well.

In conclusion, we must consider the implications of Peter's madness. We find that, like Lear, he speaks reason in madness; obsessed with the death of his first apprentice, he cannot forget the boy's last moments, when they were 'nearly home'; and the word 'home' produces an unhappy resonance in his mind when he remembers that he has no home, and has even lost his friendship with Ellen, the 'harbour' who might have sheltered peace for him. Off stage the Borough 'posse' cry out for him, seeking revenge: on stage, with dramatic irony, he shouts his own name back at them as though rejecting his identity in a paroxysm of disgust and despair. His madness makes sense: again, in the Shakespearian manner, it represents alienation rather than meaningless abnormality. He readily accepts Balstrode's advice to sail out and sink the boat.

The ending is dramatically memorable. But is it dramatically just? Had he some real guilt to atone for, the ending would have been meaningful as well as memorable: the tragic inevitability which Crabbe manages to convey as a force behind his narrative would have lent itself to the opera. But in the absence of established guilt, Peter is accepting death merely because of the Borough's desire for revenge. Balstrode at this moment acts as the Borough's executioner; mentally weakened, Peter submits. And the Borough celebrates its easy triumph with its routine performances, in the 'cold beginning of another day'.

Clearly there is a remarkable musical power in this opera, so dominating our response that we can accept the self-contradictory figure of Peter, and imagine him to be an entity corresponding to the musical organization which we encounter. Hans Keller has rightly shown how the interludes between the scenes, as distinct from the acts, are Grimes interludes; this is where his musical personality is summed up. The storm interlude, for example, corresponds to a storm within Peter, parallel with the storm in *King Lear*: it has a natural, a pictorial, a symbolic, and a psychological meaning. We have the illusion that Peter 'lives' in this music, and in the thematic vocal material for the central part. But the music's grandeur is at odds with the neurotic failure that Peter turns out to be. Britten's music is far more appropriate when it creates, with fine economy, the loneliness of the fisherman out at sea, and, by means of the broken phrases in the bass and slow, heaving movement, the sense of the timeless ocean which rolls in and sometimes threatens the petty-minded little human settlement which dredges a living from its shore.

12 *Plausible darkness: 'Peter Grimes' after a quarter of a century*

PETER GARVIE (1972)

'To meet is to destroy', wrote Crabbe of the elements in collision, and it might stand as a summary of *Peter Grimes*. Both the Borough and Peter are caught in the 'force, tumult and wrath' in which 'the river and the ocean met': the ordered society and the disordered elements of the individual. The Borough seems to survive the threat that Peter posed. What really survives is only the non-human, the elemental. The passing bell is tugged by human hands to signify the end of human time for each of us, but the bell-buoy sounds for ever to the movement of the tides.

In 1945 we looked at *Peter Grimes* as a beginning, and tried to find hints of operatic genius in the song cycles and instrumental works that preceded it. Now we see it down the perspective of a quarter of a century and a dozen later operas. The temptation then was to see it as uniquely new; now it is to see it as uniquely conventional. It is of all Britten's operas the one which owes most to the recent past and is richest in observation of human character. The later operas which appear more conventional, more like *Peter Grimes*, are significantly different. The angle at which the drama is presented, and the relationships within, for instance, *Billy Budd*, give a new emphasis to theme rather than action. *A Midsummer Night's Dream*, the setting of a play, reveals itself as a secular parable of transformation. The chamber operas are stylized microcosms. The parables for church performance are dramatic exemplars of their perspective. What is worth exploring is whether *Peter Grimes*, reviewed in the experience of Britten's later work, is only what it seems to be: a great but final reincarnation of more or less traditional opera – once done, not to be repeated, nor even to have many echoes among Britten's later preoccupations.

If we begin by looking at *Peter Grimes* as simply as possible, we find a story presented as it happened. The events are in sequence and unmodified by any perspective such as Britten imposes upon such apparently different works as *Billy Budd, The Rape of Lucretia*, or *Curlew*

River. The opera *is* what is put before us, and we make of it what we will or can. There are no preconceptions of belief or angles of vision. It is about people whose way of life a century and half before is still familiar to us in so far as it is preserved in small communities. The characters are detailed for us by text and music as credible human beings; blind and responsive, touching and comic, commonplace and unusual. The central situation – an individual and a community at odds – may have a tragic development, or a comic one, as in Verdi's *Falstaff*. The outcome of a comedy is a realistic reconciliation; the people are changed, but the world is not. In many tragedies we do feel that the world we know at the end is no longer the one put before us at the beginning of the play. The fate of Oedipus or Lear or Tristan makes a world without them seem a different mode of existence. In Mozart's *Don Giovanni*, a civilized society has to fill the vacuum left by the Don's damnation. In Molière's Don Juan, our last image is of the greedy Sganarelle missing his wages. The effect of *Peter Grimes* is in some ways more like that of dark comedy: the world can go on, incredibly, despite what it has witnessed and experienced.

The sequence of events begins even before the opera does. It begins in the boat where the first apprentice died. It is the interpretation of that fact, and the distortion of it into suspicion, that initiates the conflict. The action develops from what Peter does, and the way the Borough interprets his acts. Each alternately tightens the screw. In Act I, Peter gets a new apprentice, and this brings out the enmity of the community. In Act II scene 1, his failure of control is seen as habitual: 'Grimes is at his exercise'. But the next scene, the centre of the opera, is ironic in that it temporarily exonerates Peter just after the new apprentice has fallen to his death. 'Here's order, here's skill', says the Rector, quoting Borough virtues. In Act III, the screw tightens again. The finding of the boy's jersey precipitates the manhunt. The final irony is the lack of reaction to Peter's death: the gossip of the Prologue has become just 'one of those rumours'.

There is, in fact, no direct confrontation between Peter and his community. In a sense they do *not* meet. The closest to confrontation is at the inquest, but it is suppressed and oblique. That is the Borough way. Peter does get some help to pull up his boat (Act I scene 1). In the Boar, he evades the challenge. In Act II scene 1, he has left by the time the people emerge from church, and in the next scene he has left his hut before the deputation enters it. In Act III, the manhunt never finds him.

Peter does not belong to the community; his attachment is to the place:

I am native, rooted here . . .
By familiar fields,
Marsh and sand,
Ordinary streets,
Prevailing wind.

He is elemental, and Ellen Orford could never domesticate him. His notion of community is to get enough silver, fish and money, to impress them into silence, and this is in itself a kind of violence. He has to force peace and tolerance upon the Borough. Yet this is a fantasy of being alone; Peter and his community do not share enough vocabulary to confront one another. They see his strangeness as violence, and fear it; he sees their conventions as suspicion, and therefore threatening.

The absence of direct confrontation, with the possibilities of resolution by change, convinces us dramatically because of the moral detailing of the community. Ellen is no conventional heroine, but a widow past her youth, a schoolmistress, tame; she has the virtues to complement Peter, but they are the ones remotest from him. Balstrode, the most understanding of him, is the least sympathetic to apprentices – 'workhouse brats' – and a believer in letting things settle down:

We live and let live
And look, we keep our hands to ourselves.

The Borough collectively is only hostile when reacting to threats. The effectiveness of *Peter Grimes* in terms of conventional opera is in its transference of the humour, mixed motives, and self-absorption of a closed community into dramatic terms. It is when we explore the other levels and themes of *Peter Grimes* that its power is more appropriately understood, and its relationships with Britten's other music become apparent.

In terms of theatre the inquest as prologue is masterly. Drama has to begin with exposition, and the dramatist usually hides his method. But the purpose of an inquest is precisely to discover facts, and so Britten is able to convey a great deal of necessary information to us directly and rapidly. He can in a few minutes involve and characterize all the main people in the drama, and establish the central relationship between Peter and the Borough. And we should remember that, despite the insinuations, an inquest is not a trial, but a search.

The theme of searching is a key one in the opera. Fishing is searching. A new apprentice must be looked for. There are two trips of investigation after Peter. The boy's jersey turns up as evidence. Peter's image of happiness and peace is one that must be sought and deciphered. Almost the final image of the opera is of the telescope searching the sea and not confirming the coastguard report of a boat sinking. The search theme is an exploration that proceeds from the known to the unknown, from the conscious to the unconscious. The Borough needs to turn experience into fact, to find it, assimilate it, and tame it. Peter, like the elements, eludes that search, that control through knowledge, and is therefore strange and fearsome. The one fact that no one inquires about is Peter's death.

The community's need to order and conventionalize experience into acceptable fact is a pull towards confinement. The inquest packs the populace into the Moot Hall as the dance will in Act III. In Act I scene 1, the capstan is symbolically at the centre of the scene; it is the machine that by common effort recovers and makes safe the boats from the sea. In Act I scene 2, The Boar is the refuge from the elements. In the next scene it is the church.

When in Act II scene 2 we finally see where Peter lives, we find it is an upturned boat, stranded out of its element. His confinement is to be that of himself when he breaks down in the foggy small hours. At this point the Borough is least domestic, least rooted; it has become the distant hunting pack, and its voice as inhuman as the fog horn's. The posse does not stop Peter; his imagination does that. His boat returns to its element for the last time:

> What is home? Calm as deep water.
> Where's my home? Deep in calm water.

Peter says little at the inquest. He confides to Balstrode when the storm protects his truth. At this point a resolution seems possible, for Ellen has already intervened to take care of the new apprentice. But it is her compassion that he rejects when Balstrode tells him to marry her now. He will enforce the Borough's respect in Borough ways; he will fish the sea dry. Even that is a threat. When Peter comes into The Boar in the next scene, the greeting is, 'Talk of the devil, and there he is'. His strangeness confirms it, for he wants to decipher the stars, find a way out of the trap of time, and yet,

> . . . the horoscope's bewildering
> Like a flashing turmoil of a shoal of herring.

When the round starts (in communal self-protection against such strangeness), fishing is again a way to wealth. When Peter's voice enters the round, it is thrown off balance because fishing has become dragging up the dead from the bottom.

The opening of Act II, the glitter of waves and sunlight, the calm of Sunday morning, makes the storms of the previous scene, mental and physical, at first seem a nightmare survived. Ellen is all compassion. When Peter comes in, it is to take the boy off fishing, away to the elemental world: 'I can see the shoals to which the rest are blind'. Ellen challenges his dream of buying off the Borough with silver and says that they have failed. '*Peter cries out as if in agony – strikes Ellen, whose work basket falls to the ground.*' The symbol of domesticity is lost. The Amen from the Borough at church is echoed by Peter: 'So be it – and God have mercy upon me!' The heavy, accented downward phrase, like a judgement falling upon him, is repeated by the orchestra. It is to become the passacaglia bass in the next interlude, the recompense for violence.

The Borough, prompted by Boles, is at least initially motivated by concern for the boy, and Ellen tries to extend their pity:

> O pity those who try to bring
> A shadowed life into the sun.

The women's quartet focusses the compassion into a care for all men. Women must be mothers keeping 'the *bitter* treasure of their love.'

In the next scene, Peter is still obsessed by the sea boiling with silver. He breaks out of his violence – fishing as an act of reprisal – and into his dreams of life with Ellen. He echoes both the compassion of the women's quartet and his song from Act I. The stars prefigure, but sleep admits, nightmares from the past as well as dreams of the future, 'dead fingers'. Peter blames the new apprentice for this new trouble, the gossip that brings the Borough leaders to his hut. He flies for safety to the elements. The boy falls. The deputation finds no substance to the gossip. 'Will the last to go please close the door', says the Rector. The passacaglia disclaims the neat cadence, the judgement of the bass now supporting the compassion of the solo viola.

What the tide brings in is the boy's jersey, not the great shoal of fish. Peter is to call back at the posse, 'Come on! Land me!', and he remembers the round from the pub. The inversion of roles – the fisherman to be netted – goes further when he calls out to the Borough at large, 'And God have mercy upon you'. Home is now the oblivion of the sea, and Peter is the victim.

The action of the opera is measured by Peter's appearance in Act I, with Balstrode helping to winch his boat up, and his disappearance, with Balstrode helping him to push it down the shingle for the last time. The Prologue brought us a world that must take account of Peter; the last scene, as dawn comes, is almost an epilogue, a world without Peter which goes on as though he had never been.

What seems to be missing in *Peter Grimes*, and is persistently present in Britten's later music, is the sense of redemptive continuity. This continuity, a sense of meaning beyond the act, is usually expressed in Christian terms, but it may also be found as a secular transformation, an accord of the human and natural worlds within the creative imagination. (The *Nocturne* and *A Midsummer Night's Dream* are good examples.) It is tempting to think of *Peter Grimes* in terms of the end as an end, and to wonder whether it was its moral implications that forced Britten to find a response. The treatment of Christianity in *Peter Grimes* seems to bear that out. Whether it is the socially binding Anglicanism of the Rector or the evangelical zeal of Methody Boles, it is uninfluential for good. It does nothing to heal Peter or his community. The death of Peter is not in the true meaning of the term 'a sacrifice'; it does not 'make sacred'.

Peter is natural man, responsive to both the metamorphoses and the unalterable in nature. The tide is his symbol and makes his epitaph; never the same, but in its larger rhythm never to be altered. He is egocentric: 'mercy upon *me*'. The personality that defines itself only in relation to nature does not have to modify itself as it would if it were really in commerce with the human. There is something of the child in him too, especially in his easy drift between fantasy and reality, and his wilfulness. He never defines himself in terms of community, but in terms of ambition, of a self as large and powerful and undiscriminating as the natural world, that is, the unconscious self. He is as alone with his unconscious as he is with the sea.

Peter's prison is not the Borough, but his own skull. It is as though he feels enormous elemental pressures against the thin walls of bone. It is characteristic of his incapacity to tell experience from fact – the obverse of the Borough's will to reduce feeling to fact – that his beliefs are magical: he will decipher the stars, he will turn the fish into silver. He is a man of imagination, but it is not redemptive. His bad dreams do not change the past, the ghosts, the system.

Peter is fundamentally unlike Billy Budd, even when words fail both and gesture becomes the substitute. In Billy's case, as he struggles with the more complex and more attractive evil of Claggart, it is the only form that a good act can take in the shadow of his stammer. In Peter's case, his striking of Ellen, it is an act against himself and his failure, projected outwards. That Peter commits suicide by drowning is not an evasion of tragedy, but the way in which violence must be turned if it cannot be relieved.

Act II scene 1 proceeds by ironic juxtaposition – a method to be developed much further in the *War Requiem* – and is most specifically about the three levels of experience: the divine, the human, the natural. They begin in concord: the Borough at worship, Ellen and the boy, the peaceful glitter of the seascape. But even in the opening hymn the irony begins to be felt as the Borough prays to be kept free from gossip, from verbal trespass. The juxtapositions intensify:

THE CHURCH	ELLEN
Amen.	Every day I pray it may be so.
. . . strayed from Thy ways like lost sheep.	There's a tear in your coat.
. . . And we have done those things which we ought not to have done. . .	That was done recently . . .
O Lord, open Thou our lips. . .	John, what are you trying to hide?
O Lord, make haste to help us.	A bruise . . . well, it's begun.

There is a passage of resumed congruity, leading into the *Benedicite* which should be creation's praise. Peter bursts in upon it:

THE CHURCH	PETER
O ye whales and all that move in the waters.	I can see the shoals to which all the rest are blind.

'It is Sunday', sings Ellen, 'the day that belongs to God.' And Peter replies, 'This is whatever day I say it is'.[1] His final identity is to answer at the end of the opera in the voice of Davy Jones, 'Come home'. Each act ends, indeed, with an ironic sense of home: the first with the outraged Borough calling after him, 'Home! Do you call that home!'; the second with the Borough deputation accepting where he lives as home at the exact moment that the boy has fallen to his death; and the third with the Borough preferring not to notice that Peter has come home to death by water.

If there is no redemption in *Peter Grimes*, no making sacred, there is at least intercession, and its terms are Christian. The most dominant and powerful phrase that Ellen sings in the opera sweeps downward to the words, 'Let her among you without fault cast the first stone'. Peter's phrase, 'And God have mercy upon me!' moves downwards too, though more abruptly, and he has to reach up to begin it. Balstrode's key phrase in Act III, 'When horror breaks one heart, All hearts are broken!', also descends, though, true to his character, it is more constricted.

Nothing redemptive comes of this phrase in the opera, but one is tempted to say that everything does in Britten's later music – and even in his earliest music, for Variation V of *A Boy was Born* juxtaposes Incarnation and Sacrifice: man's transformation of God's birth in this world, and God's transformation of His death in this world. It is this distinction that is crucial to the *War Requiem* rather than simply the challenge to established liturgy of human experience. Nor is there as much distance as we might suppose between Britten's secular and religious works. For when it is the imagination that provides the redemptive continuity, it still operates upon an experience that takes in dream and nightmare, Incarnation and Crucifixion, and it is their transformation that turns what happens into what is healed. It is an act of imagination that must inform charity: to perceive the common wound in the individual hurt – whether in Lucretia's end or Vere's self-doubt or the governess's lullaby or the parable of the Good Samaritan in *Misericordium*. *Peter Grimes* recognizes the need, but shows no way to act, to prevent and to redeem. We need to be reminded of these normal worlds that no amount of suffering can make sacred; and to fail to experience them is to misunderstand the plausible darkness from which Britten's later music seeks to rescue us. In the words of Crabbe,

> Fairly they bought, they said, and fairly sold,
> And yet they dealt in darkness.

13 *Britten and Grimes*

PHILIP BRETT (1977)

'I am firmly rooted in this glorious county. And I proved this to myself when I once tried to live somewhere else.'[1] In this tribute to his native Suffolk, Benjamin Britten refers to his attempted emigration to America during the years 1939-42. He and his friend Peter Pears left England shortly before war was declared and hard on the heels of two friends and collaborators, W. H. Auden and Christopher Isherwood, whose departure stimulated a minor exodus of British writers and a considerable outcry in the national press. Britten, then a discouraged young composer, has described himself on arrival in the USA as 'muddled, fed-up and looking for work, longing to be used'.[2] Commissions quickly came his way, and in the next three years he wrote a number of considerable works, including the Violin Concerto in D minor, the String Quartet in D, the Michelangelo Sonnets, the operetta *Paul Bunyan* on a libretto by Auden, and the *Sinfonia da Requiem*. And it was a performance of this last piece in Boston that prompted Koussevitzky to offer him the grant that enabled him to write his first major opera. But the muddle did not clear up. If as Auden is reported as having said, 'an artist must live where he has live roots or no roots at all',[3] then it became clear that the anonymity and isolation beneficial to the poet did not suit the musician, and Britten gradually realized he must return to his native land, whatever the consequences to him as a pacifist.

The opera *Peter Grimes* has an intimate connection with the composer's decision to go back. It was in Southern California in summer 1941 that he picked up an issue of *The Listener* to which E. M. Forster had contributed an article on the Suffolk poet, George Crabbe.[4] This seems to have been the turning-point in Britten's decision not only about nationality but also locality. It was Crabbe's own Borough to which the composer repaired, no doubt with a sentence of Forster's ringing in his ears: 'Yet he never escaped from Aldeburgh in the spirit, and it was the making of him as a poet'. More important still, the article sent Britten to Crabbe's poems, which he had not previously read, and in *The Borough* he discovered not only a place to put down roots but also a series of characters and a plot for an opera.

Crabbe's Peter Grimes is one of the poor of the Borough, and though the poet grew up among the poor he did not like them. His portrait of the man whose cruelty leads to the death of three boy apprentices from the workhouse and whose guilty conscience drives him to madness and death is alleviated by few redeeming features: a bold and unusual choice for the central figure of a musical drama in the tradition of grand opera. True, there are other anti-heroes in 20th-century opera, of whom the most famous is Wozzeck. But there is no assumption of basic decency in the Grimes of the poem, and he is not so obviously the downtrodden common man pushed into crime and insanity by the savage acts of those around him. It is true, of course, that Britten and his librettist, Montagu Slater, transformed him from Crabbe's ruffian into a far more complicated figure, one who can be recognized in certain lights, perhaps, as a distant foreign cousin of Wozzeck's. At the beginning of the opera Grimes has lost only one apprentice, clearly by accident, and the death of his replacement in Act II is also patently a mishap. The new, almost Byronic, Grimes is rough, to be sure, but he is also a dreamer; and his music constantly invites compassion and concern. Yet there are still great difficulties with Grimes as the central figure, and the reaction of the critics ranges from Patricia Howard's prim little sentence, 'His is not a character with whom we can admit to identifying ourselves' (p. 23), to Eric Walter White's more sophisticated but equally unhelpful remark that he is 'what might be called a maladjusted aggressive psychopath'.[5] In a comparatively recent review, Desmond Shawe-Taylor has gone so far along these lines as to find 'a flaw in the conception of the central character'. In his opinion, 'the new Grimes is inconsistently presented. For all his visionary airs, the death of his second apprentice is directly caused by his roughness and callousness, so that the sympathetic Ellen Orford was in effect culpably wrong, and the "Borough gossips" and the much-maligned Mrs Sedley dead right.'[6]

This statement raises a number of issues. It is of course usual and right for a society to protect the innocent and helpless from harm, but it is also generally recognized that it must observe due process of the law. The accident that befalls the second apprentice occurs when Peter, who is responsibly watching the boy, has his attention diverted and his paranoia understandably aroused by the arrival of the Borough procession, which observes neither due process nor common decency. That knock at the door just before the boy's scream reminds us in a very direct way that society precipitates what it should be guarding against, and therefore shares the responsibility with the individual. To put it in Forster's more trenchant words, there is 'no crime on Peter's part except what is caused by the far greater crimes committed against him by society' (See above, p. 20). More important than what is indicated by the libretto, however, is what goes on in the score, because questions of right and wrong in opera are ultimately determined not by moral law but by music. We come away from the final duet of *Poppea* or the Liebestod of *Tristan und Isolde* believing if anything in the power of love, not the culpability of fornication, faithlessness, peremptory execution and banishment. Grimes is as undeniably sympathetic from the music he sings as Mrs Sedley, on the other hand, is sinister. But what is finally disturbing here is not only that an experienced and respected member of the profession should wield a stick he would never use to beat earlier classics of the repertory, such as *Poppea* or *Tristan*, but also that he studiously avoids any truth that lies below the most obvious surface of the action. To discover why that should be is to take a further journey into the opera.

In the most sensitive account of *Peter Grimes* to date (see chapter 5), Hans Keller, who draws usefully on psychoanalytic theory as well as a secure musical and dramatic instinct, points out that Peter 'cannot show, let alone prove his tenderness as easily as his wrath – except through the music, which, alas, the people on stage don't hear. Thus he is destined to seem worse than he is, and not to be as good as he feels. *Peter Grimes* is the story of the man who couldn't fit in.' It is this theme that Peter Pears explored in an article directed to the opera's first radio audience (see chapter 8):

> Grimes is not a hero nor is he an operatic villain. He is not a sadist nor a demonic character, and the music quite clearly shows that. He is very much of an ordinary weak person who, being at odds with the society in which he finds himself, tries to overcome it and, in doing so, offends against the conventional code, is classed by society as a criminal, and destroyed as such.

This is a clear explanation, so far as it goes, and rather more helpful than Britten's own statement that 'in writing *Peter Grimes*, I wanted to express my awareness of the perpetual struggle of men and women whose livelihood depends on the sea' (above, p. 149). One of the greatest strengths of the opera is of course its vivid portrayal of the moods of the ocean – owing much, I suspect, to Britten's re-encounter with the Suffolk coastline. But, as in Crabbe, the natural detail is secondary to the human drama played out against it and which it sometimes reflects (e.g. in the Storm Interlude). In approaching this human drama, however, we need to go further than Keller's psychoanalytical abstractions, further too than Pears perhaps felt able, into the idea of the outsider, Grimes the unclubbable. His tragedy is of course relevant on a universal scale in our age of alienation, but I am interested in a particular interpretation that I believe solves some of the problems that have been raised.

It is clear from the music of the opening scene that Peter is not only telling the truth about the death of his first apprentice but also that he really is at odds with the Borough, and seeks in his own inner life a means of averting the harshness of his condition. All this can be heard in the orchestral motif played as he steps into the witness box, in his first words – sung on the same note as those of the bullying coroner but harmonized differently, and also in the way he cadences so frequently, not on the tonic, like Swallow, but on the seventh of the supporting chord (Ex. 34). Peter cannot reply in the worldly manner of the coroner, then, just as later he cannot respond immediately to the approach of his schoolmistress supporter, Ellen Orford. She sets him off on a paranoid outburst that is literally out of tune with her E major blandishments, and when she does bring him round to her key, what they sing together

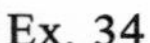

Ex. 35

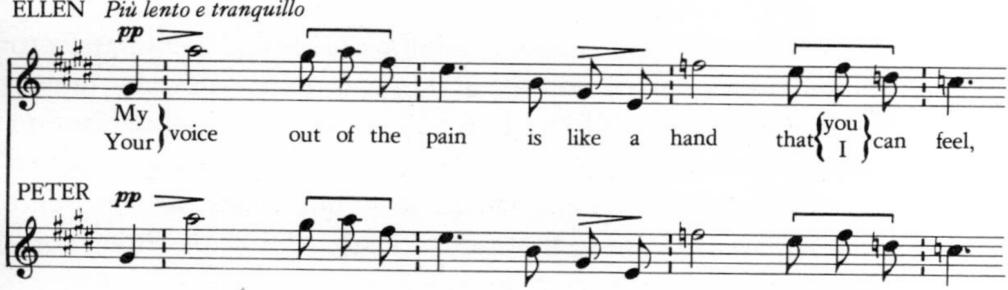

centres upon the minor ninth, the interval most associated with Peter's loneliness and his private fantasies, of which she is the unrealistic focus (Ex. 35).

'I have my visions, fiery visions, they call me dreamer', sings Peter (in Act I scene 1). And the tonal planning of the opera reflects the conflict between this fantasy-life (generally expressed in D, E or A major) and the outside reality represented by, say, the E flat of the storm and pub scene, or the B flat of the courtroom and the final manhunt. It is easy enough to point to the self-destructive force of Peter's pride and of his fantasies, and to show how even his relationship with Ellen is doomed by his seeing marriage to her as the last step on the ladder of gaining respectability and 'showing the Borough'. But this still leaves him, in a sense, as an unexplained boy-beater, and it is only by looking more closely at his relation with the chorus, representing the Borough, that a closer understanding of his nature can be reached. Eric Walter White has pointed out important distinctions between the handling of the chorus in *Grimes* and in Musorgsky's *Boris Godunov*, with which it has often been compared.[7] Britten was evidently concerned to characterize the minor figures who emerge now and then in order to emphasize that the crowd is after all a collection of individuals, each of whom, like Grimes in Crabbe's memorable phrase, 'is at his exercise'. Yet the most powerful moments are undeniably those, like the storm fugue, the round in the pub scene, the posse in Act II, the manhunt in Act III, when everyone on stage joins the chorus, only Peter himself standing out in contradistinction to the general will, which at one point, in the round, 'Old Joe has gone fishing', he almost overcomes musically singlehanded. There is no other relationship so important in the opera: the boy doesn't utter a word; and Ellen – well, as we have seen, marriage with her is out of the question, and her parental response when she discovers a bruise on the boy's neck prompts her to a judgement which Peter can only interpret as desertion. The failure of their relationship leads to another and crucial step in Peter's decline. It is expressed musically in the second most important motif in the opera, a downward thrusting figure in which Peter, so to speak, accepts his fate (Ex. 26).

But the break with Ellen is only symbolic of his final capitulation to the values and judgment of society at large, a point ironically underscored by the final 'Amen' of the Borough at prayer. The congregation emerges, and starts a different chant: 'Grimes is at his exercise' – set to the very notes of Peter's self-surrender. Is it quite clear at this point why the Borough people are so incensed? Clearly no-one but Ellen combines moral fervour with sufficient human warmth to be unduly concerned about the misfortunes of a workhouse brat. It is Peter himself who rivets their hypocritical attention. He is an outsider not merely because of the unpleasant sides of his personality either, but because he is 'different' – a difference accounted for on the surface level of the plot by his visionary side. His difference of nature – proud, aloof, rough and visionary – poses some sort of threat to the narrow ordered life of society struggling for existence against the sea, and therefore he is subjected to persecution, which is part of the ritual societies devise, whether subtly or in this case brutally, to maintain the bounds of what is socially acceptable.

The action of such a society upon an individual or minority in such a manner is simply stated as oppression. The word is overworked, but there is nothing better to describe the essence of a tragedy conceived long before the writings of the 1960s taught us the mechanics of the phenomenon outside purely political spheres. The dramatic treatment of this subject in earlier ages tended – as in, say, Milton or Handel's *Samson* – to dwell on the heroic aspects of the destructive but ennobling anger it can generate. But the anger of the non-heroic Peter is directed not towards some cataclysmic showdown with the crowd, but more dangerously against the defenceless boy, and still more dangerously, against himself. The moment when oppression becomes crippling and leads to tragedy is when it is accepted and internalized. And once we hear Peter falling under the spell of the Borough's values, we know that he embraces his own oppression and sets his soul on that slippery path toward self-hatred that causes the destruction of the individual.

First, it cuts off his means of escape: he is rooted, not only 'by familiar fields, marsh and sand', as he admits to Balstrode in Act I, but also 'by the shut faces of the Borough clans'. Second, it leads him to think he can vindicate himself by making money, setting up as a respectable merchant, and even more unrealistically by marrying Ellen. Balstrode perceives clearly enough that a new start with a new apprentice will lead only to the old tragedy again, and Peter's acceptance of this unpalatable truth an act later is the pivotal moment of the drama (see Ex. 26). And yet the most terrifying dramatic realization of his self-hatred is reserved for the last scene when, after recalling fragments from the opera in his delirium, he catches the sound of his persecutors calling his name through the fog. The Borough by this time has become a surrealistic caricature of itself as an oppressive society engaged in that ultimate fantasy of the oppressed – the manhunt. And Peter's response is to shout back at them, not abuse, but his own name – first in anger, but then as his energy subsides, in the self-loathing that longs for dissolution and death. On the appearance of Ellen and Balstrode he curls up, as it were, into the womb-like state he associates with Ellen in his fantasy, and sings the melody first heard just before the Storm Interlude in Act I. This time the optimistic orchestral accompaniment is replaced by the fog-wreathed voices of his distant hunters, and he completes the descent from the rising ninth previously left unresolved.

Easily unnoticed, but highly significant, is the staccato figure (Ex. 36) separating the lyrical arcs – modified in this last statement to emphasize the pathetic minor seconds more strongly. It is audibly an inversion of the angry crowd's motif in the courtroom Prologue. Bearing in

Ex. 36

mind that Britten combines an unconscious melodic gift with a highly conscious and responsible working-out of thematic connections, this can be taken not merely as a sign of Grimes's alienation but as a musical clue to his perverse relationship with the Borough through the inverting and turning inwards of the outward forces of oppression. The true tragedy of Grimes, then, can be heard in his most eloquent moment of fantasy.

With this in mind, we can return to the question of why critics like Shawe-Taylor tend to be so uncomfortable about Grimes. Hans Keller provides one answer by observing that there is something of a Grimes in each one of us, though most have outgrown or outwitted him to the extent that they cannot or will not recognize him (see chapter 5). Perhaps there is a more specific reason. The situation that gives rise to the oppression of Grimes – poverty and the 19th-century British apprentice system – is hardly relevant to opera-going audiences today, and it is consequently underplayed in the libretto. Instead, Peter's dreaming, visionary side is played up. We can safely take him as a symbol and the story as an allegory.

If Britten had been black, or had been a woman composer, he might well have addressed himself to the oppression of these groups. As a pacifist, he must have been engaged in the questions dealt with in *Owen Wingrave*, though 1945 would scarcely have been a good time to raise them, even in heavy camouflage. No, *Peter Grimes* is about a man who is persecuted because he is different. We may recall Peter Pears's explanation that Grimes 'is very much of an ordinary weak person who . . . offends against the conventional code, is classed by society as a criminal and destroyed as such'. To which he adds as a final line, 'There are plenty of Grimeses around still, I think!'. There is every reason to suppose that the unspoken matter is what in 1945 was still the crime that hardly dare speak its name, and that it is to the homosexual condition that *Peter Grimes* is addressed. At any rate, if we look at the opera in this allegorical way, the problems (both moral and dramatic) about Grimes's character fall away, the viciousness of the Borough's persecution becomes more explicable, and Peter's own tragedy, that of guilt and self-hatred, all the more poignant and relevant to people today.[8]

A number of Britten's other operas deal with male relationships, some of them – *The Turn of the Screw*, *Billy Budd* and *Death in Venice* – in a more specifically homosexual context than *Grimes*. Yet none of them is so vivid or urgent in quality. This can be understood in a variety of ways, not least in terms of the composer's youthfulness, but I should like to explore its connection with the circumstances of his removal to America in the wake of Auden and Isherwood. The reasons for their emigration have been explained in a number of ways, usually in broad terms embracing the decline of European civilization, the threat of Nazism, the stifling, censorious moral and artistic atmosphere of Britain in the 1930s, and so on.[9] All these reasons are plausible, but another fundamental impulse must also have been at work: namely that desire, so common in young gay men, to seek anonymity and freedom by going to the big city, the far-off country – any place, that is, away from the home where they feel at best half-accepted. But mere removal generally solves nothing. Every homosexual man, and in particular the artist, needs to come to terms with himself as well as society, and settle the linked questions of 'roots' and sexuality in order to live, to grow, and to work fruitfully.

Let us consider the cases of two analogous British artists, both friends and collaborators of Britten's, who represent alternative possibilities at each extreme of the scale. Christopher Isherwood, who settled in the Los Angeles area where he has remained to this day, has not become any the less a British novelist for the remove. His perception of America is brilliant, but it is the view of an outsider, like the hero of his novel, *A Single Man*, who is a British homosexual man teaching at a Southern Californian State College. Yet as an exile Isherwood has been able to write freely on sexual matters. He was the only writer of his time to explore the English phenomenon of male homosexuality, as a recent critic has pointed out,[10] and it was not until Michael Holroyd's biography of Lytton Strachey that the subject so central to English intellectual life was treated in a manner, like Isherwood's, neither maudlin nor flamboyant. In more recent years, moreover, Isherwood has written and talked openly of his own experience of homosexuality, most notably in the two autobiographical books *Kathleen and Frank* (1971) and *Christopher and his Kind* (1976).[11] Maintaining a reputation as one of the most distinguished living writers of English prose, he has also taken a prominent part in the activities of the gay movement in the USA.

The case of E. M. Forster is very different, though the two writers have many values in common, particularly those of honesty, gentleness and decency. Forster's most important experience abroad comprised the two visits to India (chronicled in *The Hill of Devi*) that provided the material for his masterpiece, *A Passage to India*, published in 1924. Ten years earlier, after a lean period following the success of *Howard's End* in 1910, he had written *Maurice*, a homosexual love story. His reasons for not publishing it are often misunderstood: to quote the author's Terminal Note (p. 236): 'Happiness is its keynote . . . If it ended unhappily, with a lad dangling from a noose or with a suicide pact, all would be well, for there is no pornography or seduction of minors. But the lovers get away unpunished and consequently recommend crime.' Forster did not want to face the possibility of being prosecuted; but the book, and some of what he called his 'sexy stories', circulated among friends. The tension between society's conventions and demands on the one hand and his own wishes as a creative artist on the other finally led to the painful and difficult decision to abandon the writing of fiction for publication, as several entries in his personal diary indicate.[12] And if there should be any doubt about the price this sensitive and private man would have had to pay for what is now called 'coming out', even in his later years, then one has only to contemplate the treatment of the posthumously published *Maurice* by the British critics, whose condescension on every other aspect of the novel barely concealed either a deep-seated embarrassment at, or hostility to, the subject itself.[13]

Given Forster's love of England, then, his acceptance of himself as a homosexual had an effect amounting almost to suicide as a novelist. Britten, no less rooted in his native country, arrived at a less drastic accommodation allowing him to act upon his belief in music as a social activity. He wrote for particular people and places – a principle that began at home, so to speak, in the huge amount of music composed for his friend, the tenor Peter Pears, whose artistry and discrimination contributed enormously to Britten's own development. In addition to their work as singer and accompanist, these two men literally re-created English opera. They founded a national opera company, they initiated and successfully maintained a provincial music festival of international standing at Aldeburgh, and in their work with children and amateurs they played a large part in the dramatic transformation of English musical education since World War II. This great achievement above and beyond Britten's music would scarcely have been possible, in a country where homosexuality is tolerated as an eccentricity but not accepted as a way of life, if Britten had been as overt as, say, Angus Wilson or David Hockney.

Peter Grimes was conceived at the very moment when Britten decided to exchange uncongenial freedom abroad for unknown peril at home, when he forswore the advantage of Isherwood for a life that might entail the Fosterian sacrifice. The work therefore occupies a special place in his accommodation to society. After his return Britten always showed an affable face to his countrymen, and the artistic aristocracy lent him support and showered him with honours. I believe the other side of the coin, the dark side of his feelings as a potential victim of persecution and as an outsider in an established society, come out with tremendous force in *Grimes*. They were once again to emerge in 1953, the coronation year, when he scandalized conventional opinion by his treatment of the first Queen Elizabeth in *Gloriana*; but by the time of the *War Requiem* nine years later the voice of protest had become institutionalized in the oratorio form, and consequently muted.

In 1945, however, Britten had just returned to face unknown penalties from a repressive and embattled society on account of both his lifestyle and his pacifism. And I believe it was *Peter Grimes*, representing the ultimate fantasy of persecution and suicide, that played a crucial role in his coming to terms with himself and the society which he both distrusted and yet wished to serve as a musician. Unlike Isherwood, Britten needed to live and work where he had roots; unlike Forster he was not prepared to damp down the creative fires. Having made his choice, *Grimes* served as a catharsis, purging its agony and terror.

14 *Postscript*

PHILIP BRETT

Two statements about the opera by its composer escaped my attention when I wrote 'Britten and Grimes'; they provide different but connected ways of re-examining, in these closing pages, the concerns of the composer and his work. One of them, now frequently quoted, comes from an interview in which Britten recounts how he and Peter Pears came across Crabbe's poem and started working together on the outline of the plot:

> A central feeling for us was that of the individual against the crowd, with ironic overtones for our own situation. As conscientious objectors we were out of it. We couldn't say we suffered physically, but naturally we experienced tremendous tension. I think it was partly this feeling which led us to make Grimes a character of vision and conflict, the tortured idealist he is, rather than the villain he was in Crabbe.[1]

It was reassuring to find the composer confirming a symbolic view of the opera, stressing Peter Pears's involvement in its conception, and relating it to their personal situation. On the face of it, Britten's words contradict my view that '1945 would scarcely have been a good time to raise the questions dealt with in *Owen Wingrave*'; but, to quote Michael Kennedy, 'is it to be seriously doubted that "and homosexuals" were unspoken but implied words in that statement? [after 'conscientious objectors'] ' (pp. 123-4). Though the opera owes a good deal to the composer's experience not only as a pacifist in wartime but also as an artist in a society he considered 'basically philistine' (an expression he used twice in that same interview), its intensity must ultimately derive from the much earlier and more fundamental experience of the stigma of his sexuality, a stigma so strong that it could not be mentioned.

Peter Pears has said 'Ben had a marvellous childhood', and all one can discover of family life at 21 Kirkley Cliff Road in Lowestoft confirms this. A strict but gentle father who read Dickens to his children and took them on walks, a mother who pampered the boy and encouraged his musical talents, sisters who jumped up indulgently from the piano bench whenever he had a musical idea he wanted to try out – these were some of its happy ingredients. There was also a certain puritanism, which Britten regarded as an advantage to him as a composer because it inculcated disciplined working habits. Indeed, he remained nostalgic all his life for this ordered boyhood idyll (though when reconstructed it could prove a little stifling, as Auden pointed out to him in 1941 in a remarkable letter about 'the demands of disorder'[2]).

'His personality was outgoing, as a young child' writes Christopher Headington (p. 17). 'A later shyness came with adolescence.' Such a manifestation of the awkward age is familiar to many of us who had to confront our homosexuality while growing up in comparable circumstances. The dawning realisation of sexual feeling can rarely be a simple matter; when it is homosexual feeling and when the family tie is strong, the resulting conflict can be devastating – for it is the special characteristic of the homosexual stigma (unlike that attached to being black or Jewish) that it is almost always reinforced at home and is thus the more readily 'internalised', that is, accepted as valid and to a greater or lesser extent incorporated into the values and sense of identity of the person in question.[3] Attempting to imagine the special degree of guilt and shame he accumulated during this outwardly happy and unremarkable youth is, I think, the key to understanding Britten's sense of being an outsider, his insecurity and the resulting contradictions in his character. If imagination fails, some estimation of the damage his self-image sustained can be gained from his later attitude to his sexuality and from his hostility to the gay movement and to homosexual life-styles other than his own. According to Duncan (p. 28) 'he remained a reluctant homosexual', and Pears has said, 'the word "gay" was not in his vocabulary . . . "the gay life", he resented that'.[4]

More important, the effect on Britten's work can be seen in the themes which crop up in it with some frequency: the difficulties surrounding male relationships; the loss of innocence; and the plight of the outsider. Perhaps even the more profound issues, the doubts about life and art that surfaced with such intensity in *Death in Venice*, derived at least in part from that early and crucial self-doubt. Not that Britten was totally obsessed by these things to the exclusion of all else in his dramatic music – far from it – but the importance in his creative output of an experience of human society resulting from his sexual preference can perhaps be gauged by comparing him with other leading composers of this century who happen to have shared the same orientation. In no other case does it seem so important an issue.

There is, however, no reason to see all his work as autobiographical.

It is surely wrong, and perhaps crass, to identify Britten with any of his characters to the degree that both Davis and Vickers identify him with Peter Grimes in the literature accompanying the Philips recording. Equally suspect is the tendency to criticise the composer for failing to measure up to the implications of his plots and characters, as Peter Conrad does in his essay about *Grimes* and *A Midsummer Night's Dream.* The furthest we might go is to see Grimes as symbolic of something the composer recognised in himself. For if, as I suggested at the end of 'Britten and Grimes', he came to terms with his worst fears about the darker side of society in this opera, he may also have explored there the darker and more violent sides of his own nature.

But at this point a distinction needs to be made. My ultimate concern is the social experience of oppression and its effects in the writing of *Peter Grimes,* not Britten's sexual preference.[5] With appropriate changes to fit the conditions, I might write similarly about the social accommodation of another of England's greatest composers, William Byrd, who experienced another kind of oppression that affected his music. But the essence of Britten's sexuality or Byrd's religion is as inaccessible to criticism as the inner mystery of a work of art, 'this stuff from the bucket, this subconscious stuff' as Forster calls it.[6] Moreover, once we realise that, as several recent studies have emphasised, the very concept of 'homosexuality' as a social and psychological category distinct from the 'normal' or 'heterosexual' is of comparatively recent origin (the word itself was not coined until 1869), the phenomenon of 'homosexuality' becomes less relevant than the psychological effects of the labelling and its social consequences.[7] And Britten's preoccupation with a predominantly negative 'homosexual vision' shows how crucial for him was the effect of this labelling and the concomitant oppression. Viewed as representatives or adumbrations of the 'homosexual condition', Aschenbach, Oberon, Quint, Claggart, Vere and Grimes make a horrifying sextet; one almost forgets that the same composer wrote *Albert Herring*, that profound comedy of liberation. Furthermore, it is (to say the least) ironic that Britten, who enjoyed one of the most remarkable personal and professional partnerships in musical history, should choose for his final operatic 'testament' the story of *Death in Venice*; for though one might join Tippet in saying 'I think all the love which he had for his singer flowed into this work',[8] the fact that it centres on Thomas Mann's sad and lonely character seems to suggest that the oppression Britten sensed and internalised was much more powerfully present in his imagination than the well-regulated, shared and accepted life he led throughout adulthood.

Ultimately it is not the causes that are of greatest concern when one tries to come to grips with works of art, but the effects. While those who earlier this century sought completely to dissociate the work of art from its creator's life now appear mistaken, they did achieve what is surely the best focus for criticism. Our findings about the creator, the conception and the context of a work are put to best use only if they are projected in such a way as to sharpen our perception of its nature. The discoveries of Alfred Dürr and others redefining Bach's attitude to his work at Leipzig and Joseph Kerman's exploration of the significance of Byrd's Roman Catholicism are two examples of how radically a new interpretation of a composer's life can enhance our comprehension of his work. The taboo on all mention of composers' sexuality was of course partly a manifestation of wider repressive forces from which all of us, straight or gay, need liberating. In the case of Britten it was also an affront to critical intelligence, for it tended to force those who wrote about Britten's music into evasive tactics verging on intellectual dishonesty or, even worse, into euphemisms ('emotional immaturity' headed the list) that were themselves oppressive and insulting. On the other hand we should avoid making the simplistic claim that here lies the single key to Britten's creative personality: no inner mystery in the music is revealed by the simple acknowledgment of his homosexuality and its consequences, but the way is at least cleared for us to approach the works a little closer and with more understanding.

Britten's other statement may indeed help us in that quest. It comes from the article printed in *Time* magazine (16 February 1948) when *Peter Grimes* first opened at the Metropolitan Opera House in New York: 'Britten regards this opera as "a subject very close to my heart – the struggle of the individual against the masses. The more vicious the society, the more vicious the individual."' This raises the moral question, familiar to social thinkers of liberal persuasion in this century, about the balance of responsibility between the criminal or delinquent and society, and relates it to the character of *Grimes* in a graphic way. When, at the climax of his quarrel with Ellen, Grimes accepts society's judgment, he also implicitly accepts the role forced on him by the prejudice and inhumanity of his fellow beings. He becomes the criminal he is thought to be. The question of whether or not he is technically guilty of the second boy's death – one I now see I was over-anxious to answer – is (as Edmund Wilson saw clearly enough) beside the point. The intrusion of the posse in Act II scene 2 was not merely a strategy to exculpate Peter, but more importantly a way of further dramatising the moral question at the heart of the work.[9]

The connection between this question and the mechanics of oppression is a close one, for it is characteristic of stigmatised people to internalise society's judgment of them. This is the point Britten saw so clearly and (inasmuch as it did not gain general currency for another twenty years) so prophetically; it is also the one that critics of the opera, like Shawe-Taylor, Garbutt and Conrad, who do not discern the source of Peter's apparent self-contradictions, have consistently failed to grasp. A common result of this internalisation is that while trying to conform the person represses anger and eventually comes to distrust all feeling to such an extent that on top of the burden of insecurity and self-hatred is heaped the paralysis of depression.[10] Sometimes, however, the dam holding back the anger and guilt bursts with a resulting deluge of senseless violence. As I write, the newspapers carry two stories in which the 'Grimes syndrome' reaches horrendous proportions. William Bonin, the so-called Freeway Killer of Southern California, and Wayne B. Williams of Atlanta have been convicted in murder cases concerning the deaths of large numbers of young men and boys. Both men are reportedly homosexual; Williams, whose victims were young blacks, is himself black. 'Homophobia is the true murderer', wrote a correspondent to the *Los Angeles Times* (6 February 1982) in the wake of Bonin's trial, pointing the same moral: that society's fear of homosexuality had sentenced Bonin to death just as it had destroyed his victims.[11]

One reason why critics of the opera tend to evade this moral question is suggested by a passage in Adrienne Rich's *Of Woman Born* where she discusses a case of infanticide by an apparently devoted mother with a history of 'depression' (pp. 256-80). The experts of modern society, she points out, instead of examining the institution of motherhood to discover root causes for such appalling tragedies, prefer to label those women who erupt in violence as psychopathological. Indeed, when Eric Walter White labels Grimes a 'maladjusted aggressive psychopath' (p. 116) or Arnold Whittall finds him 'immature in the sense that he cannot conform',[12] what we hear louder than their words are echoes of the conformist post-war era, when 'unsocial attitudes', whether criminal or not, were equated with mental sickness or 'immaturity', and when the tendency of psychiatrists was to put pressure on women and gays, for instance, to adjust to the expectations of society, thus increasing their guilt, suffering and sense of isolation. No wonder Grimes seemed as prime a candidate as Wozzeck for 'treatment', because far from being the romantic, Byronic figure Slater wanted – a character with the self-possession and self-will that, as we have seen, Peter notably lacks – he is in fact, as Pears puts it, 'very much of an ordinary weak person' (see chapter 8). The successful realisation of so modern a dramatic character is one of the main reasons for the opera's wide general popularity.

A common thread in all the murders mentioned above is that the violence was directed against those who were loved or who would have been the natural objects of affection but for the reversal of feeling caused by the long process of the internalisation of society's values and the ensuing self-hatred and repression. 'It has often been suggested (though seldom in print) that Grimes's inner struggle (like Claggart's, and perhaps Captain Vere's) is against a homosexuality that neither he nor, for that matter, his creator is consciously aware of' wrote Andrew Porter as long ago as 1971.[13] Grimes's outright demand for love from the boy in Pears's Amityville draft (see above p. 50), shows on the contrary that Britten must have been very well aware of this element, which adds its own touch of psychological realism to the story. The question of why all homoerotic overtones, as well as other aspects of Peter's background, were slowly but surely expunged as the opera grew has already been explored in chapter 3. But one of the reasons not mentioned there, and perhaps ultimately of greatest practical importance, was that whereas universal meaning could have been extrapolated from the predicament of many other kinds of 'minority' hero or antihero, an obvious homosexual – even an obviously repressed homosexual – in the title role would have either spelt outright failure for the opera or caused it to be dismissed as a matter of 'special interest'. As recently as 1979 Jon Vickers could claim on the one hand that Grimes is 'totally symbolic' and that he could 'play him as a Jew' or 'paint his face black and put him in a white society', and on the other hand declare that 'I will not play Peter Grimes as a homosexual' because this 'reduces him to a man in a situation with a problem and I'm not interested in that kind of operatic portrayal'.[14]

The opera was a long time in gestation. When Britten and Pears conceived the idea in 1941 they were adrift; they had recently escaped from Auden's dominating presence, and were without immediate responsibilities to society. It took exactly four years for the finished work to reach the stage, and those years were ones of tremendous development in their lives: first and foremost there was the return to England; then Pears, from having little or no operatic experience, quickly became a leading performer in the Sadler's Wells company; Britten meanwhile in 1943 worked out the theme of alienation in a different context in *Rejoice in the Lamb*; and both men gained a tremendous success with the *Serenade* in the same year. Moreover, with Eric Crozier excused his duties with the Sadler's Wells company in order to attend meetings with

Britten and Slater in 1943, there must already have been some sense that the work might be chosen to celebrate the return to its true home of what was in effect, if not then in name, England's national opera. No wonder, then, that the homoerotic elements in the early drafts were censored.

More remarkable is the way in which Britten, in opposition to the ideas of his librettist, saw how to be true to his own feelings when turning the work into 'a presentation of a general human plight – that of the outsider at odds (for whatever reason) with those around him'.[15] For in order to make Peter so powerfully symbolic and to render the action of the opera so successfully allegorical, Britten could not allow the story to have homoerotic implications, much less an identifiably homosexual title figure. He had to desexualise Grimes, and furthermore rid him of his father-figure with all its attendant Freudian implications, in order that the work should not be misinterpreted as a 'pathological' study. In doing this he made it abundantly clear that the opera's concern, implicit in its musical structure and thematic process, is the purely social issue of 'the individual against the crowd': the one reflects the judgment and behaviour of the many even while striving desperately to remain distinct. To watch Britten arriving at that conclusion and finding a solution, bit by bit, consciously or unconsciously, is to see how mature a dramatic composer he had by this stage already become; it is also to discover anew how from private pain the great artist can fashion something that transcends his own individual experience and touches all humanity.

Notes

For full references to works cited in the text and notes by author or by author and title only, see the Bibliography.

1 Two essays on Crabbe

1 Crozier (ed.), *Peter Grimes.* This revision makes changes to accommodate a reading rather than a listening public and rounds out the picture a little more; Forster inserted an extra quotation from the death-bed scene in 'Peter Grimes', and also introduced some passages from two earlier essays on Crabbe (see Bibliography).
2 The text is reprinted from *Two Cheers for Democracy*; notes have been introduced to pinpoint the sources of quoted material, and precise references to Crabbe's poems have been interpolated from Ward's edition. 'Peter Grimes' is Letter XXII of *The Borough*.
3 Slater, 'The Story of the Opera', pp. 15-16.
4 *The Village*, I, 123.
5 A remark to his son reported in chapter IV of the latter's *Life of Crabbe*.
6 Letter of 22 July 1794 to Edward Cartwright, quoted in Huchon, *George Crabbe and His Times*, p. 205.
7 Letter of 19 January 1831 to Henchman Crowfoot quoted in chapter X of his son's *Life of Crabbe*.
8 'The Lover's Journey', *Tales*, X, 118-26.
9 See the first two quotations in the first essay for the passage as a whole.
10 As reported by J. G. Lockhart in a letter of 26 December 1833; see chapter IX of the *Life of Crabbe* and Huchon's *George Crabbe and His Times*, p. 466, Forster's original text substitutes 'bit' for 'hit'.
11 As reported by Edward Fitzgerald, claiming Crabbe's son (the biographer) as his authority; see Huchon, *George Crabbe and His Times*, p. 374 and (for further quotation) *Un poète réaliste*, p. 473.
12 'The story of the Opera', p. 16.
13 *George Crabbe and His Times*, pp. 460, 478.

2 Montagu Slater: Who was he?

1 'Presenting "Things As They Are"', p. 142. *Left Review* was edited by Montagu Slater, Amabel Williams-Ellis and T. H. Wintringham

from its inception until June 1935, when they were joined by Alick West. In January 1936 Edgell Rickword was appointed editor. His assistant editor for a brief period was D. K. Kitchin, who then became the journal's manager, Derek Kahn taking his place as assistant editor. (An editor for Scotland, Douglas Boddie, appeared for only one issue, in November 1936.) Randall Swingler (see above, p. 31) was the last editor, from July 1937 until the paper closed.

3 'Fiery visions' (and revisions): *Peter Grimes* in progress

1 I am especially grateful to Rosamund Strode, music assistant to Britten in the last twelve years of his life; as keeper of manuscripts at the Britten–Pears Library and archivist to the Britten Estate, she not only put every scrap of information she could find in front of me, but also advised me about it. She cannot be held responsible for any of the interpretations I place upon these documents, but I would have made many more mistakes without her generous and invaluable assistance. I am also grateful to Donald Mitchell and the Britten Estate for permission to see and quote from many of these documents.

2 In the BBC radio programme 'Birth of an Opera: *Peter Grimes*'. I am grateful to Sir Peter Pears for permission to reproduce this and further quotations from this interview.

3 The tiny cottage in the grounds of the clinic where Dr William Mayer worked 'was in every sense a home for Britten and Pears' during their stay in the United States, 1939-42; see Mitchell and Evans, *Pictures from a Life*, nos. 114-28, 149-53. An important figure for Britten in those years, and even more for Auden later, Elizabeth Mayer is admirably described in Carpenter's biography of the poet, pp. 275-6.

4 These papers are now in the Britten–Pears Library. Those in the hand of Pears are written on the back of draft concert programmes for his Elizabethan Singers. Another sheet in the Elizabeth Mayer collection, in Britten's hand, notes descriptions in *The Borough* of the storm (Letter I), inns (Letter XI) and the poor (Letter XVIII).

5 Lines 177-206 of Letter VIII have been marked in the Britten–Pears copy of Crabbe's *Works* (see above, p. 53).

6 These were placed in the back of a green loose-leaf folder (now in the Britten–Pears Library) containing early drafts of portions of Slater's libretto.

7 *Poetical Works* (1851), presumably A87 of Bareham and Gatrell's *Bibliography*, descended from Murray's eight-volume edition of 1834 (A48) by way of the single-volume edition of 1847 (A86). Quotations in this chapter are from A48, with line numbers from Ward's edition. Peter Pears inscribed the copy in 1978: 'I bought this book at a Los Angeles book-seller's in 1941 and from this we started work on the plans for making an opera of "Peter Grimes".' Rosamund Strode has pencilled in 'San Diego?' to reflect Pears's uncertainty. Escondido, the place where Britten and Pears were

staying in summer 1941 with Ethel Bartlett and Rae Robertson (see Mitchell and Evans, nos. 145-8), lies only thirty miles north-east of San Diego; it is over a hundred miles from Los Angeles.

8 In Act I, lines 19-22 ('Where hang at open doors the net and cork'), 55-8 ('He, cold and wet, and driving with the tide') and 87-90 ('Dabbling on shore half-naked sea-boys crowd'); in Act III, lines 291-4 ('Or measured cadence of the lads who tow') and 37-40 ('With ceaseless motion comes and goes the tide'). 87-90 and 291-4 are not marked in the Britten–Pears copy. 'To those who pass the Boro' sounds betray' is presumably derived from lines 287-90, but Slater's stanza is anything but the 'direct quotation from Crabbe' he claims it to be on p. 26 of Crozier (ed.), *Peter Grimes.*

9 The Vicar, III, 15-16; Boles, IV, 274-5.

10 Swallow, VI, 232-7 (referring to Swallow junior); Keene, VII, 257-60.

11 XX, 11-16, 152-4, 198-9, 218-9, 336-7.

12 XXII, 12-31, 40-52, 270-7, 292-7, 304-22, 324-7, 331-3; the last four passages are quoted by Forster in the second of his essays reprinted in chapter 1.

13 Walter Jones, successful but unloved (VIII, 177-206) has already been mentioned above. A passage from the story of the lofty-minded Parish Clerk who dips into the collection box, is discovered and disgraced – almost a companion soul to Grimes – may have suggested the end of Act I scene 1:

> Or to the restless sea and roaring wind
> Gave the strong yearnings of a ruin'd mind. (XIX, 272-3)

Other marked passages in Letter XIX are 54-77, 142-5, 181-2 and 274-8. Material for a real 'character' is marked out in the story (as told by the boorish Benbow) of plain-speaking, hard-drinking and generous old Squire Asgill (XVI, 61-75, 80-1, 96-103, 126-44, 150-1). In addition there are further lines marked in Letters I (228-38), IX (115-32) and XI (17-46), two passages from Abel Keene's story (XXI, 273-8, 322), the first again dealing with the despair of 'the lost soul', and three passages from 'The Poor and their Dwellings' (XVIII, 263-70, 292-304, 326-7), the first of which may have suggested the nature of Grimes's hut.

14 'Birth of an Opera' interview.

15 See chapter 2, and Mitchell and Evans, nos. 79-81, 90-1.

16 Blyth (ed.), *Remembering Britten*, p. 22.

17 Above, n. 6.

18 'Birth of an Opera' interview.

19 See 'Staging First Productions I', pp. 24-5.

20 'Birth of an Opera' interview. To this BBC programme Crozier also contributed an interview on which I base this interpretation.

21 A London coffee-house in Regent Street situated above Oxford Circus between Boosey & Hawkes and Broadcasting House.

22 Note that in *S* 'Balstrode who has come in late . . . goes to the cliff side door, looks down, then closes it carefully' before the Curtain;

in the opera he 'hurriedly climbs down the way Peter and the Boy went'.

23 'Strive' and 'weep' are reversed in *VS1945*. The reason was perhaps to save Joan Cross the discomfort of an awkward vowel on a top F. One should not perhaps underestimate the cumulative effect of such small tinkerings in Slater's decision to publish his own version.

24 See Schafer, *British Composers,* p. 116.

25 Slater allowed some of the adjustments to this into *S*.

26 All these findings about *C* are based on a collation of the manuscript prepared by Rosamund Strode with my assistance in 1980, before it was bound at the British Library. Having at our disposal copies of the separate sketch pages that survive, we were able at the same time to assign almost all of them to their original places in *C*. Sketch J (our labelling) is inscribed by the composer 'For Heather [Harper] with love & thanks for her superb Ellen – BBC TV, the Maltings, Feb. 1969. Ben B.' The others (A–H, K–T) belong to a private collection.

27 Sketch A also contains a roughed-out version of the passage leading up to Ellen's 'Let her among you without fault' – another, less important, case of revision necessitating an inserted sheet (pp. 28a-b) in *C* to substitute for the deleted parts of pp. 29 and 30. Britten rewrote the setting of the chorus stanza 'Ellen, you're leading us a dance'. Sketch B also experiments with this passage; this leaf was originally attached to the folio numbered 19-20, and its other side therefore begins with the chorus one bar after fig. 19. Sketch A, however, begins with Balstrode's 'Look, the storm cone!' at fig. 31 (and preserves a rather different version of the fugue subject of the ensuing chorus); this suggests that the new version of 'Ellen, you're leading us a dance' was an afterthought.

28 See his 'Staging First Productions I', p. 26.

29 Schafer, *British Composers*, p. 116.

30 *The Music of Benjamin Britten*, p. 114; Evans points merely to the moment just before fig. 27, but as so often in this opera the detail is reflected in the larger organisation.

31 'The Story of the Opera', p. 25.

32 'Stranger' is replaced by 'prentice' in *S*, which also deletes the ensuing dialogue (in *La*, transcribed word for word into *C*), in which Balstrode painstakingly explains to a reluctant Grimes the necessity and means of committing suicide.

33 See Duncan, *Working with Britten*, pp. 35-9.

4 Breaking the ice for British opera: *Peter Grimes* on stage

1 For the complete programme, see Mitchell and Evans, *Pictures from a Life*, no. 182.

2 Dr Thorp, or Thorpe, was the guise under which Dr Crabbe of the libretto appeared in this production; he lived on in the published vocal score. Dr Crabbe has now been restored.

3 'Staging First Productions I', p. 26.

4 As the composer himself said, according to Coleman in 'Producing the Operas', p. 107.
5 *Benjamin Britten: His Life and Operas*, p. 42.
6 Guthrie, 'Out of Touch', p. 11.
7 '"Peter Grimes": An Unpublished Article', p. 414.
8 See Forsyth, *Tyrone Guthrie*, p. 191 and Guthrie, *A Life in the Theatre*, pp. 219-20. A more historical account may be found in White's *The Arts Council*, esp. pp. 46-7, 52-4, 128-46.
9 'Benjamin Britten Talks to Alan Blyth', p. 29.
10 For substantial quotation, see Kennedy, *Britten*, p. 45.
11 *Ibid*. pp. 15, 29-30, 46.
12 *Music Review*, VI (1945), 187-8.
13 Britten had written enthusiastically about the work in his diary after a concert performance in London in 1936; see Mitchell, 'Britten on "Lady Macbeth"', p. 11.
14 'Benjamin Britten Talks to Alan Blyth', p. 29. See also Northcott, 'Since *Grimes*'.
15 The list is primarily of performances: those at Brussels and Paris in 1948 were given by Covent Garden on tour; the Los Angeles performance was given by the Met, which also performed the work in Philadelphia (1948) and Boston (1949). The opera was also performed at Stanford University in 1948 in a student production. A complete list of productions and casts is given in Pitt, *Benjamin Britten*.
16 *A Life in the Theatre*, p. 252.
17 *Ibid*. The deletion of the recitative for Auntie and Ned Keene just before the 'Great Bear' aria, reported by Keller in '"Peter Grimes" at Covent Garden', p. 47, was presumably an attempt on Guthrie's part to get rid of one of 'the little chatty passages' he disliked.
18 Cf. Pears, 'The Good Companions'.
19 Peter Pears supports the essential points of Anderson's statement and my interpretation; see Blyth (ed.), *Remembering Britten*, p. 20.
20 Letter of 17 August 1946, Library of Congress, Koussevitsky Collection.
21 'Tanglewood in Retrospect', p. 299.
22 *The Story of the Metropolitan Opera*, pp. 554, 566.
23 See Mitchell and Evans, nos. 369-70.
24 Jess Thomas and Ava June took the roles of Peter and Ellen in San Francisco in 1973, and the Chicago Ellen was T. Kubrak; the production also appeared in Dallas, December 1980.
25 The librettist himself may have suggested such an interpretation of Ellen's character; he refers to her 'We've failed' as 'Ellen's unforgivable phrase' ('The Story of the Opera', p. 23).
26 'Peter Grimes', in Blyth (ed.), Remembering Britten, pp. 14-15.
27 The text changes, which are signalled in the libretto accompanying the Philips recording (1979), are another example of Guthrie's tinkerings, as is made clear in an interview with Vickers in the same booklet. Guthrie handed them to Vickers at the time of his debut in the part at the Met in 1967; he took it on trust that they had

Britten's sanction and has not dropped them since. If the composer did approve them, he can have done so only for this one production and to please an old colleague. It is unfortunate that they persist in a recorded version.

28 *Opera News*, XXXI (11 February 1967), 16.

5 *Peter Grimes*: the story, the music not excluded

1 Beyond which the theme derives from the 2nd movement (or the 2nd part of the 1st movement) of Mahler's Fifth; see, for instance, the bassoon part 5-7 bars before the end. Britten, one gathers, had heard the symphony only once.

2 Keller refers here to Sackville-West's 'The Musical and Dramatic Structure', in which (p. 54) he characterised the fifth motif of the last Interlude as 'a grunting figure for two clarinets' without noticing its derivation from 'Wrong to plan? . . .' – an oversight first pointed out by Keller in 'Britten: Thematic Relations', pp. 332-4. (PB)

3 But see chapter 3, n. 8. (PB)

6 Act II scene 1: an examination of the music

1 I.e. the Lydian mode. For extensive comments on Britten's use of modality in *Peter Grimes*, see Evans, *The Music of Benjamin Britten*, pp. 120-1.

2 See Mitchell and Evans, *Pictures from a Life*, nos. 125, 174, 176.

3 The original plainsong setting is to be found as Hymn 254 in *The English Hymnal*. Britten used the Latin hymn twenty-four years later to open *The Prodigal Son*, but with another plainsong accompaniment – that given in *The English Hymnal* for Hymn 255, 'Come Holy Ghost, with God the Son'.

4 In the First String Quartet, for example. See my contribution on Britten's chamber music in *The Britten Companion* (Faber & Faber, forthcoming).

5 For additional comments on this passage see Evans, pp. 105-6.

6 That this is its proper ending is confirmed by the concert version of the passacaglia, where Britten used the last fifteen bars of the Act (from fig. 72) to end the piece.

10 An account of *Peter Grimes* from 'London in Midsummer'

1 G, 'a London girl whom I very much liked'; see *Europe without Baedeker*, pp. 179-85, 192. (PB)

2 I.e. *Sinfonia da Requiem*, op. 20, first performed by the New York Philharmonic under John Barbirolli on 30 March 1941. (PB)

3 Described by Wilson at pp. 10-13 of *Europe without Baedeker*. (PB)

11 Music and motive in *Peter Grimes*

1 The author quotes from the Boosey & Hawkes libretto of 1945 which, as shown in chapter 3, was out of date by the time the opera reached the stage. What Britten actually has Grimes sing here (Act I scene 1 fig. 45) is

These Borough gossips
Listen to money,
Only to money.
I'll fish the sea dry,
Sell the good catches. (PB)

2 Actually in the previous scene, Act I scene 1. (PB)

12 Plausible darkness: *Peter Grimes* after a quarter of a century

1 In all versions of the text the lines read 'This is a Sunday, his day of rest.' 'This is whatever day I say it is!' (PB)

13 Britten and Grimes

1 From a speech on being presented with the freedom of Lowestoft in 1951; quoted by White, *Benjamin Britten: His Life and Operas*, p. 92.
2 *On Receiving the First Aspen Award*, p. 21
3 Letter from Louis MacNeice in *Horizon* (July 1940), quoted in White, *Britten*, p. 30.
4 See chapter 1.
5 *Britten*, p. 116.
6 *The Sunday Times* (20 July 1975), echoing his views of thirty years earlier (see chapter 9).
7 *Britten*, p. 116.
8 A reading of the first two chapters of Altman's *Homosexual: Oppression and Liberation* will show the connection clearly enough. I am happy to acknowledge that it was while reading this intelligent book and seeing Sir Geraint Evans's moving production of *Peter Grimes* at the San Francisco Opera in 1973 that this essay was first conceived.
9 A good summary appears in Spender's *Love-Hate Relations*, pp. 252-4.
10 Heilbrun, *Christopher Isherwood*, p. 11.
11 For Isherwood's involvement in *Peter Grimes* see chapter 2.
12 See Stallybrass's introduction to Forster's *The Life to Come and Other Stories*, p. xiv.
13 The reviews of the first volume of Furbank's biography of the novelist show that concealment diminishes in proportion to the increase of embarrassment and hostility. Paul Johnson in *The New Statesman* (22 July 1976), for instance, fills almost all the considerable

space at his disposal fitting the young Forster into what might be called the 'withered-sissy' stereotype, a stupid exercise that concludes with the cruel and facetious remark, 'perhaps it would have been better for the novels if he had never found out about sex at all'.

14 Postscript

1 See Schafer, *British Composers*, pp. 116-17.

2 Published in Mitchell, *Britten and Auden in the Thirties*, pp. 161-2.

3 At that stage homosexual feeling need not, of course, be consciously identified as such for social and family judgment to be sensed and for feelings of isolation, exclusion and unhappiness to result; see Altman, *Homosexual: Oppression and Liberation*, pp. 25-6: 'In my case I had the sense of not belonging, of being excluded through some perception by my peers that I was apart from them. Like many others I had no idea why exactly that was (if it was); I put it down, as do others in similar situations, to excessive intellectualism or timidity or artistic bent, anything other than the real cause.' This common experience is still little affected by the liberalisation of social attitudes to sexual preference.

4 'The Good Companions'. The use of 'gay' as a term of self-determination (replacing derogatory epithets such as 'queer' and 'faggot' in the same way that 'black' replaced 'nigger') began in the early 1970s towards the end of Britten's life, and was initially threatening to most homosexuals (including much younger people) who had already arranged their lives in one way or another. For Britten, 'the gay life' probably signified something of the type of existence he and Pears had encountered while living under the same roof as Auden; the influence of his upbringing was, I think, decisive in his rejection of this and also, perhaps, as Auden thought, in his idealisation of 'thin-as-a-board juveniles, i.e. . . . the sexless and innocent' and in his 'aloofness' (see Auden's letter referred to above, n. 2, and above, p. 33).

5 My use of the catchword 'oppression', here and in chapter 13, follows the sense developed by feminists and formulated by Altman (pp. 30-3): 'Strictly speaking, oppression results from the fact that societies are divided along class, racial and caste lines and that some groups occupy positions from which they are able to dominate others . . . But even when one concedes that, in these terms, oppression exists, it may seem difficult to conceive of groups being oppressed for their sexuality. This is, I think, largely because our concept of oppression has tended to be based upon a crude Marxist model that envisages oppression as a class or economic phenomenon, and there are those who still seek to incorporate all oppressed groups into such a uni-dimensional economic model. It is precisely the discovery that oppression is multi-dimensional, that one may be simultaneously both oppressed and oppressor that underlies the

analysis of the sexual liberation movements . . . The oppression faced by homosexuals takes on a number of forms, and at its most pernicious may be internalized to the point that an individual no longer recognizes it as oppression.' Altman's book was enormously influential because it provided an intellectual basis for the gay movement, enabling it to reach many who had earlier remained aloof; his analysis of the various types of oppression is still retained implicitly in such important accounts as Weeks's *Coming Out* (p. 190), but his concept of 'liberation', while still basically valid, benefits from comparison with more recent directions of thought as outlined in Weeks, 'Discourse, Desire and Sexual Deviance'.

6 In 'The Raison d'Etre of Criticism in the Arts', p. 123.

7 The 'anti-essentialist' view briefly outlined here is elaborated from various vantage points in Plummer (ed.), *The Making of the Modern Homosexual.* The view of sexuality in general as a social and historical construction, rather than an inherent 'drive', has been reinforced by Foucault's *History of Sexuality*; for a good exposition in the context of modern British history see Weeks, *Sex, Politics and Society*, esp. pp. 1-16. It is a paradox of the gay movement that while offering a new sense of identity for homosexuals it also looks forward to the eventual disintegration of categories based arbitrarily on sexual behaviour or preference (see Weeks, pp. 286-8).

8 Obituary in *The Listener*, 16 December 1976, reprinted in Blyth (ed.), *Remembering Britten*, p. 71.

9 J. W. Garbutt, who (in chapter 11) seems obsessed with the question of Grimes's guilt, conspicuously ignores the significance of the Borough's intrusion into Grimes's hut.

10 A straightforward guide to such typical reactions to oppression is Clark's *Loving Someone Gay*; see pp. 22-8, 52-60, 146-9.

11 'Homophobia', a term denoting fear of homosexuals, was first employed by Weinberg in *Society and the Healthy Homosexual.*

12 'Benjamin Britten', *Music Review*, XXIII (1962), pp. 314-16, at p. 315.

13 In a note for the New York Opera production of *Albert Herring*, the substance of which is also found in '*What Harbour Shelters Peace*?'.

14 In an interview included in the literature accompanying the Philips recording. Vickers makes a more considered statement, but with little change of basic attitude, in a later interview with Michael Oliver (*Opera*, XXXIII (1982), pp. 362-7, at 364-5).

15 Porter, *ibid.*

Bibliography

The introduction to chapter 1 presents suggestions for further reading on Crabbe and *The Borough*. The most up-to-date biographical information now available on Britten will be found in Mitchell and Evans, *Pictures from a Life*, and in Kennedy, *Britten*. These will no doubt be out-dated (but since they are so fine, hardly superseded) when Dr Mitchell's biography of the composer appears. The most recent and by far the most subtle analytical and critical account of the music as a whole is that of Peter Evans, *The Music of Benjamin Britten*, but the account of this work in White's *Benjamin Britten: His Life and Operas* still wears well. The reader may also wish to consult the essays not reprinted here – by Montagu Slater and Edward Sackville-West – in Crozier (ed.), *Peter Grimes*. An account of the first performance opens Headington's *Britten*, a sympathetic and rather personal biography. A libretto will be found in Herbert (ed.), *The Operas of Benjamin Britten*, as will some of the original scenic and costume sketches and models by Kenneth Green, and some relevant essays, including one by Crozier on his experience as the director of the first production, and one by Keller which deals thoughtfully with the nature of Britten's operatic output. References to reviews of stage performances of *Peter Grimes* are not listed below but are given in chapter 4.

Dennis Altman: *Homosexual: Oppression and Liberation* (New York, 1971, 2nd edn 1973; London, 1974)

Ande Anderson: 'From the Beginning', interview with Arthur Kaplan, *San Francisco Opera Magazine* [*Billy Budd* issue] (1978), pp. 91-100

Anon: 'Opera's New Face', *Time*, LI/7 (16 February 1948), pp. 62-8

Jacob Avshalomoff: 'Tanglewood in Retrospect', *Modern Music*, XXIII (1946), pp. 298-300

T. Bareham and S. Gatrell: *Bibliography of George Crabbe* (Folkestone, Kent, and Hamden, Conn., 1978)

BBC Radio: 'Birth of an Opera: *Peter Grimes*', director M. Rose, 28 September 1976

Neville Blackburne: *The Restless Ocean* (Lavenham, Suffolk, 1972)

Alan Blyth (ed.): *Remembering Britten* (London, 1981)

Philip Brett: 'Britten and Grimes', *Musical Times*, CXVIII (1977), pp. 955-1000 [repr. with slight corrections as chapter 13]

Benjamin Britten: 'Benjamin Britten talks to Alan Blyth', *The Gramophone*, XLVIII (1970), pp. 29-30

'Communicator, an Interview with England's Best-Known Composer', interview with Elizabeth Forbes, *Opera News*, XXXI (11 February 1967), p. 16

'Introduction', in Crozier (ed.), *Peter Grimes*, pp. 2-3 [repr. as chapter 7]

On Receiving the First Aspen Award (London, 1964)

'Peter Grimes', *Opera*, I/2 (April 1950), pp. 43-4, repr. in Blyth (ed.), *Remembering Britten*, pp. 13-15

Peter Grimes [see pp. 58-60]

Humphrey Carpenter: *W. H. Auden* (London, 1981)

Don Clark: *Loving Someone Gay* (Millbrae, Calif., 1977, 2nd edn 1979)

Jon Clark, Margot Heinemann, David Margolies and Carole Shee (eds.): *Culture and Crisis in Britain in the Thirties* (London, 1979)

Basil Coleman: 'Producing the Operas', *The London Magazine*, n.s. III/7 (1963), pp. 104-8

Peter Conrad: 'The Top Line and the Sub-Text', *Times Literary Supplement* (10 July 1981), pp. 781-2

Deryck Cooke: *The Language of Music* (London, 1959)

George Crabbe: *The Poetical Works of the Rev. George Crabbe, Edited, with a Life, by His Son. A New Edition with Portrait and Vignette* (London, 1851) [the edition used and annotated by Britten and Pears; see also chapter 3, n. 7]

Poetical Works, ed. A.W. Ward (Cambridge, 1905-7)

see also under E. M. Forster

Eric Crozier: '"Peter Grimes": An Unpublished Article of 1946', *Opera*, XVI (1965), pp. 412-16

'Staging First Production I', in Herbert (ed.), *The Operas of Benjamin Britten*, pp. 24-33

(ed.): *Benjamin Britten: Peter Grimes*, Sadler's Wells Opera Books no. 3 (London, 1945)

John Deathridge: 'England: Music and Society', in *Music in the Modern Age*, ed. F. W. Sternfeld (London, 1973), pp. 193-216

Ronald Duncan: *Working with Britten* (Welcombe, Devon, 1981)

Peter Evans: *The Music of Benjamin Britten* (London, 1979)

E. M. Forster: 'Crabbe', *The Spectator*, CXLVII (20 February 1932), pp. 243-5, rev. as the Introduction to Forster (ed.), *The Life of the Rev. George Crabbe, LL.B. by His Son* (London, 1834, repr. Oxford World Classics, London, 1932)

'George Crabbe and Peter Grimes', a lecture given at the Aldeburgh Festival, 1948, repr. in *Two Cheers for Democracy* (London, 1951), pp. 178-92 [repr. in chapter 1]

'George Crabbe: The Poet and the Man', *The Listener* (29 May 1941) [repr. in chapter 1], rev. in Crozier (ed.), *Peter Grimes*, pp. 9-14

The Life to Come and Other Stories, ed. O. Stallybrass (London, 1972)

Maurice (London, 1971)

'The Raison d'Etre of Criticism in the Arts', in *Two Cheers for Democracy*, pp. 117-31

James Forsyth: *Tyrone Guthrie* (London, 1976)

Michel Foucault: *The History of Sexuality*, I, *An Introduction*, tr. R. Hurley (New York, 1978; London, 1979)

P. N. Furbank: *E. M. Forster: a Life* (London, 1976)

J. W. Garbutt: 'Music and Motive in *Peter Grimes*', *Music & Letters*, XLIV (1963), pp. 334-42 [repr. as chapter 11]

Peter Garvie: 'Plausible Darkness: *Peter Grimes* after a Quarter of a Century', *Tempo*, no. 100 (1972), pp. 9-14 [repr. as chapter 12]

Frank Gloversmith (ed.): *Class, Culture and Social Change: a New View of the 1930s* (Brighton, 1980)

Tyrone Guthrie: *A Life in the Theatre* (New York and London, 1959)

'Out of Touch', *Opera News*, XXXI (28 January 1967), 8-11

Andre van Gyseghem: 'British Theatre in the Thirties' in Clark *et al.* (eds.), *Culture and Crisis in Britain*, pp. 209-18

Ronald B. Hatch: *Crabbe's Arabesque: Social Drama in the Poetry of George Crabbe* (Montreal and London, 1976), esp. pp. 104-13

Carolyn G. Heilbrun: *Christopher Isherwood*, Columbia Essays on Modern Writers no. 53 (New York, 1970)

David Herbert (ed.): *The Operas of Benjamin Britten* (London and New York, 1979)

Patricia Howard: *The Operas of Benjamin Britten* (London, 1969)

René Huchon: *Un poète réaliste anglais* (Paris, 1906), trans. F. Clarke as *George Crabbe and His Times 1754-1832* (London, 1907)

Hans Keller: 'Britten: Thematic Relations and the "Mad" Interlude's 5th Motif', *Music Survey*, n.s. IV (1951), pp. 332-4

'Operatic Music and Britten' in Herbert (ed.), *The Operas of Benjamin Britten*, pp. xiii-xxxi

'"Peter Grimes" at Covent Garden', *Music Review*, IX (1948), pp. 47-8

'*Peter Grimes*: The Story; the Music not Excluded', in Mitchell and Keller (eds.), *Britten: A Commentary*, pp. 111-24 [repr. as chapter 5]

Michael Kennedy: *Britten*, Master Musicians Series (London, 1981)

Joseph Kerman: '*Grimes* and *Lucretia*', *The Hudson Review*, II (1949), pp. 277-84

Opera as Drama (New York, 1952)

Irving Kolodin: *The Story of the Metropolitan Opera, 1883-1950* (New York, 1953)

Stuart Laing: 'Presenting "Things as They Are"', in Gloversmith (ed.), *Class, Culture and Social Change*, pp. 142-60

Left Review (October 1934 – May 1938, repr. in 8 vols., London, 1979)

Donald Mitchell: *Britten and Auden in the Thirties: The Year 1936* (London, 1981)

'Britten on "Oedipus Rex" and "Lady Macbeth"', *Tempo*, no. 120 (1977), pp. 10-12

and John Evans: *Benjamin Britten: Pictures from a Life, 1913-1976* (London, 1976)

and Hans Keller (eds.): *Benjamin Britten: A Commentary on His Works from a Group of Specialists* (London, 1952)

Peter New: *George Crabbe's Poetry* (London and Basingstoke, 1976), esp. pp. 93-100

Bayan Northcott: 'The Search for Simplicity', *Times Literary Supplement* (15 February 1980)

'Since *Grimes* – A Concise Survey of the British Musical Stage', *Musical Newsletter*, IV (Spring 1974), pp. 7-11, 21-2

Anthony Payne: 'Dramatic Use of Tonality in *Peter Grimes*', *Tempo*, nos. 66-7 (1963), pp. 22-6

Peter Pears: 'The Good Companions', interview with Gillian Widdicombe, *The Observer* (30 March 1980) [preview for Tony Palmer's ITV film 'A Time There Was', Easter Sunday 1980]

Interview with Hallam Tennyson in BBC Radio's 'Birth of an Opera' [unedited tape in Britten–Pears Library]

'Neither a Hero nor a Villain', *Radio Times* (8 March 1946), p. 3 [repr. as chapter 8]

Charles Pitt: *Benjamin Britten: Peter Grimes* (=) *L'Avant-Scène Opéra*, XXXI ([Paris] Jan. – Feb. 1981) [includes libretto in English and French, ten articles, complete list of productions and casts, discography and bibliography]

Kenneth Plummer (ed.): *The Making of the Modern Homosexual* (London, 1981)

Arthur Pollard: *Crabbe: The Critical Heritage* (London, 1972)

Andrew Porter: 'Hero', *New Yorker* (21 July 1980), repr. in *Music for Three More Seasons, 1977-1980* (New York, 1981), pp. 564-7

'What Harbour Shelters Peace?', *New Yorker* (3 August 1978), repr. in *Music for Three More Seasons*, pp. 206-12

Adrienne Rich: *Of Woman Born* (New York, 1976)

Edward Sackville-West: 'The Musical and Dramatic Structure', in Crozier (ed.), *Peter Grimes*, pp. 27-55

Murray Schafer: *British Composers in Interview* (London, 1963)

Desmond Shawe-Taylor: 'Peter Grimes', *New Statesman* (9 and 16 June 1945) [repr. as chapter 9]

Montagu Slater: *Peter Grimes* (London, 1945, Boosey & Hawkes) [*L1945*]

'Peter Grimes', in *Peter Grimes and Other Poems* (London, 1946), pp. 9-56

'The Story of the Opera', in Crozier (ed.), *Peter Grimes*, pp. 15-26

Stephen Spender: *Love-Hate Relations: English and American Sensibilities* (New York, 1974)

Charles Stuart: *Peter Grimes*, Covent Garden Operas (London, 1947)

J. Symons: *Critical Observations* (London, 1981)

The Thirties: A Dream Revolved (London, rev. 1975)

Virgil Thomson: Review of *Peter Grimes*, *New York Herald Tribune* (13 February 1948), repr. in *A Virgil Thomson Reader* (Boston, 1981), pp. 308-9

Jeffrey Weeks: *Coming Out: Homosexual Politics in Britain, from the Nineteenth Century to the Present* (London, 1977)

'Discourse, Desire and Sexual Deviance: Some Problems in a History of Homosexuality', in Plummer (ed.), *The Making of the Modern Homosexual*, pp. 76-111

Sex, Politics and Society: The Regulation of Sexuality since 1800 (London and New York, 1981)

George Weinberg: *Society and the Healthy Homosexual* (New York, 1973)

Eric Walter White: *The Arts Council of Great Britain* (London, 1975)

Benjamin Britten: A Sketch of His Life and Works (London, 1954), rev. as *Benjamin Britten: His Life and Operas* (London, 1970)

Edmund Wilson: Account of *Peter Grimes* in 'London in Midsummer', in *Europe without Baedeker* (New York, 1947, 2nd edn 1966), pp. 186-91 [repr. as chapter 10]

Basil Wright: *The Long View* (London, 1974)

Discography

MALCOLM WALKER

PG	Peter Grimes	*S*	Swallow	*N2*	Niece 2
EO	Ellen Orford	*MS*	Mrs Sedley	*BB*	Bob Boles
B	Balstrode	*A*	Auntie	*R*	Rector
H	Hobson	*N1*	Niece 1	*NK*	Ned Keene

ⓜ mono ⓔ electronically reprocessed stereo ④ cassette
all recordings are in stereo unless otherwise stated

1959 Pears *PG*; C. Watson *EO*; Pease *B*; Kelly *H*; Brannigan *S*; Elms *MS*; J. Watson *A*; Studholme *N1*; Kells *N2*; Nilsson *BB*; Lanigan *R*; G. Evans *NK*/Royal Opera Chorus and Orch/Britten
Decca SXL 2150-2 ④ K71K33
London OSA1305

1978 Vickers *PG*; Harper *EO*; Summers *B*; Van Allan *H*; Robinson *S*; Payne *MS*; Bainbridge *A*; Cahill *N1*; Pashley *N2*; Dobson *BB*; Lanigan *R*; Allen *NK*/Royal Opera Chorus and Orch/C. Davis
Philips 6769 014 ④ 7699 089

1948 (excerpts) Act 2 scene 1 (Glitter of waves and glitter of sunlight); Act 3 scene 1 (Embroidery in childhood was a luxury of idleness); Interlude VI; Act 3 Scene 2 (Grimes! Grimes! . . . Steady! There you are!) Pears *PG*; Cross *EO*/choirs, Royal Opera House Orch/Goodall
EMI ⓜ RLS707

Four Sea Interludes, Op. 33*a* (1–4)
Passacaglia, Op. 33*b* (5)

1947	1–5	Concertgebouw/Van Beinum	Decca K1702-4 (78 rpm)
	1–4	LSO/Sargent	Columbia DX1441-2 (78 rpm) CBS (US) ⓜ ML2145
1953	1–5	Concertgebouw/Van Beinum	Decca ⓔ ECS712 London ⓜ LL917
	1–5	LPO/Boult	Pye GSGC14059 Westminster (US) WST14010

1963	1–4	Philharmonia/Giulini	EMI SXLP30240 ④ TC-SXLP30240 Angel S36215
1971	1–4	Bulgarian Radio and TV SO/Stefanov	Harmonia Mundi HMB114
1975	1–5	LSO/Previn	EMI ASD3154 SLS 5266 ④ TCC-SLS 5266 Angel S37142
1977	1–5	New York PO/Bernstein	CBS (US) M34529 ④ MT34529 (UK) 76640 ④ 40-76640
1977	1–5	Philadelphia/Ormandy	RCA (US) ARL1 2744 ④ ARK1 2744 (UK) RL12744
1978	1–4	Royal Opera House Orch/C. Davis	Philips 6527 112 ④ 7311 112

Index